Transitioning 'In-Between'

Spotlight on China

Series Editors

Shibao Guo (*University of Calgary, Canada*)
Yan Guo (*University of Calgary, Canada*)

International Advisory Board

Yanjie Bian (*University of Minnesota, USA*)
Qing Gu (*University College London, UK*)
Ruth Hayhoe (*OISE/University of Toronto, Canada*)
Khun Eng Kuah-Pearce (*Monash University Malaysia, Malaysia*)
Baocun Liu (*Beijing Normal University, China*)
Allan Luke (*Queensland University of Technology, Australia*)
Gerard A. Postiglione (*University of Hong Kong, China*)
Barbara Schulte (*Lund University, Sweden*)
Rui Yang (*University of Hong Kong, China*)
Qiang Zha (*York University, Canada*)
Jijiao Zhang (*Chinese Academy of Social Sciences, China*)
Li Zong (*University of Saskatchewan, Canada*)

VOLUME 7

The titles published in this series are listed at *brill.com/spot*

Transitioning 'In-Between'

Chinese Students' Navigating Experiences in Transnational Higher Education Programmes

By

Kun Dai

BRILL

LEIDEN | BOSTON

All chapters in this book have undergone peer review.

The Library of Congress Cataloging-in-Publication Data is available online at https://catalog.loc.gov

Typeface for the Latin, Greek, and Cyrillic scripts: "Brill". See and download: brill.com/brill-typeface.

ISSN 2542-9655
ISBN 978-90-04-50511-7 (paperback)
ISBN 978-90-04-41711-3 (hardback)
ISBN 978-90-04-50513-1 (e-book)

Copyright 2022 by Koninklijke Brill NV, Leiden, The Netherlands.
Koninklijke Brill NV incorporates the imprints Brill, Brill Nijhoff, Brill Hotei, Brill Schöningh, Brill Fink, Brill mentis, Vandenhoeck & Ruprecht, Böhlau Verlag and V&R Unipress.
All rights reserved. No part of this publication may be reproduced, translated, stored in a retrieval system, or transmitted in any form or by any means, electronic, mechanical, photocopying, recording or otherwise, without prior written permission from the publisher. Requests for re-use and/or translations must be addressed to Koninklijke Brill NV via brill.com or copyright.com.

This book is printed on acid-free paper and produced in a sustainable manner.

Sense of in-betweenness (Chinese calligraphy)
CHEN HONGJIE (Boya Professor, Graduate School of Education, Peking University)

Advance Praise for
Transitioning 'In-Between'

"There is an acute dearth of literature in international higher education on transnational programmes that do not involve the bodily mobility of students. This book provides an original and insightful analysis of the ways in which Chinese students negotiate transnational articulation programmes, and the extent to which such programmes have the potential to promote intercultural learning."
– Fazal Rizvi, Professor in Global Studies in Education, The University of Melbourne

"This timely volum reminds us of what scientists refer to as 'the knowledge illusion' in transnational higher education: We tend to believe we know more than we do. In this book, Dr Dai moves beyond appropriation of cultural resources to unravel the complexities of learning in modern transnational higher education programmes. Seeing intercultural learning as boundary crossing, he highlights the intricacies of the in-between spaces of students as agents of their life-changing experiences."
– Rui Yang, Professor and Associate Dean for Research, Faculty of Education, University of Hong Kong

"The world is facing unprecedented health crisis with the spread of COVID-19 across different corners of the globe. Well before the present global health crisis, growing debates have emerged to critically examine the future of internationalization of education, especially when people begin to question the value and benefits that international education brings. The COVID-19 pandemic again raises the issues of the future of international higher education. Would the COVID-19 adversely international education and student mobility? This book by Dr Kun Dai has chosen very important research problem, connecting the wider international research community to critically reflect the futures of internationalization and transnationalization of higher education. The present volume provides critical review, rich empirical analysis and relevant theoretical debates on internationalization and higher education. This volume is highly relevant to academics, researchers, policy makers, and postgraduate students in higher education."
– Ko Ho Mok, Lam Man Tsan Chair Professor of Comparative Policy, Vice President, Lingnan University, Hong Kong

"Articulation programs are a form of transnational education that have been largely underexplored, so it is timely that Kun Dai provides us with this highly engaging and thought-provoking book. Examining the attitudes, perceptions and experiences of Chinese students who study on a range of Chinese-Australian articulation programs, Dai shines a light on how students, as 'in-betweeners,' may experience intercultural learning and a sense of belonging with their home and host cultures. It is recognized that studying in two education systems may present students with both benefits and challenges. Dai calls upon his own experiences as a former articulation program student and expands this through the rich voices of the study's interviewees, to candidly discuss and explain the positionality of those who fall 'in-between.' This book offers valuable insights to both researchers and practitioners and may be useful for educators to consider in order to improve relevant programs and classroom practice."
– **Stephen Wilkins, Professor in Strategy and Marketing, The British University in Dubai**

"Transnational higher education (TNHE) is a significantly understudied area within the social sciences and yet its impact upon education systems is being felt around the world. This excellent book provides a valuable and detailed examination of students' experiences of transnational higher education programmes in China. We still know very little about how students actually experience TNHE, and this is a significant growth area in China in particular. This book is timely and insightful, and I look forward to using it in my teaching and writing."
– **Johanna L. Waters, Professor of Human Geography, University College London**

Contents

Foreword XI
Bob Lingard
Acknowledgements XIII

1 **Globalisation, Internationalisation, and Transnational Higher Education** 1
 1 Globalisation and Internationalisation of Higher Education 2
 2 Transnational Higher Education 6
 3 Transnational Higher Education in China 10
 4 Significance of This Study 18
 5 Research Design: A Narrative Inquiry 19
 6 Conclusion 25

2 **Cross-System Transitions across Cultures, Spaces, and Places** 27
 1 Transitioning and Learning between Cultures 27
 2 Cultural Influences Shaping Chinese Learners 30
 3 Critical Understandings of CHC and Chinese Students 33
 4 Encountering Shocks with Complicated Transitioning Trajectories 36
 5 Moving across Different Spaces and Places as Diaspora 42
 6 Conclusion 51

3 **Start the TAP Journey with Various Certainties and Uncertainties** 53
 1 Begin the TAP Journey 53
 2 Encountering Certainties and Uncertainties 59
 3 Conclusion 66

4 **A Tortuous Trajectory of Intercultural Learning** 68
 1 Positively Deal with Changes in Transition 69
 2 Being Stressful in Transition 74
 3 Shifting between Multiple Identities as Intercultural Learner 79
 4 Shaping Different Senses of Belonging as Transnational Diaspora 85
 5 Conclusion 90

5 **Mapping a Transitioning In-Between Learning Space** 92
 1 The Conceptualisation of the Transitioning In-Between Space in TAP 92

	2	ICT-Mediated Learning Space 94
	3	Transitioning between Different Assessment Modes and Cultures 103
	4	Encountering Different Teaching Strategies 108
	5	Transitioning from a Collective Setting to an Individualistic Context 114
	6	Conclusion 119

6   A Reflexive Journey as an In-Betweener 122

	1	Transitioning between Different Schools as a Domestic Diaspora 122
	2	Transitioning from China to Australia as a TAP Student 127
	3	Shifting between Chinese and Australian Contexts 133
	4	Conclusion 140

7   Critical Reflections: Becoming Compatible 141

	1	Dynamically Transitioning between Different Systems 141
	2	(Re)shaping Identity, Agency, and Belonging in Cross-System Transition 145
	3	The Contour of the In-Between Learning Space in TAP 155
	4	Intercultural Adjustment as a Way of Transitioning In-Between 160
	5	Implications 164

8   Conclusion 166

References 169
Index 190

Foreword

Kun Dai's book, *Transitioning 'In-Between': Chinese Students Navigating Experiences in Transnational Higher Education Programmes*, provides an original and insightful research-based account of the experiences, educational and cultural, face to face and technologically mediated, of Chinese students who participated in Transnational Articulation Programmes (TAPs) between Chinese and Australian higher education (HE) institutions. These mobile students are a manifestation of the flows of people across the globe, ethnoscapes in Appadurai's (1996) account of globalisation, which both reflect and express globalisation. These flows, of course, have been interrupted in the context of less porous national borders in response to national approaches to managing the Covid-19 global pandemic, which might be seen as a viral global flow. It will be interesting to see the short- and long-term effects of the pandemic on TAPs and also the impact of changing global geopolitics and China-US tensions on these flows of HE students and the continuation of such articulation programmes. The rising global status of a good number of Chinese universities, an explicit Chinese government policy agenda in HE, will also have impact on such programmes.

These articulation programmes, in this case between China and Australian HE institutions, meet the interests of both nations and both sets of participating, articulating institutions. For China, such programmes link to moves to enhance the global standing of Chinese universities and to enhance the quality of provision and international outreach. For Australian universities, there is a strong financial incentive to encourage such programmes in the context of reducing government financial support for universities and their greater dependence on other sources of funding. The latter has been very well illustrated in the financial stringencies facing many Australian universities as the pandemic has decimated the numbers of full fee-paying international HE students and particularly from China.

Dai's analysis gives voice to the students participating in articulation programmes. The study draws on interviews with a number of students participating in these programmes. Creatively, he also draws on his own experiences as a student who participated in such an articulation programme. The conjoining of the interview data with what we might see as autoethnographic insights demonstrates issues inherent in such articulation programmes. These include the different positioning and usage of the internet, websites etc in the two HE contexts, different pedagogical practices, different assessment practices, and different organisation of the classes in which the students participated, as well as broader cultural differences between the two HE systems and of course between the two national contexts. The issue of English language competency is also shown to be of real importance, especially as the students in the Chinese arm of the articulation programme focus on their English language competence so as to successfully pass the English test necessary to participate in the Australian arm of the articulation programme. English is also important in respect of HE in another way. In the context of post Cold War globalisation and the work of universities, we have witnessed the emergence of a one-world science system with English as its *lingua franca*.

While Dai's analysis utilised extant research on articulation programmes, especially the psychological work that stresses processes of adaptation or otherwise, his work also interestingly draws on more sociological, cultural studies approaches that focus on 'third spaces,' spaces in-between (Soja, 1996), in mobile individuals' experiencing of globalisation and its various flows. The internet enabled some of the students to live in-between China and Australia when negotiating the Australian arm of the articulation programmes. This is a liminal space and perhaps also precipitates something of a liminal identity. It is in effect, Dai's analysis demonstrates, the disarticulation between the Chinese-Australian arms of articulation programmes, that enables this liminality, enables this living in-between, living and learning here and there simultaneously. This is somewhat akin to how the affordances of the new technologies have supported similar experiences amongst global diasporas, very different experiences from earlier waves of migrants pre the internet. Dai hypothesises that this unintended outcome for some of the students in his study, probably well prepares some of the graduates of such programmes for participation in global labour markets and within the technical and professional arms of the new transnational class. Other less adaptive students are probably destined for their national labour markets.

This is an original study that ought to be read by policy makers and those in HE in both nations responsible for articulation programmes. The book also provides a base for future research on TAPs and on the student experience of them. It makes a very real contribution to research on the experiences of mobile students participating in these articulation programmes at a poignant moment in the context of globalisation and its associated flows and changing global geopolitics, which will surely have effects on such programmes as we move into the future.

References

Appadurai, A. (1996). *Modernity at large: Cultural dimensions of globalization*. The University of Minnesota Press.

Soja, E. (1996). *Thirdspace: Journeys to Los Angeles and other real-and-imagined places*. Wiley-Blackwell.

Bob Lingard
Australian Catholic University and The University of Queensland

Acknowledgements

In early 2020, the world encountered various historical changes and challenges due to the Covid-19 pandemic. This book has been completed during this unprecedented period and is one of the milestones in my early academic career.

I never imagined that I could write a book in English. When I started my postdoc journey at Peking University in April 2019, I thought about summarising my doctoral study. Writing a book as one of my postdoc academic products could be a good idea after publishing several journal articles. However, it is challenging for me, and I had no idea how to go through this process. Luckily, many outstanding scholars support me in this journey.

I wish to acknowledge the book series editors, Professor Guo Shibao and Professor Guo Yan from the University of Calgary, Canada. It is my honour to be one of the contributors to the book series. Then, I wish to thank my postdoc advisors, Professor Chen Hongjie and Associate Professor Shen Wenqin from Peking University. Without their support, I may not have had the opportunity to get the postdoc fellowship funded by China International Postdoc Exchange Program, which allowed me to have research and learning experiences at Peking University.

Furthermore, I appreciate the support from the following scholars and friends: Emeritus Professor Bob Lingard, Associate Professor Ian Hardy and Associate Professor Kelly Matthews from the University of Queensland, Associate Professor Vicente Reyes from the University of Nottingham, Associate Professor Michael Guanglun Mu from the Queensland University of Technology, Professor Yang Rui from the University of Hong Kong, Professor Mok Ka Ho from Lingnan University, Professor Yan Fengqiao from Peking University, Professor Fazal Rizvi and Professor Leo Goedegebuure from the University of Melbourne, Professor Simon Marginson from the University of Oxford, Professor Hamish Coates from Tsinghua University, Professor Tian Mei from Xi'an Jiaotong University, Professor Anthony Fung from the Chinese University of Hong Kong, Dr Ma Jiani from Beijing Normal University, Dr Zhang Zuocheng from the University of New England, and Dr Dely Elliot from the University of Glasgow. Due to the limited space, I may not be able to list other friends. However, I still wish to thank all friends and scholars who support me in my research journey.

Finally, I want to thank my families and friends who always support me and stand with me. Everything is impossible without family support. I wish all friends and families to have a healthy, safe, and peaceful life.

CHAPTER 1

Globalisation, Internationalisation, and Transnational Higher Education

After completing my doctoral research in late 2018, I realised that it was not enough to complete the journey by submitting a thesis and publishing some articles, which seemed too utilitarian to be a "pure" researcher. Then, I started to consider what I can systematically contribute to the research community. When I recalled my learning journey from primary school in China to the end of my doctoral studies in Australia, I realised my experiences seemed to be an adventure, which positioned me across various places and spaces. The transitioning journey potentially positions me as an in-betweener who progressively shapes a complex sense of identity, agency, and belonging. I have studied various educational contexts in either urban cities or rural areas in my school stage. After starting higher education, I have also experienced different modes of education via a transnational articulation programme (TAP). This programme is one type of educational setting in transnational higher education (TNHE). Learning via TAP has become an important pathway for many Chinese students to start their higher education. Notably, such programmes usually combine educational resources from both Chinese and international partners, positioning students between different learning experiences. Although TNHE-related research has become a hot topic in higher education and international education, few studies have illustrated students' learning experiences in detail.

Many universities have launched TNHE collaborations in China to enhance the internationalisation of higher education (HE) and raise revenue with international partners. Meanwhile, TNHE has become one significant way, which offers students different opportunities to gain international learning experiences. It seems that TNHE could be a way to achieve "triple wins" for students, Chinese universities, and international partners. The development of TNHE in China has a nearly 40 years history. However, not many studies have concretely investigated Chinese students' cross-system learning trajectory and issues in this internationalised educational setting (Qin & Te, 2016). Recently, based on an analysis of research works from 2000 to 2018 in the field of international programmes and provider mobility (IPPM), Knight and Liu (2019, p. 15) also suggest that,

© KONINKLIJKE BRILL NV, LEIDEN, 2022 | DOI: 10.1163/9789004505131_001

> More attention needs to be directed to teaching and learning issues related to the cultural backgrounds, ways of learning/knowing, and identities of students. As the world becomes more interconnected, teachers, staff, and students in IPPM programmes are bringing different values, customs, expectations, and experiences to their academic programmes and research endeavors. To date these new multicultural dynamics in all modes of IPPM is a relatively neglected area in IPPM research. The need for curriculum and applied research to be more relevant to the host IPPM country context is recognized but further understanding and knowledge of cultural and identity issues merit further investigation.

According to their analysis, those internationalised education settings create a complex picture of multicultural communications between different contexts. Specifically, TAPs, which also refer to partnership/collaborative/joint/double degree programmes, need to be further researched from different perspectives, for example, quality assurance, pedagogical practices, and related policies (Knight & Liu, 2019). From a policy perspective, the Chinese Ministry of Education (MoE) and eight other governmental departments published a new initiative in June 2020, which advocates that Chinese universities should further develop high-quality TNHE with foreign partners.

To offer some timely insights into these under-researched topics and political initiatives, I attempt to systematically illustrate my research into Chinese students' trajectories of intercultural learning in TAPs and the potential changes they gained. Meanwhile, I also examine my learning journey as an inside former student, an outside researcher, and an in-between reflexive thinker. By providing nuanced insights drawn from interviews with 20 Chinese TAP students and my reflexive narrative, I propose to address the following questions in this book. The overarching question is: *How do Chinese students experience intercultural learning in transnational articulation programmes? The two subquestions are: What changes do they experience in cross-system transition? What factors influence their intercultural learning in transnational articulation programmes?* Before further discussion, it is essential to briefly review several vital concepts: globalisation and internationalisation of HE, which could be considered as the developmental foundation of TNHE.

1 Globalisation and Internationalisation of Higher Education

The concept of globalisation is a complicated one and onerous to precisely define (Dale & Robertson, 2002), and has been critically discussed by many

GLOBALISATION, INTERNATIONALISATION, AND TRANSNATIONAL HE

scholars (e.g., Appadurai, 2000; Held, McGrew, Goldblatt, & Perraton, 2000; Knight, 1997; Marginson, 2008; Rizvi & Lingard, 2010). For example, Knight (1997) argued that globalisation means "the flow of technology, economy, knowledge, people, values, ideas ... across borders" (p. 6). This definition indicates that globalisation interweaves different elements of the world, with challenges to the nation-state's traditional working. Similar to Knight's (1997) understanding, as shown above, to further theorise the concept of globalisation, Appadurai (2000) indicated that it is about "flows and disjunctures" across national boundaries (p. 5). Specifically, flows mean the constant cross-boundary movements of different social elements, such as "ideas and ideologies, people and goods, images and messages, technologies and techniques" (Appadurai, 2000, p. 5). He calls these cross-national flows "scapes." The disjunctures between different scapes refer to the contradictions and problems that emerge from the cross-boundary movements of various social elements between different countries, ideologies, cultures, and societies because each region may have unique features that will not be entirely changed or influenced by others (Appadurai, 2000).

Later, by adopting Bourdieu's concepts, Marginson (2008) also suggested that in the global HE field, researchers need to consider two elements: cross-border flows and differences. Flows include people, knowledge, technology, financial capital, and information. However, flows in HE is dynamic and uneven between different contexts. Concerning the differences, various lateral and vertical elements influence flows, such as language, culture, hierarchy, inclusion, and unequal capacity. These flows and differences make the global HE field complex. From the perspective of social politics, Held et al. (2000, p. 15) argued that:

> Globalisation can usefully be conceived as a process (or set of processes) which embodies a transformation in the spatial organisation of social relations and transactions, generating transcontinental or interregional flows and networks of activity, interaction and power.

To summarise the core of this concept, they stated that "globalisation can be thought of as growth in the breadth, intensity, speed and impact of worldwide interconnectedness" (Held et al., 2000, p. 15). As these definitions show, globalisation can function as a double-edged sword that influences cross-boundary interactions and brings issues to different countries to some extent.

Altbach and Knight (2007) shared their views about the possible results of globalisation on world society's development. Altbach and Knight (2007, p. 291) argued that:

4 CHAPTER 1

> The results of globalisation include the integration of research, the use of English as the lingua franca for scientific communication, the growing international labour market for scholars and scientists, the growth of communications firms and of multi-national and technology publishing, and the use of information technology (IT).

According to these results, on the one hand, globalisation refers to flows of social, capital, cultural, and economic elements across borders. On the other hand, it also indicates a potential process of (re)shaping contemporary societies, cultures, ideologies. These aspects are interwoven, especially under the rapid development of technologies that are also bearers of globalisation (Rizvi & Lingard, 2010). To react to these complex changes associated with globalisation, different sectors have strategies in response to this trend relative to their particular situations (Knight, 1997). Specifically, HE is also undoubtedly influenced by globalisation. Altbach and Knight (2007) suggested that globalisation pushes HE into deeper international engagement under "the economic, political, and societal forces" (p. 290). In doing so, HE becomes internationalised.

Along with the growing international interactions, the internationalisation of HE is progressively generated. As Knight (1997) claimed, "internationalisation of higher education is one of the ways a country responds to the impact of globalisation yet, at the same time, respects the individuality of the nation" (p. 6). Later, she further indicated that "internationalisation is changing the world of higher education, and globalisation is changing the world of internationalisation" (Knight, 2004, p. 5). With the rapid development of information and communication technologies (ICTs), educational practices can be (re)shaped to open up new channels for institutions, educators, and students to internationalise their cross-cultural experience (Leask, 2004). Furthermore, using ICTs in internationalising educational services could benefit the groups that may not have opportunities to move between countries and cultures (Leask, 2004).

According to the above discussion, it is apparent that globalisation can be regarded as an activator or precipitator of the internationalisation of HE. Meanwhile, the internationalisation of HE can be seen as a reaction to globalisation and its expression. To explicitly clarify the intertwined relationships between these concepts in HE, Altbach and Knight (2007) advocated that "internationalisation includes the policies and practices undertaken by academic systems and institutions – and even individuals – to cope with the global academic environment" (p. 290).

Internationalisation in the context of HE is complicated and thus difficult to define. As Knight (2006, p. 16) suggested, it is difficult to use a "simple, unique or all-encompassing definition" to interpret the meaning of internationalisation in HE. However, internationalisation could be considered as an extension of "international." According to Bennett (2010), the concept of international in education can refer to "the movement of students, faculty, researchers, and other academics across national borders" (p. 419). This concept can echo one of the most cited definitions of internationalisation of HE proposed by Knight (1993), who identified that it is a "process of integrating an international/intercultural dimension into the teaching, research and service functions of a university or college" (p. 21). Later, de Wit, Hunter, Howard, and Egron-Polak (2015, p. 29) defined internationalisation of HE as:

> The intentional process of integrating an international, intercultural or global dimension into the purpose, functions and delivery of post-secondary education, in order to enhance the quality of education and research for all students and staff and to make a meaningful contribution to society.

Based on these explanations, it is evident that the internationalisation of HE is a systematic process conducted by different actors, institutions, and countries under the trend of globalisation. As Knight (1997) identified, "internationalisation is not only oriented to countries or nation-states but also includes the different cultural/ethnic groups within a country" (p. 8). Different educational systems and sociocultural elements continually interact with each other during this process, creating a cross-cultural context. Therefore, the internationalisation of HE occurs along with multiple intercultural communications. Notably, these definitions are based on Western discourse, which aims to capitalise HE to achieve economic growth, attract skilled migrants, and enhance the global competences of domestic labours (Liu & Lin, 2016). However, as Yang (2002) argued, this trend is an unequal process of "diffusion, either slow or fast, Western cultural values, consumer patterns and technologies to parts of the world" (p. 11). When people move from a non-Western context to the West, they potentially engage in a journey of Westernisation (Liu, 2021).

Researchers from the non-Western context (e.g., China) have critically reviewed the trend of globalisation and the internationalisation of HE. For example, Liu (2021) analysed the meaning of the internationalisation of HE from the Chinese perspective. His research found that China aims to have an equal position as the west in the global HE context. Meanwhile, China adopts non-profit oriented strategies and long-term policies to develop international education compared to the economy-driven motivation in the west. In this process, government plays a significant role in promoting the internationalisation of HE and enhancing the national identity. To summarise these features, Liu (2021, p. 241) suggested that internationalisation of HE in China can be defined as

> A nationally coordinated, institutionally integrated and comprehensive effort to import the Western-led world standards in teaching, research, management and facility development through the exposure of academic staff, students and administrators to Western practices, and to export the Chinese discourse, voice and cultural understanding in the international community through international student education in China and Chinese language/culture promotion overseas.

This definition could indicate that China has unique strategies to achieve the internationalisation of HE rather than fully accepts the Western approach. This process is a way of improving the Chinese soft power in the global context. In achieving the internationalisation of HE, an increasing number of universities have actively engaged in international collaboration through transnational education. As Rizvi (2009) advocated, "education research must therefore pay attention to the transnational spaces which are constituted by new relationalities that are necessarily non-linear, complex, open-ended and evolving" (p. 287).

2 Transnational Higher Education

In the past few decades, a growing number of scholars have explored topics related to TNHE and other relevant concepts (e.g., neoliberalism, globalisation, internationalisation, and marketisation). According to de Wit (2020), from 2010 to 2020, the number of international students has rapidly increased, and different types of TNHE (e.g., franchise operations, articulation programmes, branch campuses, and online education) have also been developed. The development of TNHE cannot be separated from the influence of globalisation. HE has been widely exported and imported between many developing and developed countries. Moreover, with the rapid development of the global economy and ICTs, especially the Internet, different cultures, societies, and countries have more opportunities to connect with others. Such close connections become an essential factor that promotes more in-depth cross-national communications in the field of education.

Transnational education (TNE) is an outcome of these developments. At the tertiary level, TNE is also known as transnational higher education (TNHE)

(Huang, 2003b). In the 21st century, TNHE has become a practical approach for achieving the educational mobility of academics, students, and resources worldwide (Altbach, Reisberg, & Rumbley, 2009). However, due to various barriers in the early stage (e.g., legal system differences), the import/export of education was not conducted very well until the outcomes of the Uruguay Round of trade negotiations from 1983 to 1993 were put in place (Hou, Montgomery, & McDowell, 2014; van der Wende, 2003).

The General Agreement on Trade in Services (GATS), one of the significant outcomes of the Uruguay Round of trade negotiations, was enacted and further implemented in January 1995. According to Ziguras (2003), "GATS is a multilateral agreement through which WTO members commit to volunteer liberalisation of trade in services, including education" (p. 89). Under the GATS policy, education has been regarded as one type of service to be traded worldwide. For instance, many countries in Asia and Latin America are actively "buying" educational services from developed countries, for example, the United States (the USA), the United Kingdom (the UK), Australia or European countries (Altbach & Knight, 2007).

Notably, Australia's HE has become increasingly prominent in the Asia-Pacific region. Since the late 1990s, many Australian institutions have actively recruited international students onshore and provided different TNHES (e.g., programme and branch campus) to several developing countries, such as China, Vietnam, and Malaysia (Sugimoto, 2006). Influenced by the trend of globalisation and neoliberalism, many Australian universities operate TNHE and recruit international students to make profits as government funding was declining, which potentially push universities to find new ways to increase income. Meanwhile, operating TNHE can also increase institutional profile in the global HE market. Although Australia has actively developed TNHE, some issues emerged as well, for example, quality assurance. Institutions need to enhance TNHE quality that directly influences students' choices. One of the critical aspects of enhancing quality is offering education by following the same standard in both onshore and offshore campuses, which may have complex impacts on students' learning experiences and university reputations. To hold TNHE students onshore, many Australian institutions adopt an integrated approach. In most cases, when TNHE students move to Australia, they attend classes like the local cohort rather than have a unique group. Thus, TNHE students can experience "pure" Australian education.

With the rapid development of TNHE, scholars (e.g., Knight, 2016) have realised that it is necessary to clarify the definition and meaning of TNHE and other similar concepts. It is worth noting that various adjectives could describe such international collaborations as cross-border, borderless, and offshore.

These terms could be used in different situations or in an interchangeable way (Knight, 2016). Among these terms, TNHE is commonly adopted to illustrate the cross-context movement of education between different countries (Knight, 2016). Notably, TNHE also refers to cross-border education (CBE), offshore, or borderless education (Huang, 2003b; Knight, 2005; R. Yang, 2008). Practically, TNHE and CBE are widely adopted in research, even though these terminologies can be used interchangeably but have different focuses (Knight, 2016). Different professional organisations and scholars have widely defined TNHE and CBE. For example, the Global Alliance for Transnational Education (GATE), defined TNHE in the following statement (as cited in Heffernan & Poole, 2005, p. 224):

> Any teaching or learning activity in which the students are in a different country (the host countries) to that in which the institution providing the education is based (the home countries). This situation requires that national boundaries be crossed by information about the education, and by staff and/or education material (whether the information and education, and the materials travel by mail, computer network, radio or television broadcast or other means).

Furthermore, according to Mok and Han (2016), the United Nations Educational, Scientific, and Cultural Organisation (UNESCO) in 2001 concisely defined TNHE as "all types of higher education study where the learners are located in a country different from the one where the awarding institution is based" (p. 20). For the concept of CBE, Knight (2007) suggested that the CBE refers to "the movement of people, programmes, providers, curricula, projects, and services across national or regional jurisdictional borders" (p. 24).

According to these definitions of TNHE and CBE, it is apparent that they have many similarities and also different focuses. On the one hand, they emphasise people's movement and educational resources, which allows them to be adopted interchangeably (Knight, 2007). On the other hand, TNHE focuses on educational provision mobility in different locations (Kosmützky & Putty, 2016). However, CBE concentrates on international cooperation's jurisdictional borders' policy and regulations issues (Knight, 2007). In this study, TNHE was adopted as the key concept, as this study aimed to explore students' learning experiences in a cross-system and cross-national setting. Although policy issues will be briefly discussed, these were not the primary focus of this study. Hence, the concept of CBE is not used in this study.

Based on the above definitions, it is evident that cross-country (or border) is a crucial characteristic of TNHE. This feature might suggest that educational

GLOBALISATION, INTERNATIONALISATION, AND TRANSNATIONAL HE 9

activities in TNHE should be conducted between different countries. Meanwhile, educational resources and people move from one to another country through various pathways. The movements of educational resources and people between different countries are fundamental characteristics of TNHE. According to the definition above, TNHE can be regarded as a broad concept that includes many interdisciplinary subfields. It combines study with various elements, such as different countries, people and ICTs. Along with the extensive development of TNHE around the world, it has been established via various modes. As the discussions of the definitions above suggest, TNHE refers to multiple elements of HE that move internationally, generating various types of TNHE, such as branch campuses, franchises, twinning, and distance education programmes (Huang, 2003b). However, Knight (2016) suggested that it is necessary to identify different types of TNHE as confusion and misunderstanding of these terminologies exist in the research literature.

According to Knight's (2016) framework, different educational modes reflecting the concept of TNE can be sorted into two types, notably, collaborative or independent provisions. Precisely, the collaborative model consists mainly of twinning programmes or other types of articulation programmes (e.g., joint, double or multiple degree programmes) between local and foreign partners. Such articulation programmes may award students one or more degrees depending on individual agreements and policies (Knight, 2016). Later, this mode has been called partnership programmes (Knight & Liu, 2019). However, this study does not focus on investigating such policy-related aspects but instead concentrates on students' learning experiences in their TAP. Hence, in this study, articulation is considered a general concept representing a research context that refers to the cooperation between universities in different nations in designing and running educational programmes of a 2 + 2, 3 + 1, or 4 + 0 kind. Students may gain one or two degrees in such partnership programmes (Knight & Liu, 2019). The most significant articulation of such programmes is collaborative design and thoughtfulness about how the two parts work together.

In contrast, the independent mode means that foreign universities offer education without cooperating with local partners, for example, creating a branch campus or instigating online learning (Knight, 2016). This book will focus on the collaborative provision, especially the study abroad via TAP, one of the critical types of TNHE in the Chinese context (Mok & Ong, 2014). Students who studied in several China-Australia 2 + 2 TAPs were recruited to share their learning experiences in this study.

In the field of TNHE-related research, researchers have conducted various discussions in the Chinese context (e.g., Ding, 2019; Han, 2019; He, 2016; He & Liu, 2018; Hu, Eisenchlas, & Trevaske, 2019; Huang, 2003a, 2003b, 2008; Mok,

Han, Jiang, & Zhang, 2018; Mok & Ong, 2014; Qin, 2021; H. Yang & Lesser, 2017; R. Yang, 2008). Meanwhile, an increasing number of researchers (e.g., Bennell, 2019; Bordogna, 2020; Dowling-Hetherington, 2020; Dunn & Wallace, 2006; Healey, 2019; Leung, & Waters, 2013; Lien & Keithley, 2020; Levatino, 2017; Moufahim & Lim, 2015; Sin, Leung, & Waters, 2019; Wilkins, Butt, & Annabi, 2017; Wilson-Mah & Thomlinson, 2018; Zhao & Xu, 2020; Ziguras, 2003, 2016) have investigated TNHE-related issues in other contexts, such as Asia, Europe, Oceania Middle East, and America. From a research focus perspective, many researchers have investigated TNHE from the macro perspectives of globalisation, internationalisation across countries, governments and policies, and institutions (e.g., Altbach, 2004; Altbach & Knight, 2007; de Wit, 2002; Jokila, 2015; Knight, 1997, 2006; Naidoo, 2009; Teichler, 2009; van Damme, 2001; van der Wende, 2003; Ziguras & McBurnie, 2011).

Distinct from the macro studies, some scholars have concentrated on examining micro aspects, such as academics' experiences, administration issues, students' motivation, intercultural adjustment, and perceptions of transnational programmes (e.g., Ding, 2018; Djerasimovic, 2014; Heffernan, Morrison, Basu, & Sweeney, 2010; Heffernan & Pimpa, 2019; Hou & McDowell, 2013; Lamberton & Ashton-Hay, 2015; Neri & Wilkins, 2019; Tian & Martin, 2014; H. Yang & Lesser, 2017). According to these different directions and topics, it seems that TNHE has become a substantial field in educational research (Heffernan et al., 2010; Knight & Liu, 2019). As one of the major countries that have imported "foreign" education, China is encouraging and experiencing the reform of HE to actively and genuinely engage with the trend of globalisation and internationalisation.

3 Transnational Higher Education in China

Having experienced rapid economic development in the past 40 years, after the instigation of the Open-Door Policy in 1978, China is seeking to increase its soft power influence through cultural communication globally. With the growing trend of globalisation and internationalisation, higher education (HE) has become one way to distribute Chinese culture to the world. Meanwhile, the HE system is also becoming a key platform for China to collaborate with international partners. After launching the "One Belt, One Road" initiative, China actively engages in international communication and collaboration via HE (Wu, 2019). Although this process might enhance educational quality and international competition, Chinese HE also encounters various historical challenges and opportunities to reform its HE system.

According to R. Yang (2016), the internationalisation of HE in China has a long history, stretching back to the Qing dynasty. However, due to the constant revolutions and social changes in Chinese society, the internationalisation of HE has faced various barriers. It was not until Deng Xiaoping's call to gear Chinese education to the world in 1983 that the Chinese central government launched the students' study overseas project (R. Yang, 2016). However, although international communication with foreign countries was being developed in this stage, it was still without enough deep and broad engagement. After joining the World Trade Organisation (WTO) in 2001, China started to play an increasingly significant role in global engagement in various areas, such as the economy and education (Huang, 2003b). From a macro perspective, the irresistible trend of globalisation has significantly influenced modern Chinese HE development. From a micro level, benefits from the accelerated growth of the economy mean that increasing numbers of Chinese families indicate a strong desire to ensure their children are well-educated, aiming to improve their global competitiveness and expand their horizons (Cheng & P. Yang, 2019). The massive demand for educational services also stimulates the HE system's reform (Huang, 2003b). Many Chinese universities are actively collaborating with international institutions to establish cross-system communication, aiming to achieve HE's development against the background of globalisation.

To foster and standardise international cooperation with foreign countries in education, the Chinese government enacted various policies. For example, the China State Council published the People's Republic of China Regulations on Chinese-Foreign Cooperation in Running Schools in 2003 (Huang, 2008). It is considered one of the most important policies for reforming and regulating the international cooperation between Chinese and foreign institutions (R. Yang, 2008). Following this policy, in 2004, the Ministry of Education (MoE) proposed another policy document, known as the Implementation Measures for Regulations of the People's Republic of China on Chinese-Foreign Cooperation in Running Schools. Based on these policies, Chinese universities established multiple types of TNHE with foreign partners. Such international articulation is well known as Chinese-foreign cooperatively running schools (CFCRS) and "Zhong Wai He Zuo Ban Xue" (中外合作办学) in Chinese (Huang, 2014).

The TNHE has become one of the essential parts of the Chinese HE system. Through establishing transnational education, both China and foreign nations get various potential benefits, such as financial income, academic interactions and even cross-cultural communications (Huang, 2011; Knight, 2004). Specifically, students and lecturers become the significant intermediaries to conduct the learning and teaching activities through different articulations (de Wit, 2002), which are regarded as valuable ways to enhance Chinese HE's quality (Mok & Han, 2016).

Many researchers have widely investigated TNHE in Chinese HE system (e.g., Bai & Y. Wang, 2020, 2021; Dai, Lingard, & Reyes, 2018; Dai, 2020; Ding, 2018, 2019; Fang, 2012; Y. Feng, 2013; Gao et al., 2012; Han, 2017, 2019; He, 2016; He & Liu, 2018; He & Wilkins, 2018; Hou et al., 2014; Huang, 2003b, 2014; S. Li & Wang, 2009; Mok & Ong, 2014; Mok & Xu, 2008; Montgomery, 2016; Qin & Te, 2016; F. Wang, Clarke, & Yu, 2016; T. Wang, 2016; Y. Wang & Bai, 2020; R. Yang, 2008). For instance, Huang (2003a, 2003b) systematically analysed the growth and development of TNHE in China. His studies reviewed the history of TNHE in China and pinpointed its features from multiple perspectives, such as programme settings, national policies, and geographical destinations. Similarly, R. Yang (2008) investigated further details of TNHE, including majors of transnational programmes, the overseas partnership, and cultural appropriateness. Additionally, S. Li and Z. Wang (2009) generally reviewed the development of the TNHE in China and canvassed potential problems from quality assurance. More recently, Han (2017) critically examined the challenge and benefits of TNHE in the Chinese context. The increasing trend of researching issues in TNHE indicates that it has become an important component of Chinese HE and a significant research topic (Xue, 2016).

In the Chinese context, as mentioned above, TNHE is called "Zhong Wai He Zuo Ban Xue" or CFCRS, which could be seen as IPPM based on Knight and Liu's (2019) framework. To explicitly demonstrate the meaning of CFCRS, Hou et al. (2014, p. 308) suggested that,

> Running schools is the English translation of Chinese 'Ban Xue' in the government regulation. It refers to the phenomenon that Chinese universities and foreign universities cooperate to set up programmes or institutions to recruit Chinese students.

TNHE emerged in China between 1978 and the mid-1980s, especially after the Open-Door Policy proposed by Deng Xiaoping (Hou, Montgomery, & McDowell, 2011; Huang, 2011). However, the development of TNHE in this initial stage was limited. Meanwhile, related policies and regulations were being constructed. After joining the WTO in 2001, China started to deeply engage in the trend of internationalisation of HE by following the agreement of GATS (Mok & Ong, 2014). As Lin and Liu (2007b) revealed, joining the WTO and conducting GATS can be considered as one of the significant motivations underpinning the development of TNHE in China. Against this background, not only does China seek opportunities to join the international platform, but foreign countries also wish to obtain benefits via exporting their educational services to China. Knight (2004) suggested that gaining financial benefits is one of the primary motivations for foreign universities to run TNHE via their developing partners cooperatively.

Furthermore, Lin and Liu (2007b) argued that along with the increasing number of students who can study in HE, the demand for high-quality education is also required. In doing so, it potentially creates a big market for both Chinese and foreign universities to cooperatively offer educational services that aim to fulfil the increasing demand for HE and to refine the structure of the Chinese HE system (Lin & Liu, 2007b). Such factors can be seen as an academic rationale for promoting the internationalisation of HE as the articulations between different countries motivate and facilitate the communications of academics, educational resources, and students (Knight, 2004).

To conduct TNHE, Chinese universities have four modes with different legal positions in the Chinese HE system. Generally, the legal position refers to whether the CFCRS has "independent" or "non-independent" legal status (Lin & Liu, 2007a, p. 3). The independent legal status of TNHE usually refers to independent universities (e.g., the University of Nottingham Ningbo China/ Shanghai New York University/Kunshan Duck University). In contrast, a non-independent legal status usually means attached (or second-tier) colleges and transnational articulation (or joint/double degree) programmes (Hu & Willis, 2017). The affiliated colleges (or institutes) are usually based in a Chinese university as an academic department, for example, Sydney Institute of Language & Commerce of Shanghai (Lin & Liu, 2007a).

For the TAPs, they are usually named "Zhong Wai He Zuo Ban Xue Xiang Mu" (中外合作办学项目) in Chinese. Chinese and foreign universities most often run them in specific majors. As mentioned above, such programmes are usually designed as 1 + 1, 2 + 2, 3 + 1, or 4 + 0 modes. Students usually need to study in China for a couple of years in the first three models and then transfer to a foreign university to complete the whole programme. Specifically, 2 + 2 and 3 + 1 are usually conducted at the undergraduate level, but 1 + 1 usually happens in postgraduate study. The 4 + 0 is a particular case for undergraduate study as students fully complete their programmes in China via learning contents offered by foreign partners without students physically studying overseas. Students may obtain their degrees from both Chinese and foreign universities, depending on programme policy. According to Lin (2016), the Chinese government has approved approximately 2,300 TNHE institutions and programmes, which higher education institutions mainly run. According to the MoE, more than 1,000 programmes and institutions offer undergraduate education or above.

Specifically, the number of programmes at the undergraduate level is higher than the postgraduate stage due to various issues such as supervision, funding and timelines, and higher recruitment requirements than undergraduate study (Gao et al., 2012). Notably, some universities have developed models that combine undergraduate and postgraduate as a degree package, for example, 3 + 1 + 1 and 3 + 1.5. Depending on agreements between partner universities, students may complete the whole or part of their undergraduate study in one country and then move to the host university to complete the rest of learning to gain both a bachelor and a master's degree.

Regarding learning in the TAPs, students usually have opportunities to learn knowledge based on the combination of Chinese and foreign contents. Practically, TAPs have become a favourite mode for many Chinese students to experience Chinese and "foreign" education (Gao et al., 2012). In this study, TAPs, especially the 2 + 2 model, are the primary research focus as, in the current landscape of TNHE, such programmes play a dominant role compared with other types (Mok & Ong, 2014). Although such programmes are popular, their development still manifests several issues.

The academic disciplines and subjects of TAPs are abundant but uneven. Hou et al. (2014) suggested that the largest group of subjects is the business and management-related areas, such as accounting, marketing and business administration. Their findings resonate with R. Yang's (2008) research finding that 61% of TAPs focus on business-related subjects. Other popular disciplines and subjects include foreign languages, engineering, information technology, economy, arts and education (Hou et al., 2014). Many programmes in business and management-related fields reflect the higher requirements of well-educated human resources under the background of the Chinese economy's growing development. Notably, after joining the WTO, many Chinese companies started to engage in international business. The increasing demands for international business graduates have stimulated the establishment of business-related programmes in universities.

The geographic distribution of TNHE education in mainland China is unbalanced. According to R. Yang (2008) and Han (2019), metropolises (e.g., Beijing and Shanghai) and eastern economic developed provinces (e.g., Shandong, Jiangsu, Zhejiang, Fujian and Guangdong) host most TAPs. Particularly, Heilongjiang in northeast China has approximately 200 programmes, which is the most substantial number compared with all the other provinces. The clustering of TNHE and TAPs in economically developed regions indicates that transnational education is affected by local financial situations and the demand for multicultural communications (Gao et al., 2012). The northeast coastal provinces have benefited from the rapid development of the economy.

Hence, growing numbers of northeast coastal residents can afford to support their children studying abroad. Therefore, universities set up many TAPs to satisfy the increasing requirements for advanced higher education and demand for international educational experiences.

The geographic distribution is also uneven. The international partnerships of TAPS are mainly hosted in highly economically developed English speaking countries (Hou et al., 2014), even though foreign partners come from "more than 30 countries and regions" (Lin, 2016, p. 229). The top three countries are the United Kingdom, the United States, and Australia. Out of the many TAPS from different countries offered to Chinese university students, approximately more than 50% of their preferences fall within the ones offered by the three countries mentioned above. Notably, these countries also dominate international students' global education market (Verbik & Lasanowski, 2007; Wilkins & Huisman, 2011). Many Chinese students also prefer to study in TNHE offered by universities from these countries.

According to the above review of TNHE in the Chinese context, it is apparent that the landscape of TNHE is complicated, which ensures that the quality of TNHE remains a problematic issue. Although many studies have systematically analysed the TNHE in China from a macro level (e.g., policy and history), it is also essential to further explore more practical issues in running TNHE from a micro perspective, for example, focusing on students' experiences. However, practically, the quality issues in a cross-system educational context are difficult to monitor and examine. This involves many stakeholders who might have different features; for example, students may experience varied learning and teaching in cross-system settings (Knight, 2006). Students can be considered as the "end users" of TNHE. Their reflections could reveal various stories, insights and issues about learning in these settings. Their voices regarding cross-system and cross-national educational settings could indicate some quality issues in TAPs. Meanwhile, due to the numbers and variety of TNHE, students' learning experiences will be varied. As such, research focusing on student voices might very well illustrate varying accounts of such students' experiences in TNHE.

Research has widely discussed the quality issues of TNHE in a cross-system context. As van Damme (2001) argued, the internationalisation trend's quality issue is essential and needs to be carefully considered. Lack of quality could significantly influence the future development of TNHE. Quality issues related to TNHE have become an attractive area for researchers (e.g., Bannier, 2016; Ding, 2018, 2019; Han, 2017; Hou et al., 2014; Liu & Liu, 2016; Ziguras, 2016). As one of the major players in TNHE, China has also conducted various strategies and enacted several policies to refine and monitor the quality of TNHE. For example, the Chinese government has started to reduce the speed of developing new programmes to emphasise that TNHE should focus on improving the quality of education rather than becoming a pathway for making profits and framing HE as a commodity (Hou et al., 2014). Although the government realises quality issues in the current TNHE, there are still many problems in practice. For example, R. Yang (2014, p. 156) indicated:

> While the central government approves or charters the establishment of joint education programmes in line with the existing legal frameworks and guidelines, a lack of consistent oversight after approval has left the responsibility for quality entirely in the hands of the dedicated teaching staff and programmes coordinators.

According to this statement, the quality of TNHE in the Chinese context reveals a complicated picture. It seems that there are many gaps between the government policy and the reactions of universities, programme designers, and lecturers in running TNHE institutions and programmes.

Furthermore, it is worth noting that various factors could influence the quality of TNHE. Different stakeholders may have different standards to evaluate quality. Existing research has suggested several approaches to monitor and enhance the quality of TNHE, for example, the establishment of quality monitoring and evaluating systems (Liu & Liu, 2016). Moreover, it is essential to consider students' experiences in such a complex cross-system education setting. They are one of the major players who deeply engage in learning and teaching practices (Knight & Liu, 2019; Mok & Ong, 2014; Pyvis & Chapman, 2004).

The quality issue set against the backdrop of globalisation and internationalisation has become an essential topic in TNHE. According to van der Wende (2003) and Hu and Willis (2017), quality assurance is an essential issue for TNHE. Specifically, one of the critical aims of running TNHE is to improve the quality of Chinese HE and offer more opportunities for Chinese students to experience high quality higher education (Mok & Han, 2016). Hence, even though quality assurance is difficult to standardise to regulate TNHE, existing research studies have acknowledged the importance of evaluating the quality of TNHE (e.g., Hou et al., 2014; Hu & Willis, 2017; Lin & Liu, 2007b; Xu & Kan, 2013).

For the Chinese context, the government has adopted various strategies to manage TNHE to ensure and improve its quality. For instance, according to Hou (2011), the Chinese government has asked institutions to run TNHE without charging unreasonable fees, which would make them expensive and perhaps suggest profit-making as the chief motivation. Furthermore, when recruiting students, institutions should use the national university exam results rather than making low standard entry benchmarks to attract students who cannot reach a required score in the national university exam. In the process of establishing TNHE, Chinese universities should seek high-level foreign partners. In teaching and learning processes, at least one-third of such programmes' content should come from foreign partners.

Some researchers (e.g., Mok & Han, 2016; Xu & Kan, 2013) have also suggested that the Chinese government and MoE must establish a quality assurance mechanism to control and monitor the development of TNHE. However, in practice, it is still challenging to measure and examine the quality of TNHE due to their complex and varied settings in cross-system contexts (Knight, 2007). Different countries have different provisions and regulations; moreover, different students have multiple experiences and views towards their educational journeys in such programmes (Knight, 2007).

Many researchers (e.g., Hu et al., 2019; Ng & Nyland, 2017; Pyvis, 2011; T. Wang, 2016b) have researched practical issues in TNHE and have revealed that the teaching and learning experiences probably reflect the quality of TNHE. As T. Wang (2016b, p. 226) suggested, it is essential to consider "the equivalence of learning experience" between home and host universities in TNHE. Due to the features of TNHE, the cross-system settings are different in respect of multiple aspects (e.g., educational system structure, teaching content, pedagogical approaches, assessment modes, and even culture and society). Consequently, these cross-system differences could be a challenge for Chinese and foreign universities when designing TNHE. These challenges might very well influence the quality of teaching and learning practices. It is worth noting that the Chinese MoE conducted a systematic assessment of the quality of TNHE and TAPS in 2018. As a result, 234 TNHE programmes or institutions were cancelled due to quality issues. Many universities charge expensive tuition fee but do not offer high-quality articulated education. Notably, many cancelled programmes were operated by prestigious universities, for example, the Peking University-University of Hong Kong dental science programme.

To deal with such challenges, educators need to consider the strategy of "both-and" (T. Wang, 2016b, p. 226), which means that home and host universities strategically manage the connections between teaching and learning in both sites. Through close communications with each other, home and host universities could offer students a smooth pathway for studying in each learning context (T. Wang, 2016b). Notably, it is also essential to avoid "educational imperialism" (Pyvis, 2011, p. 741). This means that partners in TNHE should balance the weight of educational status in running these programmes, rather than one side dominating the design and operation of TNHE.

According to these studies, it is significant to consider and explore how students learn in TAPs to unpack the essence of learning quality in this cross-system setting. As Shah, Nair, and de la Harpe (2012) argued, students' feedback on their education in TNHE is significant for evaluating and enhancing quality assurance for institutions. Although several studies have initially explored this issue, there is still limited research that has revealed Chinese students' learning trajectories in detail in the TAP settings. For example, through exploring the learning experiences of Chinese and Singaporean students in two TAPs, Wallace and Dunn (2008) found that when Australian lecturers taught in these countries, their understanding of cultural differences significantly influenced their teaching students' learning. Furthermore, Wallace and Dunn (2008) suggested that many students proposed to closely explore foreign culture to gain experiences of having fluid identities as transnational learners. However, further study must investigate how students (re)shape their identities in a cross-system educational setting (Knight & Liu, 2019).

More generally, Mok and Ong (2014) suggested that research is necessary to explore their learning experiences. Later, Qin and Te (2016) further suggested that research about students' learning experiences is still limited. Recently, Knight and Liu (2019) reviewed 364 academic publications (e.g., research papers, book chapters, reports, and doctoral theses) in IMMP/TNHE published between 2000 to 2018 suggested the necessity of exploring students' experiences in TNHE. Therefore, it is imperative to embark upon detailed research to discover students' learning in those TNHEs. In this study, students' intercultural learning in TAPs (e.g., 2 + 2 model) will be the key research focus.

4 Significance of This Study

The significance of this study is based on the following identified research gaps in the related literature. First, several researchers (e.g., Qin & Te, 2016; T. Wang, 2016b) suggested that limited studies have explored Chinese students' learning experiences in such cooperative education modes. Although there are many different types of TNHE, such as 2 + 2 or other similar modes, it is not easy to research such programmes in their entirety because of the four-year time frame and different academic settings (Hou, 2011). While this book focuses on China-Australia TAPs, the quality of TNHE is a relevant worldwide issue and one demanding further research (Bannier, 2016; Knight & Liu, 2019; Zhao, 2017).

Second, based on the first research gap, it is worth noting that the TAP setting (e.g., 2 + 2 programme) usually allows students to physically move to another country in the last two years of undergraduate study. Therefore, intercultural

GLOBALISATION, INTERNATIONALISATION, AND TRANSNATIONAL HE 19

learning spontaneously happens in these students' cross-system and cross-national learning processes. However, any intercultural learning and related changes (e.g., identity) these students may gain in the particular TAP model is under-researched (Knight & Liu, 2019). Previous research has widely discussed students' intercultural adjustment issues from different perspectives and also developed various theoretical models to theorise this process (e.g., Gill, 2007; Gudykunst, 1988; Gu & Maley, 2008; Hou, 2011). However, limited studies have examined whether or not the TAP students experienced similar intercultural adjustment aligned with these previous findings. To fill this research gap, I propose to make sense of intercultural adjustments of Chinese students' lived learning experiences in the TAP setting.

Last but not least, limited research has been conducted from the perspective of an in-betweener (Milligan, 2016). As mentioned above, I was a former TAP student who could be considered an insider in this particular setting. At the same time, I am an outsider researcher who wanted to explore other students' experiences in such an educational setting. As I completed my programme approximately five years ago, I am not familiar with the current situation. Therefore, I wish to position myself between these different roles in this study to critically reflect on my own experiences, which could be regarded as a way of understanding students' learning journeys in current TAP settings. Distinct from other researchers investigating TNHE issues as outsiders concerning students' perspectives, I attempt to adopt a reflexive-narrative to analyse and reveal students' cross-system learning experiences via the methodological position of simultaneously being inside and outside in-betweener (Milligan, 2016).

While I am an in-betweener concerning my insider-outsider researcher positioning, the concept of in-betweener has also been a useful one, but used in a different way, to show how the experiences of some of the students in my research demonstrated how the affordances of the new technologies enabled them to live and study in an in-between space and to develop new identities. This is a different usage of in-betweener, which has come from the literature on hybridity and third spaces (e.g., Bhabha, 1994; Gill, 2007; Rizvi, 2005; Turner, 1967; Vertovec, 2001). Thus, the concept of in-betweener is used in these two different ways in this book.

5 Research Design: A Narrative Inquiry

According to de Wit (2020), more qualitative research in understanding internationalisation issues is needed. To respond to his suggestion, I conducted a narrative inquiry in this study. According to Connelly and Clandinin (2006, p. 375), narrative inquiry is "the study of experience as a story"; it is "first and foremost a way of thinking about the experience." Narratives are both one type of qualitative methodological inquiries and research data (Elliott, 2005). This study explores and understands Chinese students' intercultural transitioning learning experiences in TAPs, which motivates me to focus on their subjective views towards the cross-system journeys.

A purposive sampling approach was used to recruit research participants. Purposive sampling is usually utilised in a qualitative study. It focuses on recruiting particular participants who can provide data to answer the specific research questions that framed the study (Teddlie & Yu, 2007). The research subjects are Chinese students in China-Australia 2 + 2 TAPs. Therefore, selecting participants who have suitable backgrounds and related experiences would help answer the framing research questions. I recruited participants from three Australian universities through Chinese student associations and personal networks.

Three universities located in Queensland were selected as research sites. These universities are given a pseudonym respectively, including AU-1, AU-2, and AU-3. These three universities are all comprehensive institutes with both research and teaching focuses. Meanwhile, they have many international connections with different Chinese universities. Consequently, 20 students voluntarily participated in individual interviews (see demographic information in Table 1). To protect their privacy, I gave each participant a pseudonym for this study. Notably, these students were studying in four TAPs with different disciplines, including seven from business (TAP 1), three from information technology (TAP 2), five from engineering (TAP 3), and five from multimedia design (TAP 4). Specifically, TAP 1 and 2 are operated by AU-1 with two Chinese partner universities, and all ranked as "Double First Class" universities.[1] TAP 3 and 4 are operated by AU-2 and AU-3 respectively. Notably, Chinese partners with these Australian universities are all provincial institutes that mainly focus on teaching without strong research contexts.

Student participants were also in different learning stages, including ten in their first year in Australia and ten in the second year. Having participants who studied in different stages of their Australian periods will reflect multiple views and experiences about students' learning journeys. Due to the specific academic period setting of TAPs and many restrictions (e.g., gatekeeper permission, time and funding), I could not track a group of students when they were studying in China. These students came from different Chinese universities, so it was not easy to visit them in China. In the meantime, it was not easy to recruit a large number of students in the same transnational programme

GLOBALISATION, INTERNATIONALISATION, AND TRANSNATIONAL HE 21

TABLE 1　Student demographic information

Students	Gender	Years of study
TAP 1: Major in Business		
1. Qing	Female	1
2. Liang	Male	1
3. Gong	Male	1
4. Dong	Female	1
5. Yuner	Female	2
6. Rui	Male	2
7. Minze	Female	2
TAP 2: Major in Information Technology		
8. Guang	Male	1
9. Meng	Male	2
10. Xie	Male	2
TAP 3: Major in Engineering		
11. Zhuang	Male	1
12. Qiang	Male	1
13. Xiang	Male	1
14. Diao	Female	2
15. Biang	Female	2
TAP 4: Major in Multimedia Design		
16. Shuo	Male	1
17. Hao	Female	1
18. Xin	Female	2
19. Fei	Male	2
20. Dang	Female	2

in one university. Many factors led to this issue. For example, these students usually studied in Australia without a fixed class group as they experienced in China. Furthermore, they can flexibly select courses based on individual interests and plans in Australia, rather than always study almost the same subjects with other peers, which usually happen in the Chinese context. Therefore, I recruited students from different universities pursuing different courses to enhance the data diversity.

To explore and understand such experiences in a qualitative study, I could adopt different data collection methods. According to Creswell (2009), four methods in a qualitative study gather data, including observations, interviews, questionnaires, and documents and audio-visual materials. In this study, individual interviews were adopted as the primary approach to collect data as students' voices are the primary resources that reflect and illustrate their experiences. As Seidman (2006) emphasised, research interviews seek to understand "the lived experience of other people and the meaning they make of that experience" (p. 9). The essence of experience is social, based on "contact and communication" (Dewey, 1963, p. 38). In doing so, it is vital to communicate with students to understand their experiences. Notably, interviewing individuals allows researchers to "follow up unexpected results, or to validate other methods, or to go deeper into the motivation of respondents and their reason for responding as they do" (Cohen, Manion, & Morrison, 2007, p. 351). All interviews were conducted face-to-face at universities or participant's homes and audio recorded. Each interview was between 1 and 1.5 hours. After getting ethical approval from my former university in Australia, I conducted interviews from August to December 2016. From April to June 2017, I conducted follow-up interviews with these participants to further understand their experiences based on the first round of data collection analysis.

To analyse and understand students' stories in-depth, I adopted both a deductive and inductive approach. In the inductive analysis process, I adopted Braun and Clarke's (2006) thematic analysis approach to identify potential themes found in the data, which indicate the key issues emerging from their cross-system learning. In the deductive analysis, I analysed the interview data and reflectivity regarding my individual learning experiences and interaction with Gill's (2007) transformative learning framework. I inductively ("bottom-up") analysed the interview data first and then deductively ("top-down") interrogated the meanings of this data using others' theoretical lens (e.g., Gill's 2007 transformative learning framework). Through the mixed applications of inductive and deductive analyses, I critically analysed the interview data to seek potential answers to illustrate a comprehensive picture of participants' cross-system learning trajectories.

My position in the study also influenced my understanding and interpretation of the data. The researcher's role has been widely discussed as one of the methodological debates in qualitative research and precisely and in international education (e.g., Arthur, 2010; Dwyer & Buckle, 2009; Milligan, 2016; Savvides, Al-Youssef, Colin, & Garrido, 2016). Specifically, insider and outsider concepts are vital in these arguments (Hellawell, 2006; Merton, 1972; Milligan, 2016). For example, Dwyer and Buckle (2009) systematically reviewed and compared these different qualitative studies' roles. The concept of insider refers to the researcher who has similar (or prior) experiences or characteristics with research participants (Merton, 1972). For the outsider, it is apparent that the researcher usually does not share similar (or prior) experiences with participants (Merton, 1972).

However, researchers need to reflect on their different identities during their research (Hellawell, 2006). Various researchers (e.g., Arthur, 2010; Hellawell, 2006; Merton, 1972; Milligan, 2016) have argued that the traditional perspectives of insider and outsider should be reconsidered and re-theorised. Notably, Merton (1972) revealed that researchers could have fluid identities in a research project depending on different situations, which creates a series of statuses rather than merely one status as either an insider or an outsider. Such mixed positions are a set of identities (Merton, 1972). Along with Merton's debates, Hellawell (2006) and Arthur (2010) suggested that a researcher's position should not be considered as a single role. Based on these previous arguments, more recently, Milligan (2016) pinpointed a new concept of in-betweener to reconceptualise the role of researchers in cross-cultural and international research. As an in-betweener, a researcher "can make active attempts to place themselves in between" (Milligan, 2016, p. 248). Notably, an in-betweener could have an active agency in collecting and analysing data rather than ignore themselves as a critical player in a study.

According to these theoretical arguments about the researcher's role, I positioned myself as an in-betweener in the process of data collection and analysis. As a former TAP student, my background and experiences were interwoven with the participants' experiences, which became apparent when I communicated with them in research interviews. This process allowed me to explore their experiences and enabled me to reflect on my own narrative experiences. Therefore, my role was marked by fluid identities, such as a former TAP student, a Chinese citizen, and a researcher. Such a mixed role locates researchers between different perspectives (Dwyer & Buckle, 2009), which allows them to negotiate their own experiences with participants' stories.

In collecting and analysing data, I shifted my identities in the "space between" as an in-betweener in a cyclical and constant mode. For instance, when I interviewed different students and heard their stories, I usually recalled my own experiences as an insider who had a similar learning journey with participants. Meanwhile, I usually compared each student's experiences to explore in-depth meaning via comparisons as an outsider who was doing a research study about investigating others' learning experiences. In doing so, I adopted a reflexive approach in my data collection and analysis with a consistent and flexible role as an in-betweener. Notably, as an analytical approach, reflexivity has been widely adopted in intercultural educational research and qualitative studies (Blasco, 2012; Savvides et al., 2016). Reflexivity has various meanings; it is a process of self-analysis and self-awareness (Beck, 1994). However, the application of reflexivity in international education with transnational contexts is still under-researched (Savvides et al., 2016).

Researchers have critically defined reflexivity. For instance, Beck (1994) suggested that it assesses researchers' individual experiences in their contexts and situations via comparison with others. More specifically, according to Alvesson and Sköldberg (2000), it is about "interpreting one's interpretations, looking at one's perspectives from other perspectives, and turning a self-critical eye onto one's authority as interpreter and author" (p. VII). By adopting reflexivity, researchers can potentially enhance the communications between him/herself, collected data, and research participants in a flexible approach (Savvides et al., 2016). In this process, a researcher could critically shift between insider and outsider positions concerning the research as an in-betweener to continually negotiate with data, self-experiences, and participants' stories to critically interpret potential meanings of research results (Savvides et al., 2016). Therefore, it was vital for me to critically view my data and own experiences in this study from dynamic roles as an in-betweener, whose experiences could add further insights into the data analysis and illustrate the vivid pictures of students' learning in TAPs. To illustrate the vivid picture of students' learning journey and my own experiences in TAPs, I proposed to present the data in a narrative style. In this study, I used my research notes and diaries as additional resources to help me analyse the collected data.

Meanwhile, I critically analysed my learning journey from school to university, indicating various types of "intercultural adjustment" as an in-betweener. By reflecting on my experience, I compared the similarities and differences between my journey and participants' stories. My notes and diaries were written during the process of my data collection and analysis. When I collected data, I also took notes to help me recall relevant experiences.

Ethical considerations are important in all educational research projects. As mentioned earlier, this study aimed to investigate Chinese students' intercultural learning experiences in their TAPs. Thus, the ideal participants for this study are Chinese students in TAPs. The human is the most critical object in a qualitative study, so it is significant for qualitative researchers to consider ethical issues in each step of the research (e.g., data collection, analysis and finding presentation) (Creswell, 2007). Before starting the data collection, I applied for ethical permission, which the research committee approved of my former university in Australia.

Moreover, as with all qualitative research, it is crucial to establish the trustworthiness of the study. According to Lincoln and Guba (1985), four aspects should be considered to establish the trustworthiness of research: credibility, transferability, dependability, and confirmability. Many techniques can be used to effectively meet these criteria, such as triangulation and member-checking for credibility, thick descriptions for transferability, and confirmability (Lincoln & Guba, 1985). In this study, I adopted several approaches to ensure the trustworthiness of the research. For instance, I tried to establish credibility. As Lincoln and Guba (1985) advocated, credibility means the confidence that the qualitative researcher has towards their findings' veracity. To achieve this goal, I adopted triangulation and member-checking. To conduct this checking, I invited experienced PhD peers to help me examine the collected data. After completing analyst triangulation, I emailed both Chinese and English transcriptions and translations of interview data to each participant to let them check whether or not their meanings and experiences were presented accurately. As Creswell (2007) indicated, research participants play essential roles in verifying qualitative data because they are the data's co-producer. Furthermore, I also invited one of my advisors, who was firmly engaged in my research design and data analysis, to review my translated data and discuss the research issues. Through adopting the above strategies then, I completed the process of establishing the trustworthiness of this study.

6   Conclusion

This chapter has introduced the background and rationale for this research study. It has also documented the gaps in the cognate research, which the study reported here attempted to fill in a small but significant way. Furthermore, this study's significance was outlined, namely that the research moved beyond psychological adaptation and intercultural adjustment models of TNHE students and diasporas' experiences. The critical research aim, to explore how Chinese students experience learning in their TAPs, was proposed with three research questions.

As the research background indicated above, with the growing trend of globalisation (e.g., the "flows" of people, technology, economy, and many other elements) and internationalisation of HE, China began to actively engage in international communication and cooperation more broadly as part of a soft power strategy. Specifically, in response to these trends, increasing numbers of Chinese universities established various types of TAPs with foreign partners, aimed at enhancing the quality of education in China and improving Chinese HE's competitiveness in the world. With the development of TNHE in China, many Chinese students could select TAPs as their learning pathways in HE.

However, many existing studies related to TNHE and intercultural learning have not focused on investigating Chinese students' lived learning experiences in TAPs. As students are perhaps the major stakeholders in these programmes, their voices need to be heard to fully understand how these programs work and how effective they are. Understanding student experiences could contribute to improvements in the design and delivery of these programmes. Based on students' actual experiences, universities, educators, and policymakers might be able to reform TAPs further to fulfil students' demands better and achieve the purported goals of such programmes. The next chapter will provide critical analysis of theoretical concepts and frameworks related to intercultural learning and adjustment. The research reported throughout the book seeks to build on and move beyond these approaches.

This book has eight chapters. The first chapter outlines the background, significance of this study, and research design. In Chapter 2, vital theoretical concepts/frameworks and empirical literature are discussed, respectively. From Chapters 3 to 6, findings will be presented. Specifically, Chapter 3 will focus on illustrating students' motivations and initial concerns in their TAPs. Chapter 4 will map their trajectories of intercultural learning and adjustment, especially as experienced in the Australian context, and compare their experiences in China. In Chapter 5, key factors influencing students' intercultural learning and adjustment in TAPs will be analysed. My reflexive analysis as an "in-betweener" will be provided in Chapter 6 to compare my experiences with participants' journeys critically. In Chapter 7, I will systematically discuss the findings and attempt to propose a new conceptual lens to understand different types of "intercultural learning and adjustment" in a cross-cultural context and at a micro-political level. The last chapter, Chapter 8, will conclude this book by pointing out the limitations of the reported research and providing future research suggestions.

Note

1 "Double First Class" is an initiative proposed by the Chinese government in 2015, which aims to develop elite universities and faculties into world-class by the end of 2050. In 2017, the first list of universities was published. This plan replaces the previous 985–211 project. Practically, most 985–211 universities were selected into the new "Double First Class" initiative. When this research was conducted, universities were still ranked by the previous 985–211 plan. However, to follow the new initiative, the author used "Double First Class" in this book.

CHAPTER 2

Cross-System Transitions across Cultures, Spaces, and Places

This chapter introduces the key theoretical concepts and frameworks relevant to investigating Chinese students' experiences in TAPs. As students usually need to move from China to another context (in this case, Australia), they may encounter various issues during transitioning from one sociocultural context to another. This chapter first analyses the concept of culture. Then, a comparison of different cultural features in learning between the Chinese and western contexts is presented. At the end of the chapter, issues related to cross-system transitioning and intercultural learning from the perspectives of spaces and places are discussed.

1 Transitioning and Learning between Cultures

With the growing trend of internationalisation of HE across the world, students' international mobility potentially increases the communication and interaction between different educational systems and cultures. Many researchers have investigated topics related to international student mobility and their transitioning experiences to understand the influences of such mobility between different countries and sociocultural contexts (e.g., Brooks & Waters, 2011; Dai & Garcia, 2019; Gill, 2007; Gu, Schweisfurth, & Day, 2010; Heng, 2017, 2018a, 2018b, 2018c, 2019; Ward & Kennedy, 1993a; Yan, 2017). Along with the ongoing research in this field, several concepts were proposed to conceptualise and theorise issues of such cross-countries mobility, such as "intercultural," "cross-cultural," "adjustment," and "adaptation" (Zhu, 2016).

Practically, the uses of such terminology and concepts became complicated. These concepts have been adopted interchangeably when researchers explored students' learning and life experiences in a new context (Zhu, 2016). However, "they are not mutually exclusive," but "they embrace different focuses" (Gu et al., 2010, p. 10). Hence, it is essential to clarify these concepts because specific terms influence research directions and focus.

Culture is a complex concept and is difficult to define. Various researchers have defined it depending on their understandings (e.g., Hofstede, 1980;

© KONINKLIJKE BRILL NV, LEIDEN, 2022 | DOI: 10.1163/9789004505131_002

Kroeber & Parsons, 1958). For instance, Kroeber and Parsons (1958) identified that culture is "transmitted and created content and patterns of values, ideas, and other symbolic-meaningful systems as factors in the shaping of human behaviours and artefacts produced through behaviours" (p. 583). To refine the above definition, Hofstede (1980) further defined it as "the collective programming of the human mind that distinguishes the members of one human group from those of another. Culture, in this sense, is a system of collectively held values" (p. 24). These scholars provided abstract definitions of culture.

Considering the relationships between people, culture, and other elements of society (e.g., technology), Sarbaugh (1988) suggested that "when we say persons belong to a similar culture, we are saying they share certain psychological, sociological, and technological trappings" (p. 27). According to this explanation, it seems "culture provides tools, habits, and assumptions that pervasively influence human thought and behaviour, and the task of learning does not escape this influence" (Tweed & Lehman, 2002, p. 89). Concerning the connections between culture and learning, McLoughlin (1999) claimed that "culture and learning are interwoven and inseparable" (p. 232). Culture, technology and education have strong interconnections with each other, which manifest in particular ways in different cultural contexts. When learning happens in multiple contexts, culture and learning generate further multifaceted relationships.

Culture is the critical focus among the different usages when prefixes such as multi-, trans-, cross- and inter-are conjoined. The addition of the prefix modifies the meaning of culture. To systematically summarise and comparatively define several culture-related terms, Bennett (2010) proposed different concepts, such as multicultural, cross-cultural and intercultural. He further explained the meanings of each concept, which potentially reflect their differences. Specifically, multicultural refers to "a particular kind of situation, one in which there are two or more cultures represented" (Bennett, 2010, p. 420). This concept emphasises the existence of various cultures in one setting.

In contrast, cross-cultural indicates "a particular kind of contact among people" who come from different cultural backgrounds (Bennett, 2010, p. 420). This concept indicates a strong sense of connection between people from different cultural cohorts. Last but not least, he suggested that intercultural refers to "a particular kind of interaction or communication among people, one in which differences in cultures play a role in the creation of meaning" or "the kind of skills or competence necessary to deal with cross-cultural contact" (Bennett, 2010, p. 420). This definition shows that "intercultural" highlights people's sensemaking ability in different cultural contexts. The intercultural concept is echoed in the current study that tries to make sense of students' learning in a cross-system, cross-cultural settings.

With regard to learning from intercultural perspectives, many researchers have proposed and defined intercultural learning. For instance, Alred, Byram and Fleming's study indicates that intercultural learning refers to "both the experience of encountering two or more different cultures and the learning that occurs through such an encounter" (as cited in Gill, 2007, p. 168). Based on these definitions, it seems that students could experience intercultural learning during their TAPs, which allows them to move to a new context after having experiences in their own cultural and educational contexts. Their movements from home to host partner institutions potentially make learning intercultural. More specifically, Bennett (2009) suggested that intercultural learning refers to:

> Acquiring an increased awareness of subjective cultural context (worldview), including one's own, and developing greater ability to interact sensitively and competently across cultural contexts as both an immediate and long-term effect of exchange. (p. s2)

This definition suggests that students' understanding of the cultural differences and their capabilities to deal with these differences were also vital for them to experience intercultural learning. Students may have both inter and cross-cultural experiences when they study and live in a new context that may be multicultural. Students usually experience tensions generated from the different cultural contexts in this complicated learning process, especially when these two systems have dramatic differences (Engeström, 1987). Engaging in intercultural learning may help students to develop intercultural competence (Otten, 2003). As Deardorff (2006) defined, intercultural competence is "the ability to interact effectively and appropriately in intercultural situations, based on one's intercultural knowledge, skills and attitudes" (p. 247).

To experience intercultural learning and develop intercultural competence, students may have various attitudes and strategies. Many concepts have been adopted to describe the transferring processes of international students into a new context. According to Zhu (2016), a series of terms usually appears in multiple research studies (e.g., communication, education, and psychology) that investigate students' intercultural learning, such as adjustment and adaptation. However, being similar to intercultural and cross-cultural features, these concepts can be used interchangeably in practice, which also makes people confused. Therefore, it is necessary to make sense of the meanings of these terms.

Researchers (e.g., Anderson, 1994; Shaffer & Shoben, 1956; Young & Schartner, 2014) have widely discussed the meanings, similarities, and differences between adjustment and adaptation. For instance, Shaffer and Shoben (1956) suggested that *adjustment* refers to "the reduction or satisfaction of (short-term) drives, whereas *adaptation* is that which is valuable for (long-term) individual or racial survival" (as cited in Anderson, 1994, p. 300). Through comparing different authors' definitions, Zhu (2016) indicated a similar finding with Shaffer and Shoben (1956), who found that adjustment usually stresses short-term intercultural experiences. However, in contrast, adaptation usually refers to long-term changes from one to another cultural context. However, no matter the short- or long-term foci, all these concepts indicate "the achievement of a fit between the person and the environment" (Anderson, 1994, p. 300).

Compared to these time-based differences, Young and Schartner (2014) identified that adjustment is a process of change, which can be explored over time, while adaptation can be considered as a measurable outcome of this process. This study investigates Chinese students' intercultural transitioning and learning adjustment experiences in their TAPs with initial explorations of their adaptations from Chinese to Australian academic environments based on these differences and features of adjustment and adaptation.

2   Cultural Influences Shaping Chinese Learners

The setting of TAPs positions students in two learning contexts that may have specific educational, social, and cultural features. As mentioned above, in this study, the TAP setting is based on China and Australia. These countries (e.g., China and Australia) have dramatically different social and cultural features. The existing framework of national cultural differences proposed by Hofstede (1984) does not include mainland China as a research subject. However, Hong Kong and Taiwan, which share a similar cultural heritage with mainland China, are examined by comparison with many other countries (e.g., Australia, the UK and the USA).

Hofstede's (1984) national cultural framework suggests that culturally western countries have various multiple differences from culturally eastern countries. Specifically, five dimensions are proposed to theorise the differences, including power distance, uncertainty avoidance, collectivism vs individualism, femininity vs masculinity, and long-term versus short orientation. For instance, people from a collectivist culture (e.g., China) usually do not confront others but prefer to show their harmony and respect, indicating a sense of dependence (Tan, 2013). In learning, many students in a collectivist culture may be used to a teacher-dominated model. In contrast, students from individualist contexts usually prefer to directly present their minds and ideas, which show highly independent features. Through learning in this context, students may be used to a more flexible model.

Although these concepts help people recognise the different cultures among different countries theoretically, there are still some potential issues. For instance, it has been critically argued that such stereotyped classification is not suitable for examining individual cases, as each person could have different reflections about their contexts (Montgomery, 2010). To refine the framework, Hofstede, Hofstede, and Minkov (2010) further explained that although individuals have differences, national cultures' features might also always be reflected in their personalities and behaviours.

In the field of cross-cultural education, many researchers have critically investigated the characteristics and influences of Confucian Heritage Culture (CHC) on students' overseas study experiences (e.g., Biggs, 1998; Chan, 1999; Kember, 2016; Li, 2003a; Samuelowicz, 1987; Volet & Renshaw, 1996). The CHC is recognised as a dominant cultural ideology in Chinese society and even in other Asian countries (Tan, 2016). It is worth noting that CHC has been considered a label representing East-Asian cultures and nations, primarily when people use it to compare it with so-called Western culture (Biggs, 1998). Other researchers also support this understanding. For example, Park (2011) suggested that CHC is "described by education research communities as a group of Asian nation-states with their motherland and overseas diasporas who share Confucian values, which consistently reflect in their social behaviour and practices, including academic outcomes and learning approaches" (p. 381). In this study, CHC is considered a broader concept (or a well-accepted label) to represent the general Chinese culture rather than referring to the thoughts, ideas, and sayings exactly and initially as proposed by Confucius. Understanding the differences between cultural terminologies is not the primary focus of this book.

The CHC is intensely embedded in Chinese history and esteemed in different fields, especially in education (Mu, 2014b). Mainly, the educational ideology of CHC has profound influences on Chinese students' learning approaches (Li, 2003a). Along with the increasing interests of Chinese and other Asian students who are culturally influenced by CHC (Marginson, 2010; Tan, 2017a), arguments about their learning features also become necessary to critically understand intercultural adjustment issues, especially when they move various English-speaking countries. According to Otten (2003, p. 12), "giving students an intercultural dimension in education is one of the many goals that guides present internationalisation strategies."

According to Henze and Zhu (2012), many studies of Chinese students' cross-cultural education reveal the negative aspects of their learning approaches and attitudes. These negative features include rote and passive learning, repetition and memorisation, and surface learning (Henze & Zhu, 2012). For instance, Samuelowicz (1987) investigated international students' learning experiences at an Australian university and suggested that many CHC students relied excessively on their lecturers, who were considered the authority in the classroom. Many students avoided asking critical questions in learning processes and preferred to listen to instructions without enough active engagement in interactions. From Western scholars' perspective, Volet and Renshaw (1996, p. 205) summarised that:

> These students are described as having the following features: respectful of the lecturer's authority; diligent note-takers; preoccupied with fulfilling the expectations of the lecturers; uncritical of information presented in the textbook and by the lecturers; seldom asking questions or volunteering to contribute to tutorial discussions; and unaware of the conventions regarding acknowledging quotes and referencing sources and therefore unwittingly guilty of plagiarism.

Similarly, Chan (1999) found that CHC emphasises lecturers' authority and role in the classroom, where teachers should control teaching and learning. In doing so, many Chinese students influenced by CHC prefer to pay attention to receiving and listening to information rather than putting their ideas forward. Suppose a student argues with the lecturer about the content taught during the class. The challenge could be considered discourteous behaviour, which implies that the student may not respect the lecturer (Cheng, 2000).

To some extent, these cultural influences could limit the self-motivated learning desires of Chinese students, who are already accustomed to a teacher-centred environment, exam-directed and passively rote learning (Tu, 2001). Accordingly, these learning habits potentially mean Chinese students become quiet when studying in foreign university classrooms. The lecturers usually encourage and guide peers to discuss topics and learn with each other critically and creatively (Biggs, 1994). Therefore, many CHC students could feel challenged when adapting to Western learning settings (Chan, 1999).

By comparing teaching and learning differences between Chinese and British lecturers and students, Cortazzi and Jin (1996) proposed various sides' features. For instance, in the Chinese context, learning content comes from instruction and textbooks; learning means repeated practices and memorisation; students are usually listeners who usually rely on lecturers or other people. In contrast, in the UK context, individuals have more room to study as independent learners; lecturers and students have more communications and interactions. These features seem to generalise the significant differences in teaching and learning practices between China, a CHC dominant society, and Western countries.

CROSS-SYSTEM TRANSITIONS ACROSS CULTURES, SPACES, AND PLACES   33

Influenced by Hofstede's cultural frameworks, Cortazzi and Jin (1997) further developed the culture of learning theory from Chinese students' perspective. When students study in an environment that is shaped and influenced by different cultures, they "not only carry cultural behaviours and concepts into the classroom but that they also use the specific framework of their cultures to interpret and assess other people's words, actions and academic performances" (Cortazzi & Jin, 1997, p. 77). Their learning framework and theory could reflect a series of cultural differences in teaching and learning between China and the UK. Precisely, their summarised features of teaching and learning preferences in the Chinese context echo the findings of many other studies (e.g., Chan, 1999; Cheng, 2000; Tu, 2001) that explored the influences of CHC on shaping Chinese students' learning strategies.

When individuals move to countries with dramatically different features than their home country, cultural differences could partly influence their actions, thoughts, and views in the new context. In this case, individuals could face differences in the transition from their home country to another, which may generate several barriers that make intercultural learning a struggle to some extent. However, these findings do not signify that Chinese students' learning cannot be successful in culturally western contexts and that CHC always has passive influences on Chinese students' learning. For instance, although Cortazzi and Jin (1996) have summarised various teaching and learning differences between Chinese and British contexts, using this framework to label Chinese students' learning practices is not fully reliable. As T. Wang (2008) argued, it is necessary to acknowledge that Chinese students' learning in a cross-system context is far more complicated than what people usually understand by holding several stereotyped Chinese students' views, especially in the TNHE context. Various scholars have challenged these stereotyped views of CHC and Chinese students, which tend to essentialise Confucianism (e.g., Biggs, 1994, 1996a, 1996c; Cheng, 2000; Kember, 1996). As Grimshaw (2007, p. 308) argued, "When seeking to understand the behaviour and attitudes of Chinese students, we should not allow ourselves to be led by our own preconceptions but should instead pay attention to what those students actually do and say." Hence, it is necessary to reconsider Chinese students and their cultural background rather than holding stereotyped preconceived views (Grimshaw, 2007).

3   Critical Understandings of CHC and Chinese Students

With the increasing number of Chinese students who achieve outstanding academic outcomes in universities in Western countries, their learning performances make scholars critically reconsider their conventional understandings of Chinese students. Accordingly, many researchers identified the positive influences of CHC on Chinese students' cross-cultural learning experiences. Biggs (1994) started to challenge stereotyped views of Chinese students' learning approaches (e.g., surface learning, rote learning, and memorisation). He identified that Chinese students could achieve so-called deep learning via surface approaches, rote-learning, and memorisation (Biggs, 1996b).

Furthermore, some scholars suggest that CHC inspires students to learn with each other and study hard, emphasising the role of effort. For instance, Cheng (2000), Marton, Dall'Alba, and Tse (1996) suggested that CHC encourages students to learn with their peers and think in an in-depth way. Many CHC proverbs indicate that students need to study, communicate with other peers, and critically analyse knowledge (Cheng, 2000; Li, 2003a). For example, Confucius advocates "San Ren Xing, Bi You Wo Shi" (三人行, 必有我师), a well-known saying in CHC that means "among three persons, there must be one who can be my teacher" (Cheng, 2000, p. 440). This CHC philosophical idiom encourages people to have an open mind to learn from informal education and everyday life. Furthermore, Cheng (2000) demonstrated a well-known motto of CHC, "Qin Xue Hao Wen" (勤学好问), which means that students should study diligently and have a great curiosity to ask questions. According to these traditional sayings, it is evident that CHC does not ask students to follow whatever lecturers teach in the classroom without applying any critical thinking (Tan, 2017b). These sayings also imply that students need to communicate and learn with other people rather than merely study independently (Li, 2003a).

CHC encourages students to think deeply and understand and memorise course content during the study, which is indispensable for knowledge development (Tan, 2015). Marton et al. (1996) and Tweed and Lehman (2002) argued that even though CHC background students are in favour of rote passive learning and memorisation, it does not mean that they do not understand the content and think critically. Instead, "they see memorisation as a path to understanding and vice versa" (Tweed & Lehman, 2002, p. 93). For instance, through both in-depth critical investigating and memorising formulas, CHC background students often achieve better learning outcomes than Western students in some subjects, such as mathematics and science (Biggs, 1994; Mu, 2014a). These learning strategies have become a universal identifier of Chinese students (Biggs, 1994). Based on the literature review, it is apparent that CHC has complex influences on Chinese students' learning styles, attitudes and approaches.

Notably, several studies (e.g., Briguglio & Smith, 2012; Renshaw & Volet, 1995) have shown Chinese students' adaptation to Australian education settings and the changes in their study habits. By conducting a mixed-methods study, Renshaw and Volet (1995) examined the learning performance of a group of CHC students in one Australian university. They noted that these students preferred to consult with peers, explore the textbook's knowledge, and communicate with their lecturers in learning processes. Through intercultural learning, CHC background students adapted to the Australian learning setting and achieved their academic goals (Renshaw & Volet, 1995).

These findings partly challenge some stereotyped views that many CHC students always prefer to passively follow instructions in learning without enough actively personal explorations (e.g., Samuelowicz, 1987). Moreover, these findings also resonate with the results found by Cheng (2000), Marton et al. (1996), and Tweed and Lehman (2002). They concluded that: CHC advocates that learners adopt different approaches to study in international contexts, depending on learning requirements rather than mainly utilising traditional methods. They could adopt memorisation and repetition as valuable strategies to help them genuinely master knowledge (Kember, 2000).

Based on the constant arguments about CHC and Chinese students, more recently, Kember (2016) claimed that it is impossible to merely define, label and compare the features of Chinese teaching and learning strategies with so-called western perspectives by using thick, surface or other terms. This is because "there is never homogeneity within a cultural group" (Kember, 2016, p. 185). In contrast, it is important to make sense of different situations via different ever-changing perspectives because "there is a rich and complex tapestry of variations arising from cultural distinctions, individual variations and background circumstances" (Kember, 2016, p. 185).

Through discussing the features of CHC and debates about Chinese students, it is evident that culture and students' identities as learners, who may have different learning strategies in different contexts, could have significant connections. Several researchers (e.g., Hall, 1992; Jenkins, 2008; Lave & Wenger, 1991) have discussed the relationships between identity and culture, society and learning. For example, Hall (1990) suggested that identity is a fluid concept concurrent with the changes in history and culture that people experience in life, which means that there is no fixed identity. However, "perhaps instead of thinking of identity as an already accomplished fact, which the new cultural practices then represent, we should think, instead, of identity as a 'production,' which is never complete, always in process, and always constituted within, not outside, representation" (Hall, 1990, p. 222). Hence, it seems that when Chinese students move to/between different contexts, they may (re)shape their identities to position themselves to fit into a particular environment. As Jenkins (2008) argued, "identity is constructed in transactions at and across the boundary" (p. 44). Consequently, students' sense of belonging could also be (re)shaped depending on their experiences across different contexts. There is an idea here of identity as always becoming.

Meanwhile, as numerous studies indicated, many Chinese students can achieve outstanding outcomes in their study at foreign universities, as referenced above. This finding indicates that they may feel empowered in dealing with learning issues in a new context, which shows a positive sense of agency. However, it is worth noting that when people engage in cross-system settings, they may reflect different senses of agency towards social, cultural, and educational differences from the perspective of interconnections between mental intentions and physical performances (Park, 2018). Hence, developing a capacity for the agency is a complicated process that involves multiple social and cultural interactions (Bandura, 2006). This process needs people to realise "causal relations between environmental events, through understanding causation via action, and finally to recognising oneself as the agent of the actions" (Bandura, 2006, p. 169).

Through this critical review of different arguments about CHC and Chinese students' various features, it is apparent that students' learning is a complex process. The application of stereotypes here is not at all practical. Importantly, it is necessary for researchers to comprehensively consider individual situations and differences in different cultural and educational contexts (Gieve & Clark, 2005). According to Park (2011), "CHC has evolved, is evolving, and is always immersed in a context that is situated in space, time, history and social structures" (p. 382). Therefore, it is essential to critically examine the potential influences of CHC on students' transition between different spaces, contexts, and societies. Cultural features may become deeply immersed in students' understanding and constructions of their identity, agency, and belonging when facing potential cross-system differences. As mentioned above, in existing research, limited studies explored Chinese students' learning experiences by attempting to make sense of their journeys in TAPs. In doing so, this study proposes making sense of Chinese students' learning stories and perspectives in TAPs by considering the cultural features reflected in their lived experiences.

4 Encountering Shocks with Complicated Transitioning Trajectories

The influences of cultural differences on people can be considered as "shocks." Zhou, Jindal-Snape, Topping, and Todman (2008) have suggested that shock could be seen as "the stimulus for the acquisition of culture-specific skills that are required to engage in new social interactions" (p. 65). Shocks could be complex as different people could have diverse reactions to a new environment that they are not familiar with. When people move to a host sociocultural (unfamiliar) context that has more differences compared with their home (or familiar) cultures, they may encounter more difficulties in the process of transition (Searle & Ward, 1990; Ward & Kennedy, 1992, 1993a, 1993b).

As Gu (2016a) summarised, various shocks represent the complex issues in intercultural learning and adjustment, such as culture shock, learning shock, language shock, and role shock. Explicitly, culture shock could be considered as an overarching concept to conceptualise people's sense of unfamiliarity in cross-system or cultural transitions. Other kinds of shock seem to be different subsets of reflections on the culture shock that provides a space for individuals to experience specific differences in a cross-cultural setting (Zhou et al., 2008).

Culture shock is a well-documented concept to explain the cross-cultural issues in the transition from a familiar context to another unfamiliar one. Extensive research related to culture shock has been conducted for many decades (Adler, 1975; Furnham & Bochner, 1986; Gullahorn & Gullahorn, 1963; Lysgaand, 1955; Oberg, 1960; Smalley, 1963; Ward, Bochner, & Furnham, 2001; Winkelman, 1994). Various researchers have proposed definitions of cultural shock. According to Oberg (1960), culture shock is a sense "precipitated by the anxiety that results from losing all our familiar signs and symbols of social intercourse" (p. 142). Similarly, Schumann (1986) advocated that it can be considered as "anxiety resulting from the disorientation encountered upon entering a new culture" (p. 383). According to these definitions, it is apparent that culture shock may lead to a struggling sense of intercultural adjustment. To understand the process of experiencing intercultural adjustment under the influence of culture shock, various researchers have proposed particular conceptual frameworks.

In the early stage, research studies have been conducted mainly from the medical perspective of mental health. For instance, Lysgaand (1955) proposed the famous U-curve to illustrate the new context's adjustment process. The U-curve theory suggests that people could initially feel it is easy to adjust to the new context. However, they usually notice the barriers in adjustment, making them struggle; with the constant changes, finally, people could integrate into the new context successfully.

Based on the U-curve theory, Oberg (1960) developed a further model to conceptualise intercultural adjustment processes. He suggests four stages that people experience in their adjustment process to a new context, including the honeymoon, culture shock, recovery, and adjustment. Based on the U-model and culture shock concept, Gullahorn and Gullahorn (1963) developed a W-curve to extend the U-model. The W-curve suggested five stages of adjustment to a new context, which are "Honeymoon," "Culture Shock," "Initial Adjustment," "Mental Isolation," and "Acceptance and Integration." Specifically, the honeymoon refers to people's sense of excitement when they move to a new place. Culture shock means the stress people may have when facing different social, cultural, and educational contexts. The initial adjustment suggests that people start to develop their confidence to adjust to the new context and try to overcome cross-system barriers in their transitions. Mental isolation refers to a lack of a sense of belonging, making people recall their previous life in their home countries. In this stage, the new context's values and customs are still not integrated into their minds. Finally, after staying in a new context for a long time, people may adjust to the new context, which is the last stage of the W-model as acceptance, integration and connectedness.

Adler (1975) critically proposed five stages of transnational adjustment to refine these existing models, including contact, disintegration, reintegration, autonomy, and independence. These frameworks initially conceptualise the process of intercultural adjustment from examining a person's mental development. Although they established fundamental knowledge of understanding the process of intercultural adjustment, they are somehow limited in identifying only specific examples of shocks in learning processes.

Influenced by these early culture shock theories, researchers started to investigate more particular types of shock in the process of intercultural adjustment and adaptation. For instance, Gu (2009) identified that many students might experience a series of learning shocks in the process of intercultural adjustment. According to Gu (2009), learning shock means that when students start learning in an unfamiliar learning context, they might have difficulties and stressful feelings dealing with learning issues. Their difficulties could lead to long-term non-adaptation to the new context, which could cause further unpleasantness in respect of their life and study if they cannot adapt to the new environment (Gu, 2009). The cause of learning shock could be due to both internal and external factors, such as unfamiliarity with the new environment, different teaching and learning strategies, language barriers, and individuals' personality (Cushner & Karim, 2004; Schumann, 1986; Yan, 2017).

To deal with different shocks, students could adopt different approaches, have various attitudes towards cross-system differences, and achieve different results through experiencing intercultural adjustment processes. Their changes could become far more complicated than they were in their home contexts. Thus, it is necessary to examine changes in students' identity when they study in multiple cultural and educational contexts (Gieve & Clark, 2005). Furthermore, their agency indicating capabilities and preferences to deal with cross-system differences and their sense of belonging is significant to make sense of their intercultural learning and adjustment (Gu, 2016b).

CROSS-SYSTEM TRANSITIONS ACROSS CULTURES, SPACES, AND PLACES   39

Research has widely discussed the trajectory of intercultural adjustment. As mentioned above, many theoretical models (e.g., the U-shape and the W-shape) have been proposed to conceptualise adjustment issues. The process of intercultural adjustment is primarily to develop intercultural competence. It is "an adaptive capacity based on an inclusive and integrative worldview that allows participants to effectively accommodate the demands of living in a host culture" (Taylor, 1994a, p. 154).

In a cross-cultural learning context, Kuh and Love (2000) argued that when students move to a cultural context that differed from their previous environment, they will encounter various challenges to adjust to the new context. Influenced by previous models, several researchers (e.g., Bennett, 1986; Berry, 1997; Gill, 2007; Heng, 2018c; Kim, 1988, 2001; Kim & Ruben, 1988; Kuh & Love, 2000; Mezirow, 1991; Searle & Ward, 1990; Taylor, 1994b; Yoshikawa, 1988) further developed their theories and frameworks to understand the trajectory of fostering intercultural competency from multiple perspectives, which is known as intercultural adjustment or transformation (Kim & Ruben, 1988; Taylor, 1994a). In adjusting to the new context, students usually experience culture shock or other kinds of barriers, as previously mentioned.

Notably, most of these researchers (e.g., Bennett, 1986; Gill, 2007; Kim, 1988; Kim & Ruben, 1988; Yoshikawa, 1988) have argued that students can actively deal with shocks in the process of intercultural adjustment and finally develop their positive intercultural competence — an outcome of intercultural learning. Intercultural competence is "a long-term change of a person's knowledge (cognition), attitudes (emotions), and skills (behaviour) to enable positive and effective interaction with members of other cultures both abroad and at home" (Otten, 2003, p. 15).

Specifically, to theoretically conceptualise this process, Kim (1988, p. 308) proposed a three-fold processes framework, which is well-known as "stress-adaptation-growth." In her explanation, "stress, as such, is a manifestation of the generic process that occurs whenever the capabilities of the individual are not adequate to the demands of the environment" (Kim, 2001, p. 55). Stress usually exists in the initial stage of entering into a new context. Facing stress, students start to seek different approaches to help them overcome problems and then fit into the new context. Finally, students become familiar with the new context and then achieve development, which is a positive direction or result of intercultural adjustment and transformation.

Notably, Kim (1988) advocated that this adjustment process is dynamic and circular. The stress-adaptation-development is a spiral cycle rather than a linear and one-way process. This is because "looking backwards to the original culture" is an unavoidable process in intercultural learning and adjustment (Kim, 2001, p. 56). Importantly, many people measure the new context via their old lens. In this case, various tensions and judgments have emerged to conduct self-reflexivity of experiencing different cultural contexts.

Through this spiral cycle, newcomers might engage in the new context with complex internal cognition, as some features of the new culture potentially become incorporated into their mind. Finally, they could have "a subtle growth" as they may create ways to deal with cross-system barriers (Kim, 2001, p. 56). After overcoming stress and adapting to the specific situation, newcomers may face different stress types and then restart this process (Kim, 2001). Although the stress-adaptation-growth model has been widely adopted to examine intercultural/cross-cultural adaptation issues, researchers further developed this framework to enhance the existing model to explore Chinese students' intercultural adjustment processes.

Influenced by several researchers' intercultural adjustment models as mentioned above (e.g., Adler, 1975; Kim, 1988; Oberg, 1960), Gill (2007) proposed a transformative framework to theorise the cyclic development of Chinese students' intercultural learning and adjustment based on interviewing several Chinese students in the UK context. This framework has three major dimensions, namely "intercultural adaptation, developing intercultural competence, and the reconstruction of self-identity, all leading to personal growth" (Gill, 2007, p. 171).

Similar to Kim's (1988, 2001) stress-adaptation-growth model, this framework also suggests that students start with various stresses when they learn in an unfamiliar context that may be dramatically different from their original environment. To avoid disequilibrium, students might actively engage in and interact with the new context by adopting multiple strategies (e.g., establishing new networks). During this process, they develop intercultural competence and change their thinking, values, and attitudes. They experience transformations such as changes in their perspectives, indicating how they critically consider the relationships between individual roles and the context (Mezirow, 2000).

Consequently, their identity as students who experience intercultural learning could be reshaped and different from their old identities (Gill, 2007). Considering the change of identity, Yoshikawa (1988) specifically argued that people could actively move between home and host countries with different senses of identity, which could be in-betweenness or liminality among different contexts. In this situation, they may gain various features from both contexts during their intercultural adjustment and learning.

To theorise these changes, Gill (2007) suggested that intercultural adaptation is parallel with intercultural learning. Students' experiences are about their changes and perspective transformation. They make sense of their own vibrant and cyclical trajectory of adjustment to the new context that has significant influences on shaping students' changes. As Gill (2007) further suggested, students' experiences of interactions with the new context and their reflections potentially create an intercultural space for them to accommodate different cultural, social, and educational factors dynamically. Notably, when people engage in the process of adjustment to a new context, their changes could be categorised into two types: sociocultural or psychological adjustment (Searle & Ward, 1990). The former means social skills that people develop to help them fit into a new context. The latter refers to their psychological satisfaction or well-being in a new culture. These two types of adjustment are somehow interrelated but have different foci, as the above definitions indicated.

More recently, based on the investigations of Chinese international students' experiences in the USA, Heng (2018a, 2018b, 2018c, 2019) has developed a "hybrid sociocultural framework" by combining different theoretical concepts and psychological views, anthropological and postmodern perspectives. Several tenets were proposed to understand Chinese students' experiences in a new context. For instance, it is essential to understand the relationships between "human behaviour, learning and development" and "their sociocultural context," conceptualised as the first tenet. For the second tenet, Heng (2018c, p. 1144) suggests that "humans engage in different sociocultural contexts and that their engagement, values, and attitudes change with context and time – highlights the multi-dimensionality of human experience when people cross contextual boundaries." The third tenet indicates that people are agents "who act upon their own choices – asserts that humans are continually adapting or challenging values and beliefs" (Heng, 2018c, p. 1144). In general, this framework recognises Chinese international students' experiences are multi-faceted, which is "vis-à-vis their complex and changing sociocultural contexts and encourages some of us to withhold our ethnocentric judgments of them" (Heng, 2018c, p. 1144). In the process of dealing with cross-system differences, they might develop a sense of fluidity with multiple identities along with shaping agentic potential.

Notably, the trajectory of adjustment is not linear; in contrast, it is a process of "uneven ascent" with back-and-forth negotiations with different types of struggles, which is illustrated as a "zig-zag" line (Heng, 2018c). Through this process, many students will have positive development in the intercultural learning journey through dealing with barriers and struggles. However, Heng further suggests that more than one type of change happens: horizontal or a downward zig-zag line could reflect different trajectories.

In the process of cross-system movement, many students "experience a sense of boundary or 'otherness' when confronted with conflicting values and beliefs" (Gu & Maley, 2008, p. 225). As Bhabha (1994) indicated, the boundary is a site that allows different cultures to be interactive. He further suggested that sociocultural interactions are complex. Importantly, different cultures keep negotiating with each other, which creates a space of cultural hybridity (Bhabha, 1994). According to several studies related to cross-system adjustment (e.g., Gao, 2006; Gu & Maley, 2008; Gu et al., 2010; Heng, 2017, 2018a, 2018b, 2018c, 2019; Ward & Kennedy, 1993a; Yan, 2017; Zhu, 2016), Chinese students usually experienced a series of difficulties and shocks with culture, learning, society, and language when they moved and studied in a new context. The elements together created these shocks in the transition between different contexts. Students' dynamic changes in the intercultural learning process also reflect how they approached adjustment issues in TAPs that enable them to experience various changes regarding agency, identity, and belonging.

To date, very few studies have adopted the framework of stress-adaptation-growth to illustrate the trajectory of Chinese students' intercultural learning and adjustments, especially in TAPs. The dominant studies focus on students who usually complete four years of undergraduate study in China and then study overseas for other advanced degrees (e.g., Masters or PhD). Although they experience intercultural learning and adjustment, the contexts and mode of going overseas are different from the TAP setting that is officially run jointly by Chinese and foreign university partners.

The aims of designing and offering such TAPs are multiple, for example, offering different educational experiences for students, increasing the internationalisation of Chinese universities, and enhancing HE's quality in China via engaging in cooperation with foreign partners (Mok & Han, 2017; Yang, 2014). When students study in TAPs, they usually need to physically move from one (e.g., the Chinese) context to another (e.g., the Australian) to complete the whole programme. In this mode, students need to engage with the Chinese educational system and the Australian one. In such a learning process, they may also need to adjust to each context through their explorations and understandings of educational, cultural, and social features in the two different systems. Although the goal of such TAPs (e.g., the 2 + 2 mode) is not solely for students to experience intercultural adjustment during their study, students will most likely face such adjustment issues in their transitions from the home to the host contexts. What such intercultural learning and adjustment look like in TAPs is under-researched. Thus, this study proposed exploring Chinese students' learning experiences from the perspective of transitioning and intercultural adjustment in TAP rather than investigate other aspects.

5 Moving across Different Spaces and Places as Diaspora

As Gill (2007) indicated, mobile international students have an intercultural space to engage in cross-system learning and adjustment. This space is a

CROSS-SYSTEM TRANSITIONS ACROSS CULTURES, SPACES, AND PLACES 43

mediation of experiencing intercultural adjustment and a bridge to learning across different contexts. Along with understanding students' intercultural learning experiences and adjustment, it is also essential to explore in what kind of context they engage in potential changes during their cross-system learning processes.

Globalisation motivates constant physical and virtual movements of people, culture, education, information and many other social elements worldwide (Appadurai, 1996). According to Rizvi, Louie, and Evans (2016), long-stay international students can be seen as an essential component of what they refer to as diaspora, which initially comes from the Greek as a concept to describe people who leave their home country and settle in a new land. Moreover, the diaspora initially describes groups of people who leave their homes due to different catastrophic incidents or situations (Brubaker, 2005). Later, the concept has been extended to broadly define "a system of personal networks, shared culture and language, and an imaginary relationship to the homeland" (Kapur as cited in R. Yang & Welch, 2010, p. 594). With regard to TAP students, as they do need to move to another country to complete their study, they could be a specific group of the diaspora because their learning activities happen across two settings under several so-called institutional collaborations, which enables them to have constant connections between home and host contexts. The concept of diaspora highlights the importance of continuing influences of students' homeland on their lives during the overseas study and the continuing interactions between home and host countries (R. Yang & Welch, 2010). Such interactions could be seen as a state of in-betweenness, which means that people could be "neither here nor there; they are betwixt and between the positions assigned and arrayed by law, custom, convention, and ceremonial" (Turner, 1969, p. 359).

The ongoing wave of globalisation and internationalisation of HE makes learning space much more complex across different cultures, societies, and educational systems. Notably, several researchers (e.g., Bhabha, 1994; Feng, 2009; Soja, 1996) from the postcolonial perspective propose the concept of "third space" to conceptualise the complexity of space changes across culture, societies, and countries. Bhabha's (1994) concept of third space has been widely adopted to analyse cross-culture related studies. Bhabha (1994) argued that a third space makes the nation's concept become blurred, and people could move physically and psychologically between their own and host cultural contexts, which is also considered an in-between space. In such a space, people do not try to "seek consensus, but rather one in which to open up possibilities" (Kelly, 2016, p. 69). In doing so, cultural hybridity is progressively developed. People could experience "something different, something new and unrecognisable, a new area of negotiation of meaning and representation" (Rutherford,

1990, p. 211). Consequently, people could immerse in an in-between status with dynamic and multiple perspectives towards sociocultural differences (Bhabha, 1994).

Based on Bhabha's concept of third space, Feng (2009) investigated several Chinese students' learning experiences in the UK context. By adopting interview and observation for data collection, Feng (2009) found that Chinese students' classroom performance and lecturers' teaching indicated differences that challenged some stereotyped views of the learning and teaching features between different countries with specific cultural and social traditions. Feng (2009, p. 75) suggested that there is a third space that:

> ... not only challenges traditional views of the elusive notion of culture but more importantly problematises our 'normal,' polarised or binary perceptions of the relationships between, for example, the West and the East, intercultural and intercultural communication, education and training, and deep learning and surface learning ...

According to this argument, "the concept of third space is particularly insightful when we study the experience of internationally mobile students" with "its strong proposition to contest binary or polar opposites such as Confucian and Socratic cultures of learning" (Feng, 2009, p. 87). The different potential cultures of learning reflect the cultural differences between national contexts (Planel, 2016). Therefore, it is significant for researchers to continually consider and negotiate differences of learning from a fluid position of insider and outsider of the research context with flexible views towards different social, cultural, and education contexts (McNess, Arthur, & Crossley, 2016; Planel, 2016). This is because the essential elements in education (e.g., lecturers, students, learning, and assessment) may have different meanings in different educational contexts (Planel, 2016). In this case, the concept of third space becomes vital to construct new views about intercultural transitioning and adjustment.

The third space concept could be abstract "new spaces and places" (Leander, Phillips, & Taylor, 2010, p. 329) for people to see the essence of the visible "appearance of solidity" (Lefebvre, 1991, p. 92). "The third space is neither inside nor outside but pivots across the differences between being outside and being inside" (McNess et al., 2016, p. 27). Students may live between the new and old contexts (McNess et al., 2016). For most international students, the transitioning from the homeland to other countries can be "a movement from a known place into something at first unknown—a space—which with time itself becomes known as a place" (Burnapp, 2006, p. 83). Although the third space has been theoretically used to describe something different and

CROSS-SYSTEM TRANSITIONS ACROSS CULTURES, SPACES, AND PLACES   45

abstract, it is essential to discuss these and related concepts' original conceptualisations, which could reveal the original root of third or in-between space.

The concepts of space and place have been widely discussed from both empirical and theoretical perspectives in and across various academic fields, such as philosophy (Casey, 1997; Deleuze & Guattari, 1987), sociology (e.g., Amin, 2002; Brennan, 2006; Gieryn, 2000; Latour, 2005; Rizvi, 2000, 2005; Rizvi & Lingard, 2010), culture-related studies (e.g., Bhabha, 1994; Feng, 2009; Gill, 2007; Rutherford, 1990), learning perspectives (e.g., Ellis & Goodyear, 2016; Kolb & Kolb, 2005; Matthews, Andrews, & Adams, 2011; Savin-Baden, McFarland, & Savin-Baden, 2008; Temple, 2008), and geographical studies (e.g., Leung & Waters, 2013; Relph, 1976; Tuan, 1977). For instance, Tuan (1977, p. 6) attempted to clarify these two concepts:

> The ideas 'space' and 'place' require each other for definition. From the security and stability of place we are aware of the openness, freedom and threat of space, and vice versa. Furthermore, if we think of space as that which allows movement, then the place is a pause; each pause in movement makes it possible for a location to be transformed into place.

As this explanation indicates, space and place sit in a tight relationship with each other. According to Lukermann (as cited in Relph, 1976), the notion of place is a complex concept that integrates natural and cultural features of specific locations. Different places are connected by the movement of different social subjects (e.g., people and goods). The movement of different objects from one place to another potentially generates the flow of ideology, materials and many other elements. Such movements might create various spaces that allow people to engage in constant negotiations with different cultural, social, and educational contexts.

The concept of space is much more abstract than that of place. Relph (1976) indicated that "space is amorphous and intangible and not an entity that can be directly described and analysed" (p. 8). Tuan (1977) explained the relationship between place and space. In everyday life, people interact with the physically real places they stay in and develop their understanding of the places in their minds, which generate abstractly intangible space for themselves (Tuan, 1977). In doing so, people may integrate their views, ideas, and feelings with the abstract space's construction process (Tuan, 1977).

Similarly, according to Brennan (2006), it seems that the concept of place is more "solid" or "fixed" than that of space, which is more "abstract." As Brennan (2006) argued, space could be a virtual room that allows different cultures, histories, and activities to interact without boundaries. Brennan (2006, p. 136) suggested that "space is more abstract and ubiquitous: it connotes capital, history, and activity, and gestures towards the meaninglessness of distance in a world of instantaneous communication and virtuality." In contrast, the place is more about one's experiences on or at a particular site that has certain boundaries, which connotes "the kernel or centre of one's memory and experience-a dwelling, a familiar park or city streets, one's family or community" (Brennan, 2006, p. 136). Although these researchers make several distinctions between space and place, some philosophers (e.g., Casey, 1997; Deleuze & Guattari, 1987) provided their specific interpretations about the two concepts' relationships from a philosophical perspective.

In *The Fate of Place*, Casey (1997) comparatively analysed the different views of place and space proposed by several philosophers, for example, Deleuze and Guattari (1987). They critically illustrated the interconnections of the above two concepts in their monumental work, *A Thousand Plateaus*. In chapter 12 (Treatise on Nomadology: The War Machine) of their book, Deleuze and Guattari interpreted place and space by using the relationships between royal king and nomad and then different types of science (e.g., the comparison between mathematics/physics and metallurgy/hydraulics) as metaphors. According to Casey (1997), mathematics/physics is a form of "royal sciences" that are foundational for other related fields (e.g., metallurgy/hydraulics) and universal across the world. In contrast, for example, metallurgy/hydraulics are "nomad sciences," which have the flexibility and follow specific fixed rules from royal sciences. For instance, engineers could use hydraulics knowledge to design sewer systems for city A and city B. In practice, they usually need to consider using specific knowledge from nomad science to design a specific system for these different cities with unique geographical features. Although they may propose different plans depending on their nomad knowledge, they may also need to use the same math knowledge to calculate the length of a pipeline to ensure that it fits into a proposed installation position. As this example indicates, nomad science is usually applied in different places with different approaches, and precise calculation is complicated (Deleuze & Guattari, 1987).

In contrast, royal science (e.g., math) is universal and measurable but abstract without specific meanings if it is not linked with nomad knowledge to some extent (Deleuze & Guattari, 1987). It is worth noting that such nomad and royal science have suitable and meaningful applications when used in certain situations and places (Casey, 1997). Otherwise, they may lose practical value, and one could not work without the other's support. This example might indicate that a place is essential for such nomad knowledge to become something real, needing many interactions or cooperation with abstract royal sciences at the same time (Deleuze & Guattari, 1987; Casey, 1997).

Within a place, each science usually operates in a "smooth" and "striated" space, depending on its features (Deleuze & Guattari, 1987). Casey (1997) provided a detailed explanation of the differences between these two spaces. In a smooth space, most elements are flexible and heterogeneous with various qualitative features. The movement of elements in this space is also multiple without particularly fixed pathways. According to Casey (1997, p. 304), "smooth space provides room for vagabondage, for wandering and drifting between regions instead of moving straight ahead between fixed points." Therefore, "one must continually find one's way by determining the appropriate direction" (Casey, 1997, p. 306). However, in striated space, elements usually move from one point to another by following "linear striation by precise paths" (Casey, 1997, p. 303). When social or natural elements move across different places, they follow certain "local operations." For example, geometrical routes and proposed directions (in a striated space) have unexpected or unpredictable changes in movements, depending on different circumstances (in a smooth space). Hence, movement occurs in a local place but with dynamic and infinite changes between different spaces with no clear boundaries. In this process, "local operations of reply must be oriented by the discovery (and often the continual rediscovery of direction); otherwise, these operations would be in vain" (Casey, 1997, p. 306). To discover something new, nomads must experience a local place by "legwork" to explore that context. In this process, according to Casey (1997), such movement or exploration continually shifts between smooth and striated spaces across different places. Practically, these spaces are "not entirely independent of one another" (Casey, 1997, p. 308) and have many interactions with each other. As Deleuze and Guattari (1987, p. 474) suggested, "smooth space is constantly being translated, transversed into a striated space; striated space is constantly being reversed, returned to a smooth space." In short, these two spaces usually mix in reality (Deleuze & Guattari, 1987). Human activities always happen between these spaces, but also in certain local places. Different features of spaces and places have indefinite influences on human activities as well. In shifting between different spaces and places, people are on the way of becoming, which means that people consistently engage in different transformation types via cross-spaces/places movement (Deleuze, 1994, 2006; Deleuze & Guattari, 1987). According to these explanations of the concepts of place and space, it is apparent that they are integrated but also have their particular focuses.

Under the trend of globalisation and enhanced computational capacities, time, space, and place have been compressed (Harvey, 1999; Rizvi & Lingard, 2010). This trend motivates people to have an increasing awareness that the world seems to have become one place, as many aspects seem to be connected interactively and labelled by the concepts of "global" or "world," for example, global higher education or world economy (Rizvi & Lingard, 2010).

According to the above discussion about space and place, we might think that globalisation makes human activities and movements much more complex, which are also always accompanied by exploring different smooth and striated spaces across global places. As Amin (2002, p. 387) suggested, the increasing trend of globalisation in the contemporary world "might be interpreted as a spatial process elevating the tension between territorial relationships and transterritorial development." In this process, human and social elements are all positioned in a global networked space, along with complex changes through cross-system and cross-territory mobility and connections (Amin, 2002). In this networked space, everything becomes interdependent. Meanwhile, everything is mixed and connected through either visible or hidden ways, which possibly combine "multiple spatialities of organisation and praxis as action and belonging at a distance" (Amin, 2002, p. 395). Notably, to some extent, we might also be able to argue that the new ICTs help people overcome this space/place distinction, at least to some extent, while acknowledging that face-to-face encounters remain different from technologically mediated ones. This is Amin's central point that under the conditions of globalisation and with powerful computers, the distinctions between space and place have been somewhat elided; as well, each place is now inextricably linked with other places through networked space. Through such a mixture and combination of different elements under the trend of globalisation and the development of ICTs, place and space are also restructured continuously. Human activities occur in certain local places and different spatial contexts with more complicated situations, mainly through substantial computational capacities (Amin, 2002). The computational enables individuals situated in a specific place to occupy an in-between space simultaneously, which is in-between their current place and home. In short, an "in-between transnational space" emerges (Rizvi, 2005, p. 177).

Based on the differences between the place and space considered above, it is essential to discuss the potential distinctions between the two adjectives: third and in-between, mainly when used to describe a new space. According to Bhabha (1994), the third space could be seen as a unique and abstract concept to describe a unique context (e.g., C) that is independent of two other cultural and social systems (e.g., A and B). In the third space (C), people may develop their particular understanding or ideology, which leads to changes of identity as a third party different from but at the same time being connected with other systems (A and B). As a result, the third space may become highly independent. In contrast, the concept of in-between may emphasise the indeterminate

CROSS-SYSTEM TRANSITIONS ACROSS CULTURES, SPACES, AND PLACES   49

position between two systems (A and B). In this in-between space, people continuously shift between A and B to find a suitable room for them to engage in cross-system transitioning, communication and interaction, rather than remaining independent from these systems. In this case, they may not belong to A or B but instead belong to the "transitioning in-between space."

Furthermore, they may also not establish something entirely new as a third space (C) in their movement across different systems. In the process of transitioning in-between, people move between different places. Meanwhile, they may also need to negotiate with different striated spaces and then have their own smooth space, which allows them to flexibly deal with cross-system differences as nomads, in Deleuze and Guattari's (1987) terms. In this process, different places, smooth and striated spaces are connected and combined with people's constant (re)negotiations and transitions, which see these places and spaces as also being (re)shaped continuously (Deleuze & Guattari, 1987).

According to the above discussion about theoretical differences and connections between space and places, Chinese students studying in the TAP setting need to physically transition from China to Australia. However, at the same time, they remain connected across places through networked space. Thus, the TAP setting objectively positions students in different places than other more usual learning pathways that only need students to study in one country without such articulated collaboration. However, students may establish their individual spaces in the process of experiencing the change of places. Furthermore, they may face various issues in the transition and have different strategies to deal with places' change. In this process, students may (re)shape their identity, agency, and belonging as a diaspora in the movement between different places and construct individual spaces using ICTs. Such spaces might reflect their reactions to changes in places. These matters are the focus of this book.

Considering the learning space in higher education, researchers and educators have become an essential aspect to understand. It significantly influenced students' learning experiences and their university life engagements (Matthews et al., 2011). Concerning the meaning of learning space, Savin-Baden et al. (2008) suggested that "there are diverse forms of spaces within the life and life world of the academic where opportunities to reflect and critique their unique learning position occur" (p. 221). In a learning space, students usually realise that their understandings of learning, teaching, and identity "are being challenged" and "they have to decide on their responses to such challenges" (Savin-Baden et al., 2008, p. 221). This statement probably echoes the reality that learning space usually creates a sophisticated platform for students to interact with different tasks, shaping their learning styles in particular educational settings (Kolb & Kolb, 2005). Various factors likely influence students' learning experiences in a learning space, such as teaching strategies, assessment, and curriculum design (Kolb & Kolb, 2005).

Research related to the construction of learning space through multiple elements in a university context has become a required field in higher education, yet is still under-researched (Ellis & Goodyear, 2016; Temple, 2008). Specifically, exploring the potential connections between the learning space and students' learning experiences, activities, and outcomes via qualitative interviews with different stakeholders (e.g., students and teacher) are important research directions in contemporary HE (Ellis & Goodyear, 2016). Understanding how these stakeholders make sense of their learning and teaching activities is significant for reflecting the quality of specific constructed learning spaces and programmes (Ellis & Goodyear, 2016).

Ellis and Goodyear (2016) proposed a rationale to explain why attention should be paid to the learning space. For instance, they argued that students' mobility results in universities becoming diverse. Students also have higher education expectations, which means that the university context becomes much more complicated than before. Furthermore, with the rapid development and application of digital technologies, learning approaches have compressed time and space (Harvey, 1999). By adopting multiple technological tools, students can break the boundaries of learning and mix the physical place and virtual space depending on the individual requirements that they encounter.

Many researchers have investigated students' use of different digital technologies in different contexts (e.g., Corrin, Bennett, & Lockyer, 2010; Henderson, Selwyn, Finger, & Aston, 2015; Jones & Shao, 2011; Shao, 2012). For instance, Corrin et al. (2010) investigated approximately 550 Australian students' applications of Internet-based tools in their first-year daily life and study at an Australian university. They found that most students widely adopted various tools (e.g., desktop computer, mobile phone, and laptop) for life activities (e.g., sharing photos, chatting, and playing games), but they were not frequently used support learning activities.

Similarly, by conducting a survey-based study that investigated approximately 2950 Chinese students' uses of Internet-based tools at a Chinese private university, Shao (2012) also found that most research participants generally used such tools for entertainment rather than learning purposes. It is interesting to note that along with the development of digital technologies, many students, who are considered so-called "digital natives" (Prensky, 2001), seem to be still outside the technology-assisted learning cycle. It is worthwhile to examine what factors lead to the inefficient use of technology as learning mediation tools. Although many studies explore students' usage of digital technologies

CROSS-SYSTEM TRANSITIONS ACROSS CULTURES, SPACES, AND PLACES   51

in different contexts, limited studies have explored Chinese students' uses of
Internet-based tools in a cross-system context, bringing some new narratives
and insights.

Finally, along with the construction of new complex learning spaces, differences between countries, cultures, and societies potentially mean that education becomes fragmented, which requires educators to carefully consider how
to manage these disparities to help different students achieve learning goals.
Ellis and Goodyear (2016) suggested that researchers need to explore students'
perspectives and investigate what kinds of variables play vital roles in shaping
learning spaces, especially the following issues: (1) what students do in complex learning spaces; (2) how they make sense of their learning across different
spaces; (3) what kinds of space they prefer.

Based on the above analysis, it is apparent that learning in a TAP setting happens in a combined model, which is framed by different cultural, social, and
educational features. As Leung and Waters (2013) suggest, researchers need to
consider the significant role of space and place in exploring issues related to
transnational education. Students, as key stakeholders, may have vivid learning trajectories with either shared or individual reactions to the cross-system
setting. However, in the existing literature, as reviewed above, limited studies have investigated what kinds of learning spaces students experience their
intercultural learning adjustment in TAPs and how they make sense of themselves as learners who may shift between different spaces and places. Therefore, it is necessary to comprehensively explore Chinese students' learning in
such a cross-cultural context and further illustrate their trajectories by adopting the existing theoretical models of intercultural learning/adjustment to
reveal the essence of the TAP setting's learning space.

6   Conclusion

This chapter has reviewed vital theoretical concepts and frameworks relevant
to the analysis of Chinese students' intercultural learning and adjustment in
their TAP transitioning journeys. The more sociological and socially oriented
approaches to understanding mobile international students' experiences see
how the new digital technologies' affordances enable an in-between experience in a third space. The more psychological theoretical frameworks illustrate
clearly the trajectory of intercultural adjustment and learning. Nevertheless,
the focus on inter-cultural understanding is framed by social theory. The more
psychological framework function based on several assumptions: people do
need to adjust and then adapt to the new context; transition and change usually

happen from one context to another; after experiencing stresses and adjusting to a new context, people finally will achieve development and adapt in their intercultural transition. However, when engaging in the transitioning journey, how do students perceive themselves as TAP learners, what they encounter in the cross-system journey in learning transition, and what kind of strategies do they adopt to deal with potential transition problems? What might intercultural adjustment and learning be in TAPs? Is it similar to traditional trajectories summarised by existing theoretical models? Moreover, this study probes factors influencing their academic adjustment in TAPs from beginning to the end of the intercultural transition.

CHAPTER 3

Start the TAP Journey with Various Certainties and Uncertainties

It is the first step that costs troublesome.
万事开头难

∵

This chapter first illustrates student participants' motivations to choose TAPS as the starting point of their higher education journey. Key factors that influence students' choices are discussed. Then, various certainties and uncertainties encountered when they started their learning journey in each context are presented. This exploration will help readers understand Chinese students' initial views towards cross-system transition and reveal how they start their intercultural adjustment in TAPs.

1 Begin the TAP Journey

Students shared various factors that influenced them to select TAP as a pathway to start their higher education journey. Distinct from students who study overseas directly, TAP students usually need to study in China first and then transfer to a foreign host university. This cohort could be a unique group of international students. According to Bochner (1972), factors that motivate international students to study overseas are complex and diverse. Thus, it is essential to understand the motivations of each cohort depending on specific situations. Several key factors are identified, including improving competitiveness, to be a Chinese university student, programme features, and parental influences. Notably, in China, students need to attend the university entry exam (Gao Kao) to be admitted to an institution when they complete their year 12. This exam is highly competitive, which makes many students stressed in preparing for the exam. If a student cannot get a high score, he/she will not be admitted to a top-ranked Chinese university, which will influence future development. Many students may have more options and opportunities to

© KONINKLIJKE BRILL NV, LEIDEN, 2022 | DOI: 10.1163/9789004505131_003

access high-quality HE by enrolling in TNHE programmes, which may require a lower score in the Gao Kao (Liu, DeWinter, Harrison, & Wimpenny, 2021). Thus, these programmes become popular for some students who may not get a high score in the Gao Kao but have motivations to gain a good quality of international education.

1.1 Improving Competitiveness for Future Development

Improving personal competitiveness through studying in Chinese and a foreign context is the reason why most students wanted to study in such programmes. Through learning in different sociocultural contexts, many participants (e.g., Ting, Dong, Liang, Rui, Shuo, and Zhuang) expected to improve personal competitiveness in the future, especially in the job market. This expectation can be clearly seen in what Zhuang said:

> I feel I have high pressures on Chinese university because the environment is very competitive. Graduated students are challenging to find a good job, and I think I did not have such a strong ability to compete with other students. Therefore, I wanted to go overseas to learn more skills and improve myself comprehensively. Finally, I wished to go back to China after graduation. Meanwhile, I think I can gain an opportunity to experience different cultures and societies. (Zhuang)

Shuo commented on how the TAP programme would enhance his capacities and also widen his horizons.

> I know that many programmes could award two degrees if students can complete the transnational programme. It is worth using four years to obtain two bachelor's degrees from Chinese and foreign universities. Meanwhile, studying in both Chinese and foreign contexts, which could improve personal abilities and expand horizons.

Qing thought that TAP would provide her with a wonderful pathway. However, in making that point, she also acknowledged that some Chinese employers would not know lower-ranked foreign universities. In that case, a Chinese degree might be preferable, she thought. Here she stressed the importance of learning at Chinese university and the foreign university of TAP.

> Having learning experiences and gaining a degree in China will help future job hunting, I think. Having a bachelor's degree from a recognized Chinese university could indicate the student approved their abilities in

START THE TAP JOURNEY WITH VARIOUS CERTAINTIES AND UNCERTAINTIES 55

> Chinese higher education. Many Chinese people believe that most students who did not have a good score in the university entry exam (Gao Kao) select to study overseas directly to obtain a degree. So, I think it is necessary to prove my ability. Furthermore, many Chinese companies may not know many mid or lower-level foreign universities. In this case, they may prefer to employ students who have a local degree. If the student did not graduate from a top foreign university, their degrees might not be beneficial to find an excellent job than students who have a Chinese degree. At least, companies can know students' educational background directly. My programme allows me to have both Chinese and foreign degrees for good ranking universities in China and Australia, a pathway to gain both Chinese and foreign experiences.

These examples indicated that many students believed that they could improve their labour market competitiveness after having international learning experiences. It seemed that, in many students' minds, having international education experiences has become a meaningful way to improve their abilities. Furthermore, as Shuo and Qing suggested, students could obtain two degrees after completing the programme, giving students a solid academic background.

Particularly, Qing had a unique idea about learning via TAPs. She identified that it was necessary to have a Chinese degree to find a job in China rather than only hold a foreign degree. Her comment suggested that studying in a Chinese university could indicate students' achievement in Gao Kao, which was an essential factor in showing personal ability in the Chinese context. Moreover, getting a Chinese degree could be better than only having a degree from an unknown foreign university when students try to find a job in China.

1.2   To Be a Chinese University Student

Although some students had strong motivations to study overseas to improve their competitiveness, some identified that it was also necessary to have Chinese higher education experience to get a more in-depth understanding of Chinese society. For example, Shuo, Qing, Liang, Hao and Diao argued that the TAP provided students with an opportunity to experience different higher education settings. There is no doubt that such educational modes combined Chinese and foreign education.

> Importantly, as a Chinese student, if he/she does not have a learning experience in a Chinese university, it could be regret in their lives. They do not have the opportunity to gain knowledge or experiences through

the Chinese higher education system and lost traditional Chinese traditions. Two years of Chinese learning experience could help students to have in-depth understandings of Chinese society and culture. This ability also helps Chinese student to experience Australian context and let them have own views on new conditions.

Learning at a Chinese university could help students gain much social and cultural knowledge about the Chinese context. Similarly, Yuner did not want to study overseas directly after graduating from high school. She wished to experience Chinese and foreign higher education.

I needed to experience Chinese higher education as a Chinese student. I grew up in China, and all my educational stages before higher education were completed in China. Therefore, I wished to explore and experience a Chinese university. Furthermore, to prepare the Gao Kao, I spend three years of my life on it. So, I did not want to give up this opportunity to study at a Chinese university at the beginning of my higher education stage. The TAP programme was the best choice for me as it allowed me to experience Chinese and foreign higher education.

According to these examples, it is evident that such transnational programmes provided an opportunity for these students to experience Chinese higher education and society. Some students believed that it was vital for them to understand Chinese higher education because they were fully educated by the Chinese educational system before learning at university and had succeeded in the highly competitive Gao Kao. If they did not study at a Chinese university, they might feel regret as a Chinese student. Therefore, some students believed that it was worthwhile to have higher education experiences in the Chinese context.

1.3   *Programme Features*

Lower academic entry requirements were an important factor that made many students who did not gain a high score in Gao Kao study in TAPs. As Qiang reported in his story, he did not get a competitive score in the Gao Kao.

My academic score was not very competitive in Gao Kao. It is difficult for me to study in a top-ranked university or popular majors. My programme does not need a high score, so I selected it to study at a recognized university in my province.

START THE TAP JOURNEY WITH VARIOUS CERTAINTIES AND UNCERTAINTIES   57

Learning in TAP could enable Qiang to study in a university without high academic barriers. Similarly, Rui identified that his programme also did not have a high requirement for Gao Kao.

> I did not get a high score in the Gao Kao. So, I want to find a programme and graduate soon.

These comments suggest that some TAPs provide opportunities for students who wanted to study at a university without a high academic requirement. Students could take this shortcut to study at a recognised university.

Distinct from the above experiences, Diao shared that her programme had her major, Engineering, and let her experience top-ranked Chinese and Australian universities.

> To be admitted into such a prestigious university programme, I achieved a competitive score in Gao Kao. Studying in a TAP allows me to let me have such a rare opportunity to study at both top Chinese and Australian universities. So, why not?

Moreover, some students suggested that TAPs offer their favourite majors. Xin mentioned that her programme had her interested major.

> I am interested in an Arts-related major; however, I did not want to study Fine Art, and I prefer to study something new. My programme is about multimedia design, which is an up-to-date field. So, I selected this major.

According to these extracts, students briefly described programme factors that influenced their choices. Low academic requirements for studying in some transnational programmes offer opportunities to students who wish to study in a recognised university without high scores in Gao Kao (Liu et al., 2021). However, other interviewees did not mention this point. It is essential to notice that different programmes have different policies, making the academic requirements, learning arrangements, and other related issues unique and complicated. The issues that are relevant to programme policy were not the focus of this study. Therefore, limited data was reported. Considering the disciplinary factors, most students also did not mention their interest fields when they selected programmes. It seemed that many students might not genuinely have their learning plans and goals in a major study. Data about their learning goals at Chinese learning periods will be illustrated in this chapter as well.

58   CHAPTER 3

1.4   *Parental Choices*

Parental choices played essential roles in students' selection of programmes and majors. According to interview data, students' parents seemed to have various motivations to select TAP as their children's learning pathway. For example, Minze's parents believe that having an international learning experience has become one of the important aspects of higher education, especially for young Chinese students.

> When I was in high school, my parents started to plan my international learning issues. They wished me to study overseas to gain various experiences. I also wanted to live and study in a different context. I knew I would go overseas, so why not I did it early. I did not want to study overseas after undergraduate graduation. Furthermore, an increasing number of Chinese students choose to study abroad in recent years. If I did not have such experience, I might not have enough competitions in the future.

Studying overseas seemed to become an important stage in Minze's higher education. Before deciding to study in a China-Australia TAP, Minze and her parents travelled to Australia.

> My parents and I travelled to Australia when I was in high school. After the trip, we all loved the natural and peaceful environment. So, my parents encouraged me to study at an Australian university. I also wished to study there.

To select a suitable place and programme for Minze, they travelled to Australia before making a choice. Minze's experience indicated that her parents' attitudes toward international study experience could influence her educational programme choice. Similarly, Guang and Diao have also mentioned their parents' influence on their choices of programme. For instance, Diao suggested that her parents wished her to have an overseas learning experience.

> My parents wanted me to study overseas, and they thought I could gain multiple learning and life experience.

According to the above extracts, TAP was an excellent choice for Minze to fulfil her learning requirements. Therefore, Minze finally decided to select a TAP to start her higher education study. Similarly, Guang's parents wished him to be independent and have different life and learning experiences.

> My parent wished me to be independent as an adult. Learning via a TAP is my first time living in other contexts.

This quote indicates that parents play a significant role in students' selections of a learning pathway (Bodycott & Lai, 2012; Liu et al., 2021). According to the above extracts, many students wished to improve their competitiveness through having international learning experiences. Some students identified that it was also important for Chinese students to experience Chinese higher education rather than study overseas without a learning stage in the Chinese context. Notably, unique interview data showed that the low academic requirements of some TAPs could be a significant factor that influenced students' choices to study in such a mode. Moreover, some students mentioned other factors that motivated them to select such programmes. For example, Minze, Guang and Diao reported that their parents seemed to support their children studying in transnational programmes.

To sum up, this section has illustrated a complex picture about factors that motivated students to study in TAPs. When students select their learning pathways, they considered not only their "life-guiding principles but also more specific situational objectives that are shaped by their situation in the home country, relationships with families, and future career goals and other conditions" (Chirkov et al., 2007, pp. 204–205). As many students expected, they have prepared for the TAP with solid confidence and different expectations; what they will experience as TAP students? Does the reality meet their expectations?

2 Encountering Certainties and Uncertainties[1]

Students encountered various certainties and uncertainties when they started the TAP journey. They seemed to be various in-between differences. The in-between in this case means students' constant negotiations with different programme settings and learning focuses on their TAPs. The Chinese stage is considered as a period for preparing to go overseas. As these students need to go overseas in the future and study in TAPs, they engaged in many unique classes (e.g., English training courses) or activities (e.g., guest lecturers from partner universities) cohorts. Chinese universities seemed to systematically organise their learning pathway and issues related to their application to Australia. In contrast, after coming to Australia, many students reflected that they seemed to ignore it. Several issues (e.g., unclear course arrangements, English requirements for major study) were pointed out, which made them stressed in

60   CHAPTER 3

intercultural transition and reflected complex attitudes towards the Australian setting.

In this process, students revealed multiple and varied senses of agency towards different settings and tasks. Specifically, many students could positively react to different educational tasks and cross-system differences with progressive attitudes. In contrast, some students felt that it was difficult to deal with their learning issues in TAP learning processes. Students engaged in different academic focuses and tasks at each stage, and they also needed to study in two systems, which positioned them in several rounds of adjustment. Generally, the first round occurred at the beginning of the TAP in China. The second round occurred when these students began their Australian learning stage. In each stage, students reflected various responses to the educational context.

2.1   *The Chinese Stage: A Period of Preparing to Go Overseas*

Many students started their TAP in the Chinese stage without a clear understanding of learning in this particular setting, which led to a sense of uncertainty towards future discipline study. Such feelings were mainly reflected in students' uncertainty towards their learning goals. For instance, Xie shared experiences about the initial uncertain feelings:

> I did not have a clear understanding of my programme and what I will learn. However, I knew I will go to an Australian university and pass the IELTS exam as a compulsory task.

Gong further suggested:

> I did not have a clear goal because I was young and did not understand majors and my learning interests. My family helped me to select my major. They thought that area would have high potential in the future. Therefore, they suggested me study Business.

According to these extracts, when these students started their TAPs, they seemed to be "strangers" in HE. Although they had unclear directions regarding their discipline study, they shared a common goal: to pass IELTS and then go to Australia to continue their study. As Xie mentioned, even though he had no clear understanding of his major, he knew the TAP rule regarding the required IELTS score. Similarly, other participants also indicated the importance of IELTS and their capabilities to deal with it. For instance, Hao shared:

> I focused on English learning because it determined whether I could go to Australia after two years of study in China. The IELTS was difficult for

me, so I spend much time on it. I proposed to get an overall 6.5, and each subject was 6 at least.

Distinct from other students who study in mainstream programmes, TAP students have to pass the IELTS to continue their undergraduate study in the partner nation. To achieve the English requirement, many students indicated different senses of agency. Hao further shared her learning experiences and how she dealt with the IELTS test requirements. As she mentioned,

> I did not hear about IELTS before when I was in high school. When I enrolled to my programme, I knew I need to pass IELTS, but I had no ideas about what it is, how I learn it, and whether I can achieve the required scores within the two years in China.

Hao's extract may suggest that she initially did not have an empowered sense of agency in her mind to deal with IELTS. In other words, she mentally felt uncertain about achieving the IELTS. To learn IELTS effectively, Hao suggested various strategies:

> It took me a long time to become familiar with IELTS and master the relevant knowledge. My university offered IELTS classes for TAP students, and it was beneficial. Meanwhile, I also went to the IELTS training centre to learn practical skills.

Hao's experience indicated that the IELTS requirement of her programme seemed to make her very stressed in the Chinese stage. Although Hao felt it was challenging to prepare for the IELTS test, she subsequently achieved the required scores through her efforts. As she said, "Finally, I achieved my goal. I got the required score."

Similarly, other students in the study (e.g., Diao, Dong, Biang, and Yuner) also achieved the IELTS requirements in China. When sharing her successful experiences in IELTS, Diao indicated that foreign lecturers specifically taught English in her programme, which helped her improve her English proficiency. As she mentioned, "we had English courses to help TAP students to practise English skills with foreign lecturers. Particularly, I felt my speaking improved quickly." More specifically, Biang shared that most discipline courses were taught by English speakers, making him feel somewhat empowered towards English at the Australian university.

> My Australian university waived my IELTS because my previous study was in English, and most lecturers come from English-speaking countries

at my Chinese university. So, I did not worry about the language issues ... As many courses were taught in English, I felt I did not have any concerns about language issues at my Australian university.

Biang's English-based learning experiences indicated that he had enough confidence regarding his language capability to adjust to the Australian learning context. According to these students' experiences (e.g., Hao and Biang), they started to connect with the host context via learning IELTS and studying with foreign lecturers on the Chinese stage. These students seemed to be empowered to deal with the IELTS and English learning in the Chinese stage.

However, many students argued that it was difficult for them to manage the preparation for IELTS and at the same time learn in the discipline courses. To effectively deal with these tasks, they constantly shifted their learning focuses. Specifically, many felt disappointed when preparing for IELTS, which took more time and energy to study. In contrast, learning discipline courses and passing exams became easy tasks for many students. For instance, Biang noted that there was an imbalance between learning IELTS and the discipline course.

In China, most of my energies focused on the IELTS, my primary goals and tasks. If I cannot pass it, I needed to learn English at the Australian university and spent much money. In this case, learning major courses or related knowledge became less critical compared to IELTS. I did not pay too much attention to major courses because I knew the exams were not hard to pass. At the end of each semester, I just needed to review and remember the contents highlighted by lecturers, which could ensure that I can pass exams easily.

Biang seemed to be empowered to ensure the success of passing discipline exams by adopting his particular strategies while he struggled to deal with IELTS. In doing so, he paid more attention to learning IELTS rather than focusing on discipline knowledge in his daily study. This phenomenon was not unique. Xie also mentioned in his interview:

I usually started to learn my discipline courses by the end of the semester. During the semester, I did not pay much attention to my discipline study as I struggled with learning IELTS, which is much more complicated than discipline knowledge. Therefore, I did need more time to learn it.

Their experiences suggested that although they could manage the different learning tasks by adopting their strategies, they felt empowered and handled

START THE TAP JOURNEY WITH VARIOUS CERTAINTIES AND UNCERTAINTIES 63

these tasks without stress. Moreover, many students suggested that they usually needed to study several courses delivered by foreign lecturers from partner universities, which could be a way of experiencing intercultural learning in advance. For example, Shuo described:

> My TAP regularly arranged roundtables or other activities that combine TAP and international students in the university. Taking these opportunities, TAP students could communicate with the international cohort. Such kinds of activities could help us practice English and also get familiar with communicating with foreigners. I think both cohorts could gain mutual benefits.

Similarly, Zhuang further mentioned:

> In each term, I have one course taught by lecturers from the Australian partner university. Although it is only one course in this mode, students can experience something different in the Chinese stage. I am not sure whether such a course could help us understand the Australian context or not. At least, this arrangement opens a door of intercultural learning for students, especially for most of us without any international travel or study experiences before.

Moreover, Diao shared:

> My university has arranged several staff for the TAP students. The university international office staff helped students apply for offers from the partner university and arranged visa application. I think my university provides enough support to TAP students. Compared to other cohorts, students in TAP did not need to contact foreign universities via agents. TAP makes learning overseas convenient.

These experiences suggest that their Chinese universities have strategically provided various support for TAP students in the Chinese stage. It seemed that the TAP partly extended the intercultural learning experiences from the host county to the home country. As these students mentioned, they had learned from foreign lecturers in either English class or discipline courses in China. Furthermore, although learning IELTS was a barrier for many participants, some could initially learn about the international context. Such experiences could be considered as a process of intercultural learning in advance to some extent. The intercultural adaptation started at the beginning of TAP in China.

64   CHAPTER 3

This process could be an extension of Gill's (2007) concept of intercultural adjustment that usually happens when Chinese students move to another context. Students needed to reach the requirement of IELTS in this pre-departure learning stage and needed to pass discipline courses. Such multiple task-based learning could motivate students to learn how to manage their studies and adjust to this particular programme setting. Facing IELTS pressures and discipline knowledge learning, many students constantly shifted between different learning focuses. In this process, they indicated a different sense of agency towards different learning tasks. After completing two years of study in China, most students started their actual intercultural study at Australian universities, where they experienced the second round of uncertainty.

2.2 *The Australian Stage: Transition with Uncertainties*

As Gill's (2007) transformative learning framework showed, many Chinese students studying abroad experienced three transformation stages in their intercultural learning process. They started with stress in the new context as an intercultural stranger. After studying and living in the new environment for a period, many students can develop their intercultural competencies to adjust to the new system. Consequently, they could become "another person" through an adjustment to the cross-system changes. During this process, they may experience several rounds of spiral changes depending on the different tensions and issues at different learning stages.

Compared to the experience of language achievers in the Chinese stage, some students (e.g., Dang, Shuo, Qing, Xie, Liang, Rui, and Zhuang) also described their tortuous English learning experiences in Australia. These students did not reach the IELTS scores that allowed them to start their discipline courses in Australia. Their experiences indicated a disempowered sense of agency toward the IELTS and English profoundly. For example, as a student who had strong negative senses and experiences of learning IELTS, Shuo shared his experiences.

> I would not say I liked IELTS. It was so difficult for me to achieve an overall 6.5. I started to learn IELTS in professional school at the beginning of the second year at my Chinese university. I left university and stayed in the language school for three months to learn IELTS. However, I felt so stressed. After completing three months, I took the IELTS exam for the first time. However, I only got 5. I felt uncomfortable and lacked confidence, but I still wished to achieve the requirement. Then I took the exam another four times. Although my scores improved, there always one subject that cannot reach the requirement. Finally, I decided to stop trying and to study English first at my Australian university.

START THE TAP JOURNEY WITH VARIOUS CERTAINTIES AND UNCERTAINTIES   65

Although Shuo took the IELTS test several times, his results made him upset. Zhuang also shared his views towards the IELTS preparation and English-related learning issues.

> My programme usually arranged some activities for TAP students to communicate with international students and lecturers at my university to let us know more about foreign contexts and prepare for IELTS. However, due to my limited English skills, I felt it was not easy to obtain helpful information because learning IELTS and English was not just exam skills. It is more about another culture. When rethinking my experiences of taking IELTS exams, I can feel many questions related to the UK or Australian contexts. Therefore, when I was in China preparing for the IELTS, I started to connect with a new culture. However, I did not realise it until I came to Australia. I can notice that many questions came from real life in Australia.

Due to individual different English proficiency levels, the IELTS could be a challenging task for many students. Based on my experiences, Shuo and Zhuang's experiences were shared. When I prepared for the IELTS, I experienced similar feelings and pressures; for example, I studied in both the university and professional training centre and took individual classes. I can understand that when students paid considerable attention to learning English and wished to achieve the required standard, once they failed, their attitudes became hostile towards the IELTS. Notably, the realisation of learning a new culture was also tricky for me. I had similar experiences as Zhuang. Once I came to Australia, I realised that many IELTS questions reflected real-life issues in Australia. However, IELTS is a necessary task for TAP students who wish to start Australian study without language test barriers. It is difficult for students studying for IELTS in China to grasp Australia's relevant cultural features that only become apparent when one lives in Australia for a time.

Moreover, many students encountered other uncertainties in learning and life. For instance, Xiang complained that his Australian university did not provide enough learning support for TAP students.

> When students moved to the Australian university, we did not get enough support compared to the previous Chinese stage. For example, when we selected courses, many academics and admin staff from my department did not know the TAP and could not tell us what courses we should select. As we have completed two years of study in China, we joined the class from year two according to the Australian setting. Thus, what we should

66 CHAPTER 3

select in each semester was dependent on ourselves, and we did not get helpful suggestions or feedback from academics here.

Similarly, Gong also mentioned that:

> I felt that many academics and staff even did not know our TAP. It seems that TAP students were in a gap. We needed to arrange everything by ourselves, and the university did not provide enough support. I felt that the collaboration between Chinese and Australian universities stopped when TAP students came to Australia. I think my Australian university did not arrange enough support for us to transit from China to Australia. I was imaging that the university would also host us by using the similar strategies that the Chinese partner adopted.

According to the above extracts, many students encountered "gaps" in transition from China and Australia. Some students supposed that their Australian universities will provide comprehensive support to them. However, unfortunately, their expectations were not the reality, which started their intercultural learning and adjustment process. Even though two partner universities operate TAPs, when students physically move from one to another context, they still face new challenges, such as language, teaching and learning approaches, and social life issues (e.g., Gill, 2007; Gu, 2016; Wu, 2015). Shifting between certainties and uncertainties could become a longitudinal situation in their cross-system transition. As newcomers in the new context, they also have various responses to the intercultural differences, which may also dynamically (re) shape TAP students' sense of identity, agency, and belonging. Their changes as TAP learners could help us understand how intercultural adjustment and learning are experienced in this specific setting.

3   Conclusion

This chapter analysed these Chinese students' motivations for choosing TAP as a learning pathway and their initial experiences in each stage. Considering their motivations, it is apparent that various factors made them choose TAP, including parental influences, individual situations and intentions, and programme features. It is worth noting that TAP provides a unique pathway for students compared to the standard model or directly studying overseas. It combines two sets in one model, which has both advantages and disadvantages. As many students mentioned, they gained intercultural learning experience in China and encountered various certainties and uncertainties in cross-system transition. How students respond and react to a complex situation is a critical issue to be explored and discussed. I will further analyse the TAP students' various changes during their intercultural learning transition in the Australian context in Chapter 4, drawing on interview data.

Note

1 Parts of this section are based on Dai, K., & Garcia, J. (2019). Intercultural learning in transnational articulation programs: The hidden agenda of Chinese students' experiences. *Journal of International Students, 9*(2), 326–383. Permission for re-use has been given by the publishers.

CHAPTER 4

A Tortuous Trajectory of Intercultural Learning

You never know how hard a task is until you have done it yourself.
事非经过不知难

∵

This chapter illustrates the research participants' dynamic learning experiences in their TAPs, drawing on relevant data sources. As Gill's (2007) framework indicated, the trajectory of students' cross-systems usually has three stages: encountering stress along with developing intercultural competence (sense of agency to deal with cross-system differences), adjusting to a new context with reshaping identity, and finally adapting to the new context with a sense of "fit-into." The narratives from the respondents point to three transformative axes: (1) changes of agency towards the academic and sociocultural differences between China and Australia, (2) profound changes in their perceptions of identity, and (3) reshaping sense of belonging.

When discussing the learning experiences in their TAPs, many students spontaneously compared their different learning activities between the Chinese and Australian contexts. These aspects include teaching and learning practices, ICTs, assessments, and academic atmosphere/culture, which generated cross-system academic tensions. Evidence from students' interviews suggested that they had different capabilities and strategies to deal with these tensions. As Pickering suggested, "within different cultures, human beings and the material world might exhibit capacities for action quite different from those we customarily attribute to them" (as cited in Ahearn, 2001, p. 113). Research participants shared various senses of agency towards the cross-system changes they experienced, which provided a series of insights about their intercultural adjustments as transnational learners. Educational changes led to a series of learning shocks for some of the research participants, even though some participants already knew about the Australian educational system's features.

1   Positively Deal with Changes in Transition[1]

Many participants indicated that they were able to adjust to the Australian learning context. However, the processes of adjustment were often quite tortuous. According to Gill (2007), when students went overseas, they could feel stress because they were unfamiliar with the new context. In this study, research participants also reflected stressed feelings towards the Australian educational contexts. For example, Ting suggested that she felt disempowered towards Australian learning and living modes when she came to Australia.

> Even though I came to Australia with some classmates and my programme staff briefly introduced the Australian context, I still had many pressures, such as language problems, different environments, no friends or family. All these factors impacted my study. I did not have enough confidence to survive in the new context. At that time, my primary goal was successful graduation from my bachelor's degree.

The contextual changes from China to Australia made Qing feel stressed. Even though she knew specific information about Australia when she was in China, the actual situation still brought initial shocks to her in the new context. As she indicated, language barriers, environmental differences, and lack of family and friends for support made her feel a lack of confidence in her learning in the new context. In this case, surviving in the new context to obtain the degree was her primary goal. A similar situation also happened in other students' experiences. For example, Biang felt that an English barrier was the primary issue that made him feel challenged to study in the Australian university's initial stage.

> As a non-English speaker, I found learning the discipline knowledge in English a challenge when I came to Australia. This was because of language and also my previous knowledge of my subject. I needed to spend more time and attention reflecting on what the lecturers taught. So, my primary goal was to pass all the courses I selected in my first semester with no failures.

Biang's experience indicated that language barriers significantly influenced his learning. The unfamiliarity with the English-based teaching context made him set up an achievable goal in his first semester. As his extract indicated, he wanted to pass all courses without failing. These experiences reflect similarities with many existing findings that many Chinese were uncertain and stressed in

70 CHAPTER 4

their life and study when they initially shifted to a foreign context (e.g., the UK and Australia) (e.g., Gu, 2016; C. Wang, Whitehead, & Bayes, 2017), due to the language barriers, study differences, and life problems. Although these stories demonstrated some adjustment issues, some students shared their different experiences in the transitioning processes.

Yuner was studying Finance at her Chinese university but changed to Business in Australia. When discussing her transformative experiences, she suggested that she was familiar with the Australian teaching and learning settings.

> I did not have particular issues when I came here because my previous university had similar class settings with the Australian university. I had lectures and tutorials in China to understand what the course will look like, and I knew what I needed to do in each course. I think this experience helped me to adapt to the Australian teaching and learning mode.

Yuner's experience indicated a particular experience related to the initial learning stress these students usually had when they started their Australian stage. Compared with other students' issues in language and different teaching and learning environments, Yuner seemed to be more confident in adapting to the new context. This experience could further indicate that the first two years of study potentially helped her adapt to the new environment.

Yuner's case illustrates different values in her programme than other participants' initial stress and other researchers' findings. The individual differences could suggest that even though these students all studied in TAPs, their programme settings related to the connections between Chinese and Australian academic contexts may have many differences, which led to students' different initial adaptation feelings.

Many participants suggested that they became familiar with these academic and sociocultural contexts after studying in the Australian context. Therefore, they wished to become academic achievers rather than only passing exams and obtaining degrees. As Gill (2007) indicated, students could start to develop their intercultural competence when they have more understanding of the new context. Consequently, they could change their views towards the intercultural learning context, their strategies to deal with issues and values by comparing the different sociocultural contexts. According to Kim (1988), students are motivated to actively adjust their strategies to adapt to the new context in an intercultural learning context. When facing the new context, they had various strategies to deal with their learning problems, such as self-efforts and strategic changes in learning approaches, seeking help from other students, and adopting ICTs. To deeply learn in the new major, Yuner critically considered the differences in teaching and learning approaches between China and Australia. Studying in the Chinese context, Yuner felt that learning lacked creativity or explorations beyond the textbook-based knowledge.

> In China, learning seemed to follow lecturers' track. For instance, they taught students to calculate 1 + 1. Then, students learn it. However, we did not have a keen ability to explore 2 + 2 or more complex calculation, which lacks divergent thinking. It seems lecturers have already set up the learning activities and goals for students. In Australia, lecturers may teach me 1 and 3 without 2. I needed to explore what the 2 is by myself by using various methods, such as Internet-based technology.

To adapt to the new teaching mode, Yuner suggested that she changed her strategies.

> I did need to preview lecture slides and other reading contents before going to a class rather than waiting for instructions. In this way, I can easily follow the lecturer in the classroom. Otherwise, I felt it was challenging to learn efficiently. Generally speaking, I needed to work harder in learning at my Australian university.

Yuner's story illustrated her experiences of intercultural adjustment and how she approached different educational issues in transition. She actively faced the different features of learning context and majors and positively changed her strategies to make her learning go along the right track. Her effective responses towards the change of majors and circumstances provide further insights to coincide with Gill's (2007) finding that intrinsic motivations help students develop their positive attitudes towards intercultural learning. According to Searle and Ward (1990), she seemed to be progressively adjusted to the new learning context from both psychological (e.g., establishing confidence towards learning) and sociocultural aspects (e.g., changing learning focuses and approaches).

Furthermore, many other students (e.g., Diao, Zhuang, Shuo, Hao, Xie, and Qing) also shared similar positive changes towards the different academic context. Although they initially faced various shocks, they actively changed their strategies and attitudes to fit into the new environment and then chase their academic goals. For instance, as a student from a top-ranked research-based Chinese university, Diao struggled in the initial stage at her Australian university because she supposed that she could adopt the Chinese learning strategies to study in the Australian context. However, she felt stressed in learning after moving to Australia.

> In Australia, when I was in my first semester, I relied on the strategies adopted in China: Studying hard before the final exam but not during the semester. However, I did not get good scores and failed one subject. The results made me upset. I realised that I could not keep doing this activity again. I needed to study hard during the whole semester.

The unfortunate experiences made Diao feel disempowered and reconsider her previous strategies. She concluded that Chinese learning approaches were not suitable for the Australian mode.

> Although I was studying at one of the top universities in China, most classmates did not pay their attention to study. Most students played together but did not have much communication related to learning. Furthermore, as I said, most students preferred to study before the exam. So, I was used to doing the same in that learning environment. We did not have such a stressful learning process as in Australia.

To make changes, Diao started to follow "active learners":

> I thought that making friends who were active learners was significant to me. Many of my friends liked to study at the library after class every day. They usually studied until the library was closed. Their learning attitudes and approaches influenced me as well. I started to follow them and study together because I knew if I did not work hard, I would not gain a good result. When I saw other students who studied very hard, I felt I also needed to learn in-depth. Otherwise, I appeared to be very strange in such a competitive university.

Diao's experience indicated that contextual environment influences students' learning motivations and their desires to study (Gill, 2007). Furthermore, she seemed to have active intentions to make some change "mentally" and then find strategies to achieve her goals "physically" (Park, 2018). The intercultural learning context changes established a space for Diao to reconsider her previous experiences and reconstruct her learning strategies, which helped her adjust to the new context.

Liang also shared his changes of agency towards study during his intercultural learning processes. As he suggested, when he was in China, he did not pay much attention to study, but he still could pass assessments by studying at the end of the semester. However, Liang realised that such an approach was not helpful any more in Australia. He did need to change his strategies to achieve his proposed learning goals dramatically.

> At the beginning of my first semester, I did not know what a tutorial was and did not know how to learn in this new context. I did not preview the course contents, and then I cannot understand taught contents. In the second week, I felt I was behind the normal process and missed important contents. In this way, after slow adaptation to here, I needed to spend more time reviewing the first week's contents. Based on this experience, I changed my learning methods. Now I usually preview course contents first and then do more reviews after class, which helps me catch up on the teaching process.

Similarly, Meng actively realised that it was vital for him to change learning strategies, making him become empowered to study rather than lose direction.

> I wish to get a Grade Point Average (GPA) of at least three because my English is not good. However, I can achieve it as I had already learned some similar content when studying at my Chinese university. Although English is a barrier for me, I can study harder to overcome such a problem. I now usually preview course content and review lecturers' recordings via an online learning system. Through such an approach, I feel I can follow lecturers as I study. I do not think it will be a problem for me to achieve my goal.

Meng's experiences demonstrated his confidence to achieve his learning goals. Moreover, concerning the role of ICTs in learning, Meng claimed: "In China, I think Internet-based technology was not very helpful to my study. However, it was imperative to my Australian study." He further shared his experiences.

> For example, I had many group works at the Australian university; group peers usually set up a Facebook discussion group. We usually discussed our topics online ... I thought this was very convenient and interesting.

According to Meng's experiences, although he felt confident about achieving his goals in Australia because he had foundational knowledge in the same subject at the Chinese university, ICTs were not supportive of his study in China. However, they became beneficial to his study in Australia. Many other students also mentioned that ICTs became much more important in learning in Australia than had been the case in China. For instance, Gong said:

> I did not use much Internet-based technology or other kinds of techno-logical tools in the learning process. Even though we have computer labs and Internet access, students and lecturers usually do not use them fre-quently in learning and teaching ... I did not think Internet-based tech-nology played an essential role in my study. It was used more for leisure and helped me to play rather than study.

These experiences indicate a disconnection between the two learning con-texts regarding the application of ICTs in learning. From China to Australia, the use of ICT become a tension that could shape and reconstruct students' ICT-based intercultural learning experiences. These students indicated active senses of agency in their intercultural adaptation processes, helping them overcome cross-system shocks. As the above extracts suggest, these students, who act as agents for themselves to conduct the intercultural learning, con-tinuously reflected and reviewed the different academic environments from China to Australia. Then, they had different actions towards the changes in learning contexts, which transformed their capabilities to adjust to the new context. These students' experiences indicated that they were in between hav-ing positive mental intentions to adjust to the new context and have different physical actions to achieve their purposes (Park, 2018). Notably, some students felt disempowered in the Australian university.

2   Being Stressful in Transition

As Gu (2009) explained, learning shock could lead to "intensive unpleasant feelings and may impose a deeper psychological and emotional strain on learners when they study abroad" (p. 42). According to the interview data anal-ysis, I noticed that not all students were able to actively start their intercultural learning adaptation in their articulation learning processes. Representatively, Fei and Dong showed pessimistic senses of agency towards the intercultural transformation. Their experiences are different from several existing find-ings that students usually experienced a gradual development process: initial strangeness to the "other" context to adjustment and finally the achievement of personal growth via experiencing transformative learning (Gill, 2007; Gu, Schweishfurth, & Day, 2010; Kim, 1988).

For Fei, the interview served as a form of catharsis because he wanted an appropriate opportunity to express his disappointment regarding his learning experiences. Fei identified himself as a successful student in the Chinese stage. As he described, "when I was at my Chinese university, I always obtained good academic results, and I was one of the top 5 students. Every year I can get scholarships." However, he did not reach the IELTS requirement in China, which negatively influenced his learning.

> I got 5.5 in the IELTS and needed to learn 15 weeks of courses. I was the best student in my programme. Most classmates needed to learn more than 20 weeks of English.

Even though Fei was the one who did not need to study 20 weeks of language courses in his class, he still did not achieve the minimum scores that allow students entry to major courses without any academic barriers.

Fei became demotivated in learning after coming to Australia due to various barriers (e.g., language, peer relations, teaching and learning, and assessments). This very apparent change in attitude made his story very different from the other cases in the study. Specifically, he suggested that his learning experiences in the language school were the beginning of the difficulties he continued to face in his intercultural study. These made him diffident towards study.

> When we did the language tests, most of my programme classmates were failed. Initially, we thought that our language ability may still not be good enough to pass the exam. However, after testing three to four times, we were still failed. If we cannot pass, we cannot start the major courses. It took a long time to stay in the language school ... As I was one of these students, I utilised various approaches to pass the language test, for example, retesting the IELTS or attending more internal exams. I did not want to keep paying high tuition for the language school. Finally, I graduated from the language school after studying there for 15 weeks. I thought they just wanted to charge more fees from us. However, I did not understand why my programme mates were failed. Other students can pass the course easily. This was not equal to us.

Although Fei finally completed his language study, his experiences indicated that he was disempowered to deal with these issues. The first learning experience in Australia made him feel cynical and mistrusting of the university.

> Although I completed such complex learning and could start my university learning, I cannot adapt to the new learning context. I felt the learning context, approaches, lecturers are entirely different from China. My learning attitudes dramatically changed. I wearied of studying.

76   CHAPTER 4

This negative attitude existed in his major course study, which made it difficult for him to study in the new context. For instance, he felt it was challenging to engage in in-class communications:

> When Australian lecturers asked questions, I felt I have lost. I did not know what they asked. In this case, I became afraid of going to class and lacked confidence in learning. For Australian students, I thought they were used to studying in such an interactive learning context, and they can actively communicate with peers and lecturers. I thought language issues were barriers for me. Even though I had robust major knowledge or new ideas, I cannot present my ideas clearly due to the language problem. Language barriers made me feel that the thinking and presenting were quite confusing.

Language issues seemed to be a significant barrier that limited his learning. However, Fei further argued that he was not comfortable studying in a teaching and learning context that motivates and demands that students become autonomous learners.

> I had one assignment that asked students to create a short animation. The lecturer did not tell us the steps and let students to creatively design their works. Many Chinese students feel it is difficult to complete as there was no clear guidance. I had the same feeling, but I still had to complete one. So, I needed to learn the use of software online step by step. Although I can learn a lot, lecturer seemed to not support me in detail. I passively became a self-directed learner.

This experiences apparently indicated his non-adaptation to the Australian context. It seems that he preferred to study in a didactical context with detailed instructions. To overcome such learning difficulties, Fei shared his strategies:

> I requested help from lecturers, and they gave me some guidance to complete my assignments. If I cannot get help from lecturers, I also asked peers and friends from China who have relevant experiences to help me deal with learning problems.

These experiences indicated that he had tight connections with his Chinese "homeland" in his intercultural study at an Australian university. According to Park's (2018) argument about agency ("to do mentally" and "to do physically"), he faced a series of difficulties that made him mentally averse to studying in

A TORTUOUS TRAJECTORY OF INTERCULTURAL LEARNING

the new context. However, he still had to study in the system to complete his degree physically. In doing so, Fei was immersed in such a contradictory sense of agency. Other participants (e.g., Shuo, Dang, Diao, and Ting) shared similar learning experiences. For instance, Dang mentioned that:

> I usually made use of the Internet to help me understand professional concepts. Many concepts are challenging to understand in English, so I searched for them in Chinese to deeply comprehend the real meaning. Furthermore, there were plenty of academic papers and resources online. It was handy for me to understand knowledge by searching for Chinese information. The Internet helped me to overcome some language problems.

Such virtual connections with the homeland suggested that these students' intercultural learning in Australia established transnational interactions of knowledge, information, and intelligence between the Chinese and Australian contexts. Although they struggled with some learning tasks in Australia, the Internet-based connections with the Chinese homeland helped them overcome some problems, which illustrates the vital role of ICTs in students' intercultural adjustment and learning. Furthermore, their experiences provide detailed insights to suggest that these Chinese overseas students, as part of an Asian diaspora in Australia, remained in touch with Chinese contexts (Rizvi, Louie, & Evans, 2016; R. Yang & Welch, 2010). According to Fei's experiences, it seemed that even though he had nearly completed his programme when he participated in this study, he still indicated a disempowered sense of agency towards the cross-system changes and pressures he experienced. In other words, he did not adapt to the Australian context after studying there. Compared with other peers, Fei did not adjust and still felt alienated even after graduation. This feeling contrasts with some of his peers, who eventually expressed positive attitudes towards their intercultural adjustment.

Like Fei's experiences, Dong also argued that she studied in Australia without a strong sense of agency due to her feelings of disempowerment, given the reality of new teaching approaches and different learning strategies. For instance, Dong comparatively discussed her different views towards learning features.

> I realised that students did not have enough practical tasks or practical tests after class in Australia. There were little test books for students to complete. It seemed that such tests were very sparse and a rarity. It was so difficult to get such practice from lecturers. Even though they gave us

some quizzes, I cannot get the correct answers in time. I thought it was challenging to master knowledge if I only relied on listening to lecturers. Furthermore, it was also challenging to find such a practice online because most were in English and needed to be bought, which was very expensive. Even though I can get some practical tasks, it was difficult to understand due to language barriers. However, I can quickly get plenty of practical exercises in China. I can use a variety of this kind of books to enhance my understanding of specific knowledge. In Australia, it seemed that most students might only rely on lecturers. If they can understand the taught contents, they may get good academic results. If not, they will be easy to fail in exams.

Dong seemed to be used to the Chinese learning strategies based on many practice tests. However, she did not experience similar educational modes in Australia, which made her feel ineffective in her study. Her disempowered feelings were also reflected in her views towards the differences in teaching approaches between Chinese and Australian lecturers. She provided an example to explain her views:

> For example, many Australian lecturers taught us fundamental knowledge, but they tested more complex knowledge, which made me need to learn extra contents by myself after class ... In this case, I really liked to study in Chinese style. Lecturers taught everything to students and gave us many practice tests. I thought the Australian context was too flexible to learn knowledge in depth. When I had plenty of time, I did not know what I needed to learn in Australia.

Fei and Dong's experiences indicated their disempowered feelings in the new learning context. Although they engaged in intercultural learning, they did not seem to be in control of their learning. Their non-adaptation to the English-speaking context and new teaching modes provided further evidence to show that not all students can successfully develop their intercultural competencies. It seemed that these students held negative attitudes towards the "others." Learning experiences on the Chinese stage played a dominant role in their intercultural adjustments or lack thereof to the Australian context.

Their non-adaptation indicated that such cross-system tensions negatively influenced their intercultural learning experiences. The learning shock made them struggle in the intercultural learning processes. Their experiences, especially in Fei's language school, suggested that they faced negative discrepancies between their expectations, achievements and actual actions, making them start to doubt themselves and feel frustrated in the intercultural learning process (Bandura, 1989). Based on such experiences, their attitudes, goals, and preferences regarding the intercultural study were negatively changed. Their experiences also suggested that these students seemed to have a sense in their minds that they could not adjust to the new context. However, to complete the learning process and obtain degrees, they had to study in a setting that positions them between "do not want to do mentally" and "have to do physically." Such an experience could add further insights into Park's (2018) suggestion about the relationships between the notions of "to do mentally" and "to do physically."

According to the analysis in this section, it is evident that these students experienced different intercultural adjustment processes during their TAPs. Most students faced stress in the initial stages in each context. To deal with stress, these students indicated multiple senses of agency and adopted different approaches. After experiencing each context, they found their ways to deal with different academic tasks with either positive or negative senses of agency. As mentioned above, in the Chinese phrase, TAPs seemed to extend intercultural learning from the host country to the home country. Although students did not physically move to Australia, their IELTS learning experiences and other related English-based learning activities potentially shaped an original intercultural context.

Due to individual differences, when they came to Australia, students reflected various senses of agency towards the changes in the academic context. Many students experienced a "stress-adaptation-development" process, but some of them struggled in the intercultural context. Such responses to the cross-system differences resonate with Bandura's (2001) social cognitive concept that sociocultural contexts influence people's agency. It seemed that some students wished to be intercultural learners, but some did not. Therefore, the intercultural learning in the TAP dynamically shapes and influences students' sense of agency. These students continually shift between empowered and disempowered towards different academic tasks.

3 Shifting between Multiple Identities as Intercultural Learner

Identity refers merely to who am I (Taylor, 1989). From a learning perspective, Lave and Wenger (1991) explicitly indicated that learning is a necessary and essential part of social development, which is a process that is always accompanied by (re)constructions of self-identity through interactions with different sociocultural elements. Therefore, the (re)constructions of self-identity can be regarded as "long-term, living relations between persons and their place and participation in communities of practice" (Lave & Wenger, 1991, p. 53). Intercultural learning can comprehensively bring various changes to Chinese students who might enhance their skills and reshape their identities (Gill, 2007).

As a group of diasporas, these students showed various changes of identities as intercultural learners in TAPs. Precisely, according to Robins (1991), diaspora usually reflects two trends of changing identities, including "tradition" and "translation." The former notion means that some diaspora members attempt to restore their original identities, especially when they are feeling "lost" in the new context. The latter term, translation, suggests that some people cannot be "pure" again after experiencing the other context; they develop hybrid identities. Based on these theoretical explanations of the relations between their interactions and different academic contexts, many students experienced the (re)constructions of their identities as intercultural hybrid learners during their cross-system transitioning journey.

From the learners' perspective, most students become knowledge explorers in Australia as distinct from their experiences as knowledge followers or acceptors in China. However, they were different explorers regarding their attitudes towards the change of academic and sociocultural settings. Specifically, many students considered themselves as independent explorers. In contrast, some were not comfortable with being independent explorer and thus demonstrated negative attitudes towards their cross-system learning. These research participants held on to their traditional identities and developed their cultural hybridity (Bhabha, 1994).

3.1   *Dependent and Demotivated Followers in China*

The changes of identity spontaneously occurred when these students started their TAPs. As mentioned above, in China's beginning stage, many students indicated that they did not have specific learning ambitions. They even had limited understanding regarding their further intercultural study and associated experiences. Such uncertain confusions perhaps reflected their immature personalities as young students. Furthermore, many students suggested that their choice of studying in TAP was influenced by their parents or other relatives, which indicate their "dependent" features even though they had their expectations. For example, Rui mentioned that his parents could help him find a job in a business-related field after graduation, so he studied business management. However, Rui did not have strong motivations to be an academic achiever. As he said, "I did not have a specific learning goal; I just wanted to pass exams and get the degree." Differently, Zhuang suggested that his parents wished him to be independent:

> My parent wished me to be a university student. Taking this learning opportunity, they wished me to go to other cities or countries to gain various learning and life experiences. This was my first time living in another

A TORTUOUS TRAJECTORY OF INTERCULTURAL LEARNING　　81

context. Before going to university, I was living with my parents without independent living experience.

These experiences show that many students were highly dependent on their parents when they started their university life. As Bandura (1989) suggested, the environmental contexts and people's behaviours had reciprocal influences on each other. Due to the previous one-child policy in Chinese society, many students were the only child in their family. Based on my experiences, most parental attention usually focused on the only child. According to these students' experiences, they were profoundly influenced by the parental dominated context, which made them reflect specific dependent features.

After starting the Chinese learning stage, many students argued that they usually waited for instructions without enough powerful motivation to explore knowledge independently. For instance, Biang felt that following lecturers and textbooks could ensure to pass exams, which was a safe way to study.

> In China, I did not need to do much more work by myself to pass exams. I think that I would not have explored something under the lecturers' guidance. They usually taught by following textbooks, and we reviewed them after class. Exams were based on textbooks as well.

These extracts indicate that many students were used to following their lecturers when studying in China. In this teaching model, they felt that it was unnecessary and vital to explore knowledge by themselves. Learning seemed to be highly dependent on lecturers and exams without strong self-expectations to explore knowledge independently. Importantly, they became demotivated in learning. For example, Xie said:

> When I was studying at my Chinese university, I was sluggish. I always prepared for the exam at the end of each semester. I did not study very hard during the whole semester.

Dong also mentioned that she was used to the same mode as Xie adopted. However, she felt that her university's context lacked an academic atmosphere, which made her become one of the students who felt idle at university.

> I was so ambitious when I started my university life ... After studying for a little while, I thought I did not have enough motivation because of the context and other peers. That environment was not suitable for academic achievement. In such a context, it was difficult to be independent of other factors.

Dong's story indicates that she experienced a change from motivated to demotivated learner influenced by the others in her Chinese university. The relaxed, non-demanding university context and peers provoked a passive attitude towards study. Such experiences also indicated that the others also profoundly influenced her identity as a student. The data suggested that these students' identity in the Chinese stage was significantly affected by the context that they were studying and living in. Their self-reflections of their identities as dependent and demotivated follower in learning can be one type of outcome of the Chinese academic system. It is worth noting that although these participants were studying in different majors and universities in China, it seemed that they had similar self-understandings about their identities. After studying in Australia, these students reflected dynamic and fluid changes of identities.

3.2 Becoming Independent and Motivated Explorer in Australia

Due to the changes in sociocultural contexts, many students reflected different identities. Most students become independent and active towards intercultural study and life. However, some of them passively became independent rather than having strong intrinsic motivations, revealing a strong sense of hybrid identity. Compared to the "dependent" and "demotivated" experiences in China, most students identified that they became independent and motivated learners in the Australian context. For instance, Hao shared that:

> The most damaging aspect was a high dependency. I remembered that I felt it difficult to adjust to such a learning context in the initial stage. I always wanted to ask my lecturers to help me do something. This thinking could be a problem, but I have solved this problem. When I started my Australian university learning, I felt lecturers did not teach detailed knowledge in the classroom, and few contents were introduced. However, there were many gaps between the taught contents and assessments. To fill the gaps, I needed to be a self-regulated and motivated learner who can use other methods to overcome these shortcomings. Internet-based technology became much more helpful to me at Australian universities.

She further explained that learning how to learn is more important than waiting to be "fed" knowledge.

> Before coming here, I did not realise I can become an active learner and loved to explore new things in this relaxed and flexible environment. Now I can do design work independently and have the ability to solve many problems. This was what I did not imagine before coming to the

Australian university. So, I was delighted with the transnational learning experience. In China, we have a well-known saying: 'It is better to teach a man to fish than to give him fish.' I thought learning at an Australian university can help me explore fishing methods rather than obtain fish without the fishing process.

Hao's comments showed supportive evidence to capture a snapshot of her changes of identity as an intercultural learner. As she mentioned, she actively developed her "fishing skills" rather than passively wait for "fish" in the Australian context. Her experience might well indicate that she changed her role from a knowledge acceptor to a self-regulated explorer. Similarly, other students (e.g., Shuo, Qing, Minze, Zhuang, Diao, Dang, and Biang) also indicated that they became independent and active towards study. It is worthwhile to note that although many students studied in different majors and different universities in Australia, they indicated similar changes of identity as intercultural learners. For instance, Minze said that she became an ICT-based active learner.

I thought I became more active when I studied in Australia because this environment and study style required me to rely on myself rather than lecturers or other kinds of solid material, for example, textbooks. Lecturers encouraged students to be creative and critical in learning rather than only mechanically remember what they taught in class. Thus, I needed to use Internet-based tools to develop my learning approaches and abilities to achieve my goal and academic requirements.

Their experiences indicated that they continuously changed their learning approaches from those they adopted in China to those utilised in Australia. In the negotiation process with different teaching and learning contexts, these students were also able to reconstruct their identities as intercultural learners. According to the above quotations, it is evident that these students became "another" person compared to their previous experiences. They also realised the importance of dynamically changing their roles in the new context rather than passively waiting for change. Their experiences also suggested that the contextual changes significantly influenced students' reconstructions of identities as intercultural learners. Such experiences indicated that these students could expand their views and learn via their experience of cross-system tensions (Engeström, 1987, 2001). Their identities were "translated," as they were, after moving to Australia (Robins, 1991).

However, as mentioned before, not all students reflected positive changes towards their intercultural learning process, but they still needed to accept the situation. In this case, they showed negative attitudes. For instance, concerning the changes in teaching and learning approaches, Xin's experiences indicated that she seemed to be a highly dependent learner struggling with Australia's new academic model.

> I still prefer to study in a traditional Chinese teaching mode. I wish lecturers can write down the important contents on the blackboard and give us detailed explanations, especially math subjects. Australian lecturers did not write essential contents on the blackboard during a class. They usually read slides and explained them orally without any writing. It felt so confusing for me to understand the taught content.

She further argued that she was a traditional learner who was not used to highly ICT-based exploratory teaching and learning model.

> I preferred to study in a non-Internet context. In such a context, lecturers will provide more details to students. We do not need to explore knowledge by ourselves. For students, this approach will save more time and energy.

To adjust to the new context, Xin said: "I force myself to study here, but I felt different studying without enough support from lecturers and other peers." Her experiences suggested a struggling picture of students' passive roles as learners in the intercultural learning process. These experiences may indicate that as a diaspora member, she had a strong "emotional attachment" (Rizvi et al., 2016, p. 8) to the Chinese educational model.

Meanwhile, some students' experiences (e.g., Dang, Shuo, Xie, and Zhuang) indicated that the new teaching model heavily influenced their identity changes to independent and active learners in Australia. The students appeared to have no choice but to make adjustments. For instance, Dang argued that:

> Many Australian lecturers preferred to teach more practical skills and knowledge. They wished students to do something by themselves through explorations rather than being taught everything. In this case, I felt it was difficult to keep following lecturers' teaching in some classes, and learning seemed to be superficial under this circle. I thought the knowledge I learned was based on my self-exploration from the Internet rather than mainly from lecturers. Therefore, I thought this was not a very good experience.

Although Dang became independent in her study after coming to Australia, her experiences indicated that her changes were not entirely dependent on her motivation. However, external factors made her passively adjust to the new context. Both the positive and negative changes illustrate a dynamic picture of students' fluid changes in their identities as transnational learners. These experiences provided further insights to show the "passively" active (re)shaping of identities in the transnational learning process, which could further refine Gill's (2007) framework. Their experiences and struggles also suggested that some students wished to be "traditional," and their "translations" were passive (Robins, 1991). Notably, the different uses of digital technologies in the transitioning journey played significant roles in (re)shaping their identities as transnational learners, which could be a socialisation process in different contexts (Chang & Gomes, 2020).

In this process, some students developed hybrid identities that enabled them to sit in between dependent followers and independent explorers. These two different experiences indicated that the Chinese and Australian educational variations had significant influences on shaping students' fluid identities, which suggests that "difference" (e.g., social culture and academic) is a basis for (re)constructing one's identities (Hall, 1990). Furthermore, these aspects could indicate that students' identities were not an accomplished fact; in contrast, their identities were continually being (re)shaped along with the changes of cultural and social conditions (Hall, 1990).

4 Shaping Different Senses of Belonging as Transnational Diaspora

As members of the Chinese diaspora, research participants had various senses of belonging to the different educational contexts during the transnational learning process. According to McMillan and Chavis (1986, p. 10),

> The sense of belonging and identification involves the feeling, belief, and expectation that one fits in the group and has a place there, a feeling of acceptance by the group, and a willingness to sacrifice for the group. The role of identification must be emphasised here. It may be represented in the reciprocal statements 'It is my group' and 'I am part of the group.'

In this study, these students reflected various preferences and belonging in the transnational learning processes. More specifically, as Chinese overseas students, a group of students enjoyed and satisfied their transnational learning

86   CHAPTER 4

process, especially in the Australian stage. Their positive senses of intercultural learning indicated their belonging as transnational learners who preferred and adjusted to the Australian learning context. However, some students believed that they did not belong to the Australian learning context. They did not adapt to the new learning situation and context and experienced loneliness, homesickness, and even isolation in the intercultural learning process. They preferred to study in the Chinese contexts as a Chinese learner rather than an intercultural overseas student.

4.1   *Transnational Learning as a Way to Adapt to a New Context*
Many participants (e.g., Gong, Hao, Yuner, Guang, Rui, Diao, Shuo, and Qiang) indicated that they were satisfied with their intercultural learning experiences. Significantly, as Chinese overseas students, they believed that they had adjusted to the Australian context. For instance, Hao mentioned that:

> Compared to my original expectations before coming to Australia, I thought my learning experience was much more significant than I thought before. I thought I have adapted to the Australian context. I was delighted with my transnational learning.

Hao's comments indicated her successful adaptation to the Australian context and satisfaction with her intercultural learning experiences. Similarly, Qiang's comments represent the group with a strong sense of belonging in the Australian context as Chinese overseas students.

> In Australia, I feel all things are kind and helpful ... In Australia, I felt I have more confidence to study and want to be an active learner to develop my ability. So, I was satisfied with my choice. I believed that I could become better in Australia.

Compared with Hao and Qiang's comments, Gong pinpointed his particular views on intercultural adaption and belonging issues.

> After staying here several months later, I adapted to the local environment. However, I thought adaptation issues were challenging because everyone had different backgrounds and the ability to accept new things. For me, I thought the most valuable experience was not how much knowledge I learned. It was an independent learning experience. I learned how I could become an independent and active learner in the Australian context.

Gong's comments show that he felt that he could adapt to the Australian context, which indicates his strong confidence in becoming another person that belongs to the new environment. These experiences are consistent with Gill's (2007) argument that "students who are motivated for changes and personal growth are more likely to develop positive attitudes, thereby enabling them to deal effectively with challenges and differences in learning within the new context" (p. 180). However, based on his comments, it is essential to understand individual differences in the Australian learning context. These experiences also suggested that although many students had not completed their learning and were studying in different stages at Australian universities, they had adjusted themselves to the new context and also achieved several developments. In contrast, some students reflected strong senses of isolation in the new context.

4.2 Homesick, Non-Adaptation, and Struggle

Amongst the research participants, some students (e.g., Fei, Biang, Meng, Xin, Zhuang, and Dong) reflected a strong sense of non-adaptation to the new context. Their experiences outlined in the above sections indicated a series of snapshots of their non-adaptation as Chinese overseas students in their transnational learning processes. Notably, when discussing their learning context preferences, they all shared that they wanted to go home after completing their study. Such experiences suggest a sense of isolation in the new environment. For example, Dong explained her understandings of why she felt passive in the intercultural context:

> The primary issue was the adaptation to Australian life and learning context. After studying here for a long time, I felt I still preferred the Chinese context. In Australia, I did not have too many friends and no family members. I wanted to live in a metropolis and to stay with my friends and family. So, I did not want to apply for PR now, and I wished to graduate successfully. Now I am planning to prepare for finding a job in China after this semester.

Dong not only felt that it was challenging to adapt to the Australian teaching and learning mode, but she also did not have support from family and friends. Such feelings of isolation made her passive and upset. Her experiences indicated a strong sense of homesickness. Compared with her experiences, Fei shared an example to illustrate his sense of isolation in learning.

> One impressive thing for me was writing an assignment in the language school. When I was learning English, I needed to submit a portfolio, which

included various written works. Before doing this assignment, I asked the lecturer a stupid question: 'I need to write by hand or type on the computer?' The lecturer appeared to be very unbelieving to me. I thought she might think that why you asked such a question? I explained that some of my Chinese lecturers wanted to avoid plagiarism and did not let us write assignments by using a computer. However, the lecturer told me that they had stopped writing assignments by hand for quite a long time. This case made me feel that I was so out-of-date and not belonging to the Australian ICT-based learning mode.

This example indicated that Fei was shocked by the ICT-based learning environment when he studied in a language school, which made him feel that he seemed to be a stranger in the ICT-based learning context. Although he tried to make some changes to adapt to the Australian model, he still felt that his transnational learning was problematic.

I preferred to study in China. In China, I did not have language and cultural barriers. Even though I study in Beijing, I can adapt to being there in a short time because there were no cultural and language issues. Furthermore, the Australian university had too many assignments and exams compared to my Chinese one, which made me feel stressed. When I could not communicate with other people effectively, I believed that studying became much more challenging.

Considering the life issues, Meng also had negative experiences, which made him feel "strong loneliness," for example, in respect of relations with peers.

I faced strong isolation from my Chinese classmates. When I studied hard, they felt I was a crazy boy, and I was very strange. Some of them said many bad things that made me uncomfortable. They thought I was not more intelligent than them. They cursed that the more I studied, the lower mark I may have. One of my classmates told me that most of my classmates did not successfully graduate from the language school and university. Such rude information makes me feel angry. Even though I spent much time studying, finally, my score may be still lower than theirs.

Meng's classmates did not have a friendly attitude towards him, making Meng feel uncomfortable when he heard such harsh words. He further complained that it was so difficult to make real friends in Australia.

> I proposed to live together with my Chinese classmates and help each other. However, the situation was entirely different. We did not contact each other much after coming to Australia. This may be because everyone had his or her things in both life and study. It was challenging to make real friends in Australia. So, I wished I can leave Australia after graduation.

The above experiences showed that many students faced various study and life issues during the intercultural learning process. However, as he mentioned, "when I faced such situations, I felt morose, but I must suffer this process to achieve my learning goal." According to his interviews, it is evident that he did not have a strong sense of belonging towards intercultural learning as an overseas Chinese student in Australia. The feelings of isolation ensured he suffered various negative experiences. According to these experiences, it is worth noting that he had already had a strong sense of isolation. Similarly, although Fei had nearly finished learning in Australia, he was still not able to "fit into" the "so-called" new context. Therefore, it seemed that having a sense of belonging is not profoundly influenced by the length of stay in a new environment; instead, each has their specific attitudes.

These experiences potentially offered some insights into the diasporic experience. These students believed that they belonged to their homeland no matter how long they stayed in the new context (Rizvi et al., 2016). Although these experiences indicated their keen senses of non-belonging and non-adaptation to the Australian context, their experiences showed a particular case of the diaspora's emotional connections with the home country (in this case: China). The negative "diasporic experiences" made them have a strong sense of belonging to their homeland. These findings could reflect Otten's (2003) opinion that "if foreign students do not develop close social relationships after a certain period, negative effects on their readiness for learning, their consciousness for relevant learning tasks, and their academic performance might occur" (p. 20).

More specifically, Meng's isolated experiences with his Chinese classmates provided a particular example different from that of Rizvi et al.'s (2016) finding that "individuals are recognised and accepted within their communities as being diaspora members" (p. 8). Although he was a native Chinese TAP student, he felt isolated from his peers in the micro-TAP community as an individual member of the TAP group. It seemed that other individuals did not readily accept him as a member of the TAP diaspora. This experience indicated that acceptance issues among the diaspora members potentially influence an individual's sense of belonging and even affect the whole intercultural learning and life experience. Although individuals can physically become members of a particular group of diasporas, they may not be emotionally and kindly accepted into such a group. Therefore, such examples of being a member of a diaspora group indicated the complexity of understanding the changes in belonging that these overseas students experienced.

This section has shown various students' senses of belonging in the new academic and sociocultural contexts. As the results indicated, not all students could deal with the intercultural barriers (e.g., language, teaching and learning, and relations with others). Although many students finally felt that they could adapt to the new context, some participants still struggled with the intercultural learning processes.

5   Conclusion

This chapter portrayed students' transnational learning experiences through adopting the transformative learning framework (Gill, 2007). The findings could offer evidence to manifest Gill's (2007) conceptual process of intercultural adjustment. Findings further indicated that students' intercultural learning process was dynamic rather than fixed as the transnational diaspora.

According to students' various intercultural learning experiences, TAPS extended intercultural learning in the Chinese stage. When they physically moved to Australia, the "real" intercultural learning journey started. However, students indicated different capabilities to adjust to the new context by facing issues and uncertainties in cross-system transition. Consequently, a group of students could actively reshape or relocate themselves as independent learners in the new context. In contrast, some students seemed to passively accept the changes as they had to complete their study. These students were suffering unfamiliarity with the new teaching and learning mode, isolation from peers and homesickness, and language barriers. Such struggles made them feel that they did not belong to the Australian context and wished to return to the Chinese system. These experiences also provided several insights to argue that not all students could potentially achieve positive adjustment and development in the process of intercultural learning, as Gill's (2007) framework suggested. Notably, many students may become immersed between "stress" and "adaptation" but may not reach development with a positive mind. After understanding the various changes that these students experienced, it is also essential to explore the situational context they had such individual changes.

As students' transnational learning experiences in Chapter 4 showed, they experienced constant changes from university novices in China to intercultural learners who hold multiple views towards the transnational learning journey. Their learning journeys can illustrate vivid pictures of global mobility and interactive transition of people, culture, and education across different places, spaces, and times. Such movement potentially enables more connections and communications between the home and host countries, which creates "new spaces and places, and new speeds and rhythms of everyday social practice" (Leander, Phillips, & Taylor, 2010, p. 329). However, the relationships between students' learning and the new spaces and places still merit more in-depth analysis, especially under the rapid development of technology (Leander et al., 2010). Chapter 5 will illustrate the key factors that map the contour of the learning space in TAP.

Note

1 Parts of this chapter are based on Dai, K., Lingard, B., & Reyes, V. (2018). 'In-betweenners': Chinese students' experiences in China-Australia articulation programs. *Scottish Educational Review*, 50(1), 36–55. Permission for re-use has been given by the publishers.

CHAPTER 5

Mapping a Transitioning In-Between Learning Space

To cross the river by feeling the stones.
摸着石头过河

∴

This chapter shows that Internet-based technology, assessment modes, teaching strategies, and the university community's setting emerged as factors that constantly influenced students' sense of identity, agency, and belonging in their cross-system transitions. These factors potentially mapped a transnational learning space for students to experience cross-system differences and then locate themselves in different positions in the transition process.

Such a special zone can be conceptualised as a third space (Bhabha, 1994). As Ellis and Goodyear (2016) highlighted, "understanding students' perspectives in researching the use and meaning of space is crucially important" (p. 153). This chapter will appropriate Bhabha's (1994) concepts of a third (or in-between) space to analyse and map the transnational learning space's contours based on participants' voices as articulated through research interviews. Specifically, the illustration of the spectrum of a learning space is elaborate, which means that it is impossible to holistically cover and analyse all potential factors that create a learning space (Ellis & Goodyear, 2016). Therefore, the analysis mainly focuses on my participants' responses in interviews. I wish to add further empirical insights into the research gap concerning the relationships between learners and learning space through this analysis.

1   The Conceptualisation of the Transitioning In-Between Space in TAP[1]

The TAP allows learners to engage in global mobility from both physical and virtual perspectives under the constant developments and changes in technology, society and culture. As students' experiences indicated, they studied

© KONINKLIJKE BRILL NV, LEIDEN, 2022 | DOI: 10.1163/9789004505131_005

MAPPING A TRANSITIONING IN-BETWEEN LEARNING SPACE　93

in China and Australia across their undergraduate period, which signified the transition of their learning and living places between China and Australia. The TAP feature is a cooperatively combined educational mode of two different "places" (e.g., China and Australia). From the philosophical perspective, TAP students started to construct their own learning spaces via experiencing movement across places, which usually have specific sociocultural and educational features and rules (Deleuze & Guattari, 1987). Notably, students may transit and shift themselves between "smooth" and "striated" spaces across different places (Deleuze & Guattari, 1987). The striated space has set up a series of regulations, principles, or routines, which people usually follow. Meanwhile, students may develop their own "smooth space" to dynamically (re)locate themselves in an appropriate position depending on individual features and situations in different places and also striated spaces (Casey, 1997). According to these philosophical debates, TAP students constantly transit and shift themselves between smooth and striated spaces in places with the development of qualitatively various senses of agency, identity, and belonging.

More specifically, considering the meaning of learning space, Goodyear (2006) suggested that it refers to an abstract metaphorical concept that people can share and evaluate their specific experiences as these happened in specific educational and life contexts. Learners have "opportunities to examine their cultural context" (Goodyear, 2006, p. 221). However, according to Bennett (2010), when researchers investigate interculturally related experiences, it is essential to strategically treat cultural stereotypes rather than label each individual by an over-generalised cultural sign. In other words, the way to conceptualise and understand the abstract space is not as simple as it is a terrain with many overlapping layers of different cognitions, sociocultural issues, and individual differences.

In the TAP setting, the transitioning in-between features became more apparent. When students studied at their Chinese universities (places), they needed to follow specific rules proposed by the university, lecturers, and other elements, which could be a striated space. Learning in striated space, students further developed their own smooth space where they potentially developed various attitudes towards the striated space. Depending on the changes of striated space, they also dynamically adjusted themselves to develop further smooth spaces. When they moved to Australia, places became different and then striated space also had its particular features. Then, each student potentially changed regarding agency, identity and sense of belonging in their new smooth spaces, which could contrast with their previous ones in China. As a result, they needed to develop new smooth spaces by continually negotiating with Australia's striated space and continued developing new smooth spaces through comparisons with

94 CHAPTER 5

the Chinese context. In this process, they are potentially immersed in a complicated in-between position. Meanwhile, the TAP setting also positioned them in-between various local places, smooth spaces, and striated spaces. Finally, a sense of in-betweenness might potentially smoothly emerge.

These TAP learning experiences reflect various cultural and educational differences between China and Australia and reshape their identity as TAP learners with varying degrees of agency to deal with cross-system barriers during their transition from China to Australia. According to Hall (1990), one's identity is constantly being (re)constructed. Identity is thus fluid via communications and exchanges between and across different cultures. As findings reported in Chapter 4 demonstrated, students' sense of agency towards the cultural and educational differences indicated their multiple capabilities and attitudes as intercultural learners who needed to deal with various barriers in the cross-system context. Many students were able to overcome barriers actively and have progressive attitudes towards the new context. In contrast, some participants felt disempowered to deal with intercultural learning and adjustment processes. Consequently, their identities and belonging were also influenced and partly changed under the transition of sociocultural and educational contexts from China to Australia.

Students spontaneously compared their Chinese and Australian learning experiences from different perspectives in studying in the intercultural context. Such comparative experiences potentially created a particular zone that is a space for students to reflect on and negotiate educational and cultural differences. Different educational and cultural features were continually and animatedly intertwined in this space, which can be the origin of producing the in-between space (Bhabha, 1994). In this space, the boundaries of different cultures become blurred, and people could have various unexpected new understandings of different cultures (Bhabha, 1994). Importantly, their negotiations of different cultures are dynamic in the in-between space, which is constantly changing and complex and challenging to explicitly understand (Bhabha, 1994). Therefore, it is essential to explore how these students' intercultural learning experiences produced the transitioning in-between space in TAPs to explain why they had various identity, agency, and belonging changes.

2 ICT-Mediated Learning Space

The learning space is complicated when the physical and virtual worlds are connected and mixed. The "physical places" mainly refers to learning contexts that do have not many ICT-assisted features and elements. The "virtual spaces" can be understood merely as ICT-assisted context. The combination of physical and virtual learning worlds is a blended context. In this study, students reflected different stories of experiencing the different learning places and spaces. Specifically, as many students suggested, using ICTs in China and Australia was dramatically different in their education.

2.1 From Physical Place to an ICT-Mediated In-Between Space

Students' learning experiences indicated their movement from a mainly physical learning place in China to a combined in-between space in Australia. Notably, the data was collected several years ago, and universities may also have different ICT infrastructures. With the rapid development of ICT and the general uses of internet-based tools, situations may be different now. Notably, with the pandemic of Covid-19 since the beginning of 2020, internet-based technology has played a significant role in (re)shaping education across the world. Education has encountered dramatic changes and uncertainties. Thus, students' experiences may not represent a generalised situation in China, and it only reflects several pieces of the whole puzzle. When I interviewed these research participants, they mainly studied in the physical place without deep engagement in the virtual world. For instance, learning focused on textbooks without many ICT-assisted experiences. Evidence can be found in many students' interviews (e.g., Zhuang, Biang, Xin, Dang, Qing, Shuo, Hao and Dong). As Zhuang shared his view:

> Textbooks were the primary learning resource ... I did not use too many Internet-based technologies in my study. Exams are based on the contents in textbooks rather than the Internet. So, I think most students still preferred to use textbooks as key resources.

Similarly, Hao shared her experiences that there were limited applications of Internet-based technologies in her study.

> I did not use many Internet-based technologies in learning at my Chinese university. If I did, it often happened when I needed to understand a concept shown in the textbook. Then I searched for relevant information. That was all. In China, Internet-based technologies were supplementary, and they did not play the core role in my learning.

Some students also mentioned their views towards the reasons why they did not have many ICT-based learning experiences. For instance, Dang attributed such a situation to course design.

I thought that the curriculum design influenced the use of Internet-based technology in the learning process. In China, I did not think that we had many courses requiring students to use the Internet for learning. All students always sit in a classroom, and lecturers taught knowledge from the front of the classroom based on textbooks or other related resources.

Rui added that the quality of ICTs influenced students' applications.

My previous university had an online course management system. This system can show necessary admin information. It did not have more functions and information for each course. Although we had such a system, as far as I knew, few students visited it. Before exams, some students may check relevant information and then pass it to other people. Such a system did not support students' learning. Most students only log in to the system two or three times to check exam information or fill a university survey every semester. Furthermore, the system usually frequently crashed, which made it more challenging to use. This situation indicated that establishing and maintaining such a system was not of high quality, and techniques were deficient. As a result, no one used it anymore because it was too terrible to be used effectively, which was trouble for learning.

However, many students suggested that the Internet was mainly used for entertainment purposes in the Chinese context. As Xiang suggested, "At my Chinese university, most students use the Internet as an entertainment tool." Dong also claimed, "Internet is just a tool for fun, for example, playing games, online shopping, and watching videos. Time spending on the Internet is wasted."

According to these students' interview data, it is evident that Internet-based technologies at some Chinese universities were not used to support students' learning. However, the Internet created a virtual space for entertainment. As a result, even when some tools were available, there were limited benefits for students' learning. Textbook-based learning potentially reduced the knowledge interactions and transformations between physical place and virtual space. Furthermore, textbook-based learning might suggest limited knowledge transformations in students' learning between China and Australia. These students did not have many learning experiences based on the Australian curriculum or delivered by lecturers from the Australian university when they were in China. Hence, most students in the Chinese context did not enter the in-between space created by the usage of both physical and virtual learning tools.

Instead, according to Brennan's (2006) distinction between space and place, their learning still happened mainly in Chinese physical places (e.g., classroom-based and textbook-focused learning modes). Moreover, such learning experiences suggest that many students seemed far from learning in the virtual space of in-betweenness, positioned between China and Australia. However, the situation was different in Australia.

In terms of their learning in Australia, students reflected different experiences. First, most learners entered a mixed learning zone of physical place and virtual space. Their learning activities had many interactions between physical place and virtual space, which made them deeply in-between. Practically, many students created their in-between learning space via both physical and virtual intermediaries. Consequently, many students pinpointed that learning would be complex if they did not have Internet-based technology for their study. For example, Hao shared her view:

> I have to use a lot of online resources in my study. Although I still used it for entertainment, I cannot study if there were no Internet-based tools ... Most learning contents were electric versions. It is essential to use the Internet to search for information to help me understand the contents.

Many other students also offered similar comments. For instance, Shuo provided detailed examples to show his engagement in the combined learning space.

> At my Australian university, every student had an account and password to login to his/her online learning platform. In such an online environment, I can find out most course contents and many tools that can help me study efficiently, such as an online time planner. Once I opened a course, much information will automatically show on the time planner, for example, location, duration, lecturers ... I can also use my account to log in to the library system to borrow books and reading online at the Australian university. My Australian university's account can access external databases and the online course's website. When I want to watch some video tutorials, I can access this kind of website without paying a fee, and it is perfect for students. If I wanted to borrow a specific book, they also can order and hold it through the online system, which was very easy to handle. The university online learning system also allowed students to select their courses, pay tuition and book meeting rooms. In general, at the Australian university, I can do most things through the university website and online learning platform. However, when I was in

China, I remembered that I viewed the university website no more than 5 times because I think I cannot find out valuable information from the university website or platform for my daily study.

These examples illustrated a general picture of the application of Internet-based tools in learning at Australian universities. These students' learning seemed to move into an in-between learning space rather than a physically dominant mode. Furthermore, they provided many examples to illustrate their learning processes (e.g., before, in, and after classes) in the in-between space of the combination of physical and virtual contexts. For instance, Meng noted that he usually previewed course contents during learning.

I usually used Blackboard to preview the course content and prepare my learning plan. It was convenient for me to get access to course information via this platform. However, I did not do this work when I was in China.

Meng's experience initially suggested that he adopted ICT-based tools to assist his preview, which potentially made his learning activities happen in a physical place and a virtual space. Considering the activities in class, many students reflected that their learning happened between physical and virtual spaces. For example, Diao provided an example:

For some courses in electric system management, many lecturers from the business school usually adopted Internet-based technology to teach, such as video, online interactive communication tools, professional websites and mobile apps ... Students could participate in learning and teaching processes with lecturers together rather than only listening.

When discussing the application of Internet-based technology after class, most students identified that it was essential to use such tools to review course contents and complete assignments. For example, Biang outlined his experience:

I usually followed the lecturers' teaching and review course content regularly. I used the Blackboard to download lecture slides. Sometimes I listened to the recording if I missed a class. I also did assignments online and searched for some math or engineering concepts that were hard to understand during the class learning process.

Biang's learning experience indicated that ICT-based tools holistically permeate his learning process. Similarly, Diao reported her learning experiences.

> At my Australian university, all learning content was uploaded to an online learning system, which helped me to review taught knowledge and enhance understanding easily. While writing an essay or doing another assignment, I needed to use Internet-based technology as the primary tool to help me complete my work, for example, searching for articles on Google Scholar.

These research interview extracts illustrate the differences in learning place and space in the transition from China to Australia. Specifically, students' Chinese experiences suggested a physically dominated learning place without in-depth virtual-based activities. In this place, learning was textbook-dominated, and ICTs were supplementary for most students. Consequently, it seems that the first two years of study were mainly conducted in a physical place with more focus on traditional learning resources (e.g., textbooks). However, as the selected data has shown above, ICTs were widely adopted to support learning and teaching in the Australian context, especially in students' daily study. Hence, learners seemed to start learning in an in-between space that combined both features of physical and virtual contexts. Their experiences showed apparent differences when compared with the Chinese context. It seemed that many students studied in a blended context that combined both physical and virtual educational settings. In doing so, students could engage in an in-between space rather than solely rely on physical contexts and resources.

2.2 ICT-Mediated In-Between Space for Knowledge Interactions between China and Australia

Many students used Internet-based tools to have close connections with the Chinese context when they studied in Australia. Internet-based tools became a vital bridge to position these students in between China and Australia. In short, although these students physically studied and lived in Australia, they had close connections with the Chinese contexts. According to Harvey (1999), time and space have been compressed via the broad application of Internet-based technologies. In this compressed virtual space, students achieved knowledge transformations and interactions between different educational and cultural contexts. Interview data demonstrated evidence to illustrate the construction of an ICT-based in-between learning space. For example, in this study, almost every student mentioned that their most significant learning stress was due to the issue of the English language. For instance, Zhuang observed: "For Chinese students whose first language is not English, the learning pressures are much higher than Australian students." Shuo also suggested that language is one of the most challenging barriers in his study.

> The hardest thing for me to overcome was the language. It took me a long time to adapt to the local learning environment. Significantly, it was challenging to find out a fast way to deal with such language problems. The only thing I can do was use the language, more reading, writing, listening and speaking.

Due to English language issues, many students made use of Internet-based tools to overcome language barriers. For example, Rui suggested, "I usually searched relevant Chinese information from the Internet to help me understand English meanings." Similarly, Dang further explained that Internet-based tools could provide a valuable platform for investigating and understanding specific knowledge in her field.

> I usually used Internet-based tools, such as an online directory, professional website, and search engine, to help me understand professional concepts. Many concepts were difficult to understand in English, so I searched for them in Chinese to help me deeply comprehend the real meaning. Furthermore, there are plenty of academic papers and resources online. It was beneficial to me to understand knowledge by searching for Chinese information. Moreover, I usually checked my grammar through online English learning platforms. Internet-based technology helped me to overcome many language problems.

These experiences reveal that Internet-based tools became supportive assistants that helped students to overcome language barriers to some extent. Specifically, some students even searched for information on Chinese resources to deal with language and understanding issues. Such activities further confirmed that technology became a vital mediation to shorten the distance between this student diaspora and their homeland (Rizvi et al., 2016). Notably, such technology connected the diaspora with the homeland and played significant roles in knowledge transformations from Chinese to English and vice versa, which created a learning space without the boundaries of places. Studying in this space, students experienced learning in "a world of instantaneous communication and virtuality" (Brennan, as cited in Rizvi & Lingard, 2010, p. 66).

ICT-based learning experiences helped students deal with English issues as mediation of knowledge transformation and created an in-between virtual learning space for many students to achieve knowledge communication between China and Australia. For example, Biang shared his experiences:

> When studying in a course concerning engineering project management, I found it difficult to understand some key theoretical concepts. Although I thought the language was not the primary problem, the discipline knowledge was challenging for me to understand in some cases deeply. To deal with these learning issues, I found a Chinese MOOC to learn something similar in my native language. So, I can learn detailed knowledge by following both Chinese and foreign lecturers. I can learn related contents from professors from different universities, which also extended my learning scope.

Other students also mentioned this cross-country ICT-assisted example. For instance, Rui indicated that he attended online courses to help him deal with learning difficulties.

> In the WeChat platform, some educational companies offer professional knowledge services, such as Accounting. I tried some courses, but I noticed many differences in knowledge between what I learned in the classroom and the online courses. However, much of the foundation knowledge was the same. So, I can learn such knowledge via these online courses to help me deeply understand taught contents.

More specifically, Gong further explained the role of ICTs in helping him acquire information in the Australian stage of his programme.

> ICTs were not very helpful when I was in China. However, I can gain much information in the Australian context. Everyone knows Google, YouTube, but Chinese students may not know how to search for information effectively in English. If you use Chinese in Google, results are displayed from Baidu. In this case, why do we use Google rather than Baidu directly?

From these research interview excerpts, it is clear that many students had close and ongoing connections with Chinese resources and people in their learning when they were studying in Australia. Importantly, they made use of different Internet-based tools to create a virtual in-between space for their study. In this in-between space, they learned knowledge in the Australian physical places (e.g., classroom and campus) via many ICT-assistances. They sought further virtual support from the Chinese side to help overcome learning difficulties and understand major knowledge. It seems that ICTs, to some extent, allow and enable a combination of space and place without any time and boundary restrictions (Brennan, 2006; Harvey, 1999).

The students' experiences indicated that their intercultural learning happened in an in-between space rather than merely moving from one country to another. The findings also suggested that the Internet became a vital mediation for Chinese students to keep in touch with the Chinese contexts. They even adopted more Chinese-based resources than non-Chinese content when studying overseas (C. Yang, Wu, Zhu, Brian, & Southwell, 2004). Furthermore, their Australian stories indicated more robust engagement in both vertical and horizontal in-between spaces than was the case with their Chinese experiences, which were mainly physically dominated without sufficient connections with the Australian contexts. Consequently, many students created their ICT-based in-between space when they studied in Australia. In this space, their learning became interactively transitioning.

Notably, influenced by the Covid-19, teaching and learning practices in physical classrooms are paused in most countries worldwide. Internet-based online learning partly replaced traditional classroom-based education during this crisis. In China and many other countries, almost all the teaching and learning activities were changed to online mode. The mobility of international students and academics was paused; however, the transfer of culture, knowledge, and information could be continued in the virtual space via Internet-based tools, such as Skype and Zoom. When international students cannot go to other countries to complete their learning, they can still access learning resources and attend online lectures. Although online-based teaching and learning may be inadequate compared to the traditional models, it still creates a virtual learning space for people from different parts of the world to have cross-cultural communications and connections.

Within this virtual learning space, different cultures and information are exchanged and interwoven. Students may attend an online lecture taught by foreign academics in their home countries. Academics meet their students who stayed in different countries. Such Internet-based international education seems to create a learning space that allows people, culture, knowledge, and information to have mutual communications and interactions. People could shift between virtual learning spaces, multicultural and international, and authentic living places in their domestic countries with unique sociocultural features and situations. In short, the physical movement across different countries and cultures is stopped, but the virtual transition and shift between

MAPPING A TRANSITIONING IN-BETWEEN LEARNING SPACE   103

different contexts become much more active. People, especially the international student group, seem to live in an in-between space where they can virtually position and transit themselves between different scenes.

3   Transitioning between Different Assessment Modes and Cultures[2]

When students were asked reasons why they had different senses of agency, identity, and belonging, most of them spontaneously linked their changes to the following keywords, such as "exams," "assignments," and "criteria." Then, I realised that assessment played an essential role in positioning students into the in-between space. As Boud, Cohen, and Sampson (1999) claimed, "assessment is the single most powerful influence on learning in formal courses" (p. 413). The assessment design can easily influence teaching and learning approaches (Boud et al., 1999). According to interview data, the different assessment modes between Chinese and Australian partners potentially changed students' agency and identity, which could be the second layer of the in-between space illustrated by comparing and negotiating Chinese and Australian modes.

3.1   *Studying in an Exam-Oriented Summative Mode in China*
An exam-dominated summative mode potentially ensured that many students engaged only in a physical learning place in the Chinese stage of their programmes. Many interviewees indicated that exams guided learning, which pushed them to focus on physical materials in the daily study without enough exploration and interaction with virtual space. For instance, Dong indicated that memorising documents and books became one of her learning skills in the Chinese stage.

> For example, my lecturers usually give us a lot of printed slides to remember before exams. I remembered that I could memorise a book within one week before the exam date and then passed tests with a high score.

Studying in such a highly exam-dominated space, Guang seemed to be weary of such an assessment mode.

> The exams of my Chinese university were very rigid. Such exams did not test academic ability, but they just tested out-of-date knowledge printed on the textbook. To pass exams, I just needed to remember textbooks and do more practices before the final test. In short, if I directly copied the contents of the textbook to my exam paper, I could pass it easily.

104   CHAPTER 5

This experience indicates that assessments shape "how much, how (their approach), and what (the content) students learn" (Scouller, 1998, p. 454). Furthermore, their experiences suggest that the "end-of-course" examination was still widely adopted as the dominant assessment approach in the first two years of undergraduate Chinese study (Dai, Matthews, & Reyes, 2020). In line with the use of ICTs in the Chinese stage, it seemed that such an assessment mode meant students had limited engagement with the ICT-based virtual space in doing their academic tasks. Consequently, their learning activities mainly happened in physical places. To illustrate the limited in-between communication in the Chinese stage, Yuner shared her experiences with assessments:

> Although foreign lecturers taught most courses in English, I feel their assessment approaches were Chinese style. They did not give us assignments or quizzes in learning progress. We usually just have mid-semester and final exams ... most courses were based on exam-directed learning and teaching.

Yuner's interview excerpt indicates an exciting issue in the TAP context. Foreign lecturers taught in the Chinese stage, which indicated the academic movement from a foreign country to China. Such a movement produced an in-between learning space for these Chinese students on the Chinese stage. Theoretically, this mode should allow students to experience different teaching and assessment approaches in advance of the move to the new system. A multi-cultural context was successfully constructed in Yuner's class at her Chinese university. However, as Yuner suggested, it seems that there were few differences in teaching strategies that foreign or Chinese lecturers adopted.

Practically, such an in-between space was not sufficient to experience different educational features in the Chinese context. Specifically, in contrast, it seemed that foreign lecturers adapted to the Chinese system. These experiences made Yuner identify that she did not engage in a transitioning in-between learning space of a combination of Chinese and real foreign education even though many lecturers came from overseas. In short, her experiences illustrate a theoretical in-between space in the Chinese context, but practically she was studying in a traditional Chinese mode.

3.2   *Experiencing the Combination of Summative and Formative Assessments in Australia*

When these students moved to Australia, they started to engage in a dynamic space of assessment. In adjusting to the Australian assessment mode, they spontaneously compared their Australian and Chinese experiences. These comparisons indicated various interactions of their thoughts and practices about the differences between China and Australia in this respect. Their views towards the assessment differences and strategies to deal with the problems in doing assignments indicated that they were motivated to study in a real in-between space in Australia, where they could adopt various approaches to solve learning barriers.

On the one hand, the combination of summative and formative assessment approaches created a dynamic space for students to engage in different tasks that they did not experience in the Chinese stage. For instance, Dong suggested that she had various assessments during learning at an Australian university, which brought more learning pressures to her.

> Compared to my previous Chinese exam-based mode, I had various tests (e.g., essay, exam, online quiz, group work, and presentation) during a semester at the Australian university. Then I needed to keep following lecturers and read lecture notes after class on the learning platform. If I did not study hard in the semester, it would be difficult for me to complete assignments and pass exams.

As Boud and Soler (2016) suggested, it is vital to position assessments into students' learning activities to build a sustainable assessment system. According to Dong's experiences, different assignments and tests were adopted as assessment methods across her learning in Australia. Similarly, Liang also mentioned that different types of tests were used in his programme.

> In Australia, the assessment had various types and many tests aimed at examining daily study. For example, we had essays, online quizzes, a mid-exam and a final exam. This assessment mode could test students' learning and academic ability from various points rather than textbook contents.

Many students seemed to pay much attention to the daily study with a stressful assessment mode rather than rely on the final review before exams. For example, Diao described her experiences:

> When I was in my first semester, I relied on working hard before the final exam. However, I did not get good scores, and one subject was failed. I noticed I could not keep doing this activity again. I needed to study for the whole semester ... In China, I was used to making a concentrated effort to finish learning quickly before each exam. Not many students

keep working hard during a semester. It was difficult for me to get a good result in Australia if I did not study hard during the whole semester. I did need to study nearly every day to review course contents and do more research. I felt I had many assignments to complete during a semester from beginning to end. Meanwhile, lecturers also let us complete mini quizzes. All such tasks pushed me to study hard actively. Otherwise, it was so hard to get an excellent academic record.

Diao's experiences indicated that her Chinese learning approaches to assessments did not work well at her Australian university. She needed to study hard to complete assessments in a highly stressful learning space to obtain high academic results. It seemed that the Australian assessment mode made her change learning strategies and attitudes for learning rather than focus on passing exams.

In particular, many students from the multimedia design and engineering field suggested that they also had other tasks rather than only creating video or web design works. For example, Zhuang claimed that he had many group-based tasks in his study.

In Australia, we have a lot of group work. When students work together, they usually have various opinions on a specific topic. I feel group work is one of the most significant learning and teaching approaches in my Australian study. However, I did not have too many experiences of doing group works at my Chinese university. So, when I came to Australia, I felt good at doing group works with other students.

More particularly, Hao argued that she needed to create her media and design works innovatively and present her ideas in class.

Through presentation, I can know other peers' ideas. Sometimes, I needed to do many peer reviews to evaluate their works based on assignments and presentations ... To have a professional presentation, it also needed me to have creative ideas to design slides by using various digital tools. I think it is constructive for me to foster my communication ability rather than only learning course content.

These experiences indicated the critical relationships between peer learning and assessments (Boud et al., 1999). Whether it is Zhuang's group work experiences or Hao's peer learning, their positive feelings indicated that peer or group types of learning activities and assessments are valuable. According to Boud et al. (1999), "peer learning values cooperation over competition and greater respect for varied experiences and background of participants can occur" (p. 415). In this mode, students seemed to have more opportunities to self-evaluate their study by interacting with other students in the classroom where different cultural backgrounds were exchanged, which potentially influenced their learning strategies.

On the other hand, many students' strategies to deal with assignment issues indicated a strong sense of in-between learning in their intercultural study at the Australian university. For example, Fei mentioned that he could seek help from Chinese friends when he faced difficulties doing assignments.

> When I was in my first semester, I had no ideas about doing assignments and totally cannot understand what I needed to do. As I said, what I had learned from Chinese university was not helpful to my Australian study. It was so difficult to let a video editor create a website, which was impossible to work. In this case, I requested help from lecturers, and they gave me some guidance to complete my assignments. If I cannot get help from lecturers, I also asked peers and some friends from China who have relevant experiences to help me deal with learning problems.

Qing further explained her understandings of academic tasks.

> Assignments or exams were always more complicated than the taught knowledge. To achieve a high mark in exams or a deep understanding of course content, I must become an investigator of knowledge and have progressive attitudes to study. Internet-based technology is one of the essential tools for me to become an active learner. I needed to strategically use the Internet in my study to acquire different resources from both Chinese and foreign websites and databases. Without Internet-based technology, I think it is difficult for me to have profound learning experiences at an Australian university.

The analysis of collected data shows that the changes in assessment modes significantly influenced many participants' intercultural learning experiences. The different assessment features of China and Australia created different learning places and spaces for these students. As the data showed, the Australian assessment mode made many students engage in a sophisticated learning space, which brought more stress to them than the Chinese system. Their learning strategies became dynamic in these multiple assessment modes. Meanwhile, their strategies to deal with these tasks potentially shaped the in-between space of assessment. In this space, they needed to pay more attention to daily study and have more connections with their homeland via ICTs to solve assessment problems.

4   Encountering Different Teaching Strategies

When participants discussed the role of assessment in shaping their in-between learning space, many of them also comparatively mentioned their lecturers' views in the Chinese and Australian context. According to Boud et al. (1999), assessments influenced students' learning approaches and reflect teaching features. I noticed that many teaching strategies emerged from students' intercultural learning experiences based on the data analysis. The different teaching strategies also allowed students to consider the values and issues in their study across two systems. Importantly, teaching differences offered opportunities for students to express their views concerning constructing the transitioning in-between learning space.

Research has shown the close connections between teaching strategies and learning approaches (e.g., Biggs, 1999; Marton & Säaljö, 1976; Prosser & Trigwell, 1999; Trigwell, Prosser, & Waterhouse, 1999). These researchers also summarised a series of types of teaching (e.g., teacher-centred and student-centred) and learning (e.g., surface and deep learning) approaches. However, it is difficult to say that teachers and students always adopted the same strategies in teaching and learning activities as they could change methods depending on different contexts. This section will adopt some of these theoretical ideas to help me analyse the significant features of teaching and learning in students' transnational intercultural transition. However, I will not simply label participants' experiences by using these terms. Instead, I will analyse the changes in teaching strategies from multiple perspectives (e.g., teaching and learning relations and cultural differences) to illustrate how students constructed their in-between space of teaching strategies.

4.1   *Lecturer-Centred Teaching Mode*
The role of lecturers in the Chinese stage can be summarised through keywords: teaching activity dominator, textbook-based knowledge delivery, and exam-based assessor. A series of interview extracts showed evidence of these features related to the teaching strategies of many lecturers in the Chinese stage. For instance, Yuner pinpointed her experiences about the role of lecturers in classrooms.

> At my Chinese university, many lecturers were still the centre of the class. They were in charge of teaching and learning activities. Most courses did not provide opportunities for students to do some works by themselves after class.

Dang also had a similar view that her lecturers usually dominated the learning process, and students had limited autonomy. Following lecturers in the classroom was the dominant learning mode.

> When I was studying at my Chinese university, learning was usually based on lecturers' teaching. They often controlled the learning and teaching activities. Students usually needed to follow their steps without enough autonomy.

From a specific cultural perspective, these interview extracts indicated the sense of large power distances in their Chinese learning stage. According to Hofstede (1986), power distances refer to "the extent to which the less powerful persons in a society accept inequity in power and consider it as normal" (p. 307). Some researchers have claimed that Chinese society shows considerable power distance. In education, lecturers played dominant roles in teaching and learning activities, positioning students as listeners (Hofstede, 1986).

By analysing students' English study features via the lens of Chinese culture of learning, Jin and Cortazzi (2006) found that listening and watching seemed to be the dominant way of learning for many Chinese students at school and university levels. They further indicated that students usually learn from authorities (e.g., teachers and textbooks) in the CHC context (Jin & Cortazzi, 2006). Notably, this feature was also reflected by Yuner, who identified that even though foreign lecturers taught some courses, their teaching approaches seemed to be very Chinese in style. Such experiences probably indicate that these foreign lecturers seemed to adjust to the CHC context. Interestingly, the CHC features still played dominant roles in the teaching process in many TAPs. It has constant and profound influences on these students and lecturers' understanding of teaching and learning under the TAP setting.

Concerning the role of lecturers and the application of technology in teaching, many students (e.g., Qing, Shuo, Liang and Zhuang) thought that many lecturers did not adopt various technologies to support their teaching activities. For example, Qing shared her experiences:

> Most lecturers were used to teach by reading textbooks or PPTs. The learning goal in China was to remember the key sections of the textbook

mentioned by lecturers in class and then catch these points to pass the final exam. It seemed that students mechanically followed the lecturers without doing their thinking. So, in Chinese mode, I only needed to focus on the textbook and did not need to pay more attention to other kinds of learning strategies, for example, Internet-based study. As a result, it was not easy to evaluate the role of Internet-based technology in helping students achieve their goals. Many students do not even use it for learning purposes ... Generally, Internet-based technology always seemed to be 'extra contents' in learning. The teacher was still the centre of the classroom.

Such teaching strategies indicated some features of teaching in the CHC context. For instance, Jin and Cortazzi (2006) suggested that teaching commonly refers to "Jiao Shu" (教书) or "teach the book" (p. 11). Although the concept of the book is a metaphor, it still indicates that the knowledge of books in the Chinese culture of education played an important role. The above research interview extracts partly reflected the significant roles of "books" in students' first two years of study at Chinese universities. Furthermore, it seemed that exam-directed teaching approaches guided students to study by following the line of examination. These experiences further indicated that assessment profoundly influenced teaching and learning approaches (Boud et al., 1999). In this educational context, many students could pass assessments easily by focusing on learning textbook-based knowledge.

The interview excerpts indicated a clear picture of students' views towards the Chinese teaching strategies. On the one hand, these features of the Chinese teaching style reflect various conventional characteristics of teaching and learning relationships. On the other hand, students' views towards such teaching strategies revealed that the learning space in the Chinese stage was also traditional in most TAPs. It seemed that there were limited communications and interactions in teaching between the Chinese and Australian contexts. However, their experiences illustrated a clear picture of how such teaching strategies shaped the physical and traditional space for the learners.

4.2 Studying in an In-Between Space But Yearning for the Past

Students' views towards the teaching strategies adopted by their Australian lecturers revealed differences compared with their previous Chinese experiences. By summarising the significant insights of the interview data related to teaching strategies in the Australian stage, I noticed that the following keywords described the features of many Australian lecturers' teaching, such as teaching activity facilitator, knowledge exploration guider, and practice-based assessor.

Many students identified that the Australian teaching mode offered them more spaces to explore knowledge by themselves. For instance, Biang noted that her Australian lecturers usually motivated students to actively deal with learning problems through various tools rather than directly teaching detailed knowledge.

> Many Australian lecturers usually stimulated students to think of learning problems critically and creatively compared to my Chinese lecturers. They rarely taught students how to create an animation step by step, but they liked to discuss with students about their ideas. Students needed to develop their software skills by themselves after classes by searching for online information and watching tutorial videos. Lecturers may not be interested in the steps or skills used in the creation, but they preferred to examine the design ideas. In this case, students in the Australian context seemed to be more creative. We needed to train ourselves to be more creative rather than waiting to be 'fed' knowledge by lecturers. Australian lecturers liked to ask questions or gave various small tasks during learning to let students practice their thinking and skills.

Moreover, Minze outlined her understandings of the influences of different teaching strategies on her learning approaches between her Chinese and Australian experiences.

> When I was at my Chinese university, I did not realise whether the Chinese learning strategies were good or bad for my Australian learning. We were learning through such approaches for a long time. Until I studied in Australia, I noticed the importance of self-regulated learning because Australian lecturers usually did not teach students knowledge mechanically and most of them preferred to guide students and let them think creatively. This mode motivated my brain to think and create ideas rather than rely on other people. Such learning and teaching approaches were one of the most different aspects of my transnational study experiences.

Similarly, Guang provided his opinions on the teaching approaches used by lecturers at his Australian university.

> When I came to Australia, I felt it was difficult for me to adapt to such a teaching approach because I was used to listening and following lecturers' ideas. In most Chinese students' mind, lecturers were the authority on their subjects. As students, I just needed to follow what the lecturers

112   CHAPTER 5

taught in the classroom. However, in Australia, although there were
many different principles that students needed to follow when creating
something, the idea and creativity should be unrestricted rather than
restricted by lecturers ... In Australia, lecturers did not tell students an
expected result or answer for a question. They liked to provide different
roots to students and let students complete design works creatively. Most
of them liked to discuss problems with students and let students decide
on creating their design work. They gave much room to students and let
them design their works. So, I needed to plan the idea, think about what
kind of story was in the design work, and decide what kind of model will
be used. This mode was highly creative, and students needed to do more
explorations at the Australian university.

These comments prove that many Australian lecturers did not directly "feed
knowledge" to students. In contrast, they usually provided flexible directions
for students to explore knowledge through research and investigation using different tools actively. As Rui said, "I felt my Australian lecturers liked to encourage students to think ideas creatively, but in China, more teaching focused on
the knowledge itself." According to these experiences, it is apparent that many
students had more personal space in learning at their Australian universities.
However, although teaching mainly concentrated on textbooks and exams in
the Chinese context, many students identified that lecturers usually taught in
detail and in-depth, enabling students to have a clear understanding of specific content.

Many interviewees (e.g., Shuo, Hao, Dang, Biang, Xin, Dong, Zhuang, and
Liang) critically documented their views regarding the drawbacks of the teaching strategies they experienced in the Australian context. For example, Shuo
described that many lecturers taught using design software (e.g., Adobe Creative Suits) in detail at his Chinese university, but such learning experiences
were not utilised in Australia.

Many lecturers usually taught software step by step in China and created
a model for students to follow. However, when I studied at my Australian
university, lecturers preferred to teach design concepts rather than many
details about using specific software.

Similarly, Zhuang shared his experiences:

I think lecturers usually taught knowledge in detail and explained the
origin of a certain point, especially in Math or Physics. For example, I

MAPPING A TRANSITIONING IN-BETWEEN LEARNING SPACE   113

remembered that my math lecturers usually wrote many formulas to explain how the question was to be solved and explained why specific approaches could solve such a question. After a class, the lecturer had filled a blackboard with learning resources. I felt such a learning process was very understandable. Students can develop strong foundations of fundamental knowledge. In Australia, I felt lecturers did not teach such detailed knowledge. Students usually needed to explore problems after classes.

Meng also pointed out that he had learned some content when he was in China, so he did not experience difficulties in learning, especially in his major courses.

Although learning in China was passive and rote, course content seemed to be thicker than at the Australian university. I noticed I had learned much content in some courses related to business at my Chinese university. Even though my language barriers made me slow to understand Australian lecturers' teaching, I still can know what they taught, and I did not feel such knowledge was complex.

To explicitly explain the underlying insights of different teaching styles across the TAP learning process, Dang shared that:

I did not think that I learned much knowledge in depth through the TAP, even now that I was studying at an outstanding Australian university. The knowledge taught by lecturers always seems too basic and lacked deep learning ... I think the knowledge I have learned was based on the Internet rather than mainly from lecturers. Therefore, I thought this was not a very good experience ... For instance, when I was learning the 3D model course at my Chinese university, lecturers usually introduced the software in detail ... However, Australian lecturers did not teach such detailed knowledge. I thought Australian lecturers might assume students already have such kind of skills or knowledge. Many Chinese students had feelings that taught contents were too tricky to handle sometimes ... Australian lecturers usually did not teach fundamental knowledge in detail, for example, the use of the software. In contrast, they preferred to teach more practical skills and knowledge. They wished students to do something by themselves through explorations rather than teaching everything to them. In this case, I found it difficult to keep following the teaching step, and learning seemed to be superficial under this circle.

114 CHAPTER 5

These experiences provide clear evidence that many students had critical views towards the teaching in their intercultural learning process, which indicated that they did not merely believe the different teaching was better than the Chinese style. In contrast, they were able to evaluate the advantages and disadvantages of each approach in each stage. Their critical views of teaching strategies in the Australian context suggest that if many learners complain about the quality of education, some Australian universities may become less attractive to potential international students. They fostered their negotiated views towards the different teaching styles, which facilitated them to establish a transitioning in-between space in their minds.

According to these students' experiences, no matter which major they were studying in China, their lecturers adopted similar teaching strategies, which focused on accurate knowledge delivery. After coming to Australia, students also shared some similar experiences. For instance, many Australian lecturers did not teach knowledge in detail and motivated students to do self-exploration. However, it is also vital to notice that different subjects have some differences in these respects. For example, students in the Design field (or other similar "soft" fields) thought that there seemed to be many gaps in learning content between China and Australia, making them stressed during the transition.

Meanwhile, different teaching approaches also caused some of them to struggle in dealing with knowledge gaps. Although Internet-based tools became necessary for the students, they seemed to have negative attitudes towards such changes in learning content and teaching approaches. However, students in the "hard sciences" (e.g., engineering related to math) mentioned that learning content in Australia was even easier than what they learned in China. In this case, the course content in China supported them in their study in Australia, even though the teaching strategies were also different. Based on these differences, it seems that learning in the "soft" field may face more cross-system differences and inconsistencies than those studying in "hard" sciences, which might be seen to have universal knowledge (e.g., math and physics). The above aspects are mainly about micro factors that (re)shape students' learning experiences. Moreover, the overall university context also has significant influences on their cross-system transition and learning.

5 Transitioning from a Collective Setting to an Individualistic Context

According to the analysis of interview data, I realised that learners' understandings of different teaching, learning, and assessment systems in their TAP produce a holistic picture of their transitioning in-between movements between China and Australia. All their views, experiences, and behaviours reflected how they adjusted in the transitioning in-between space. To conceptualise this holistic sense of in-between learning, I considered that the university context could be a suitable actor that might produce a network that connects different actants and places. Finally, the transitioning in-between learning space is constructed, allowing learners to dynamically experience and move between their home and host countries from physical and virtual aspects.

The university context is a more holistic concept in the transitioning in-between learning space. As Ramsden (1979) suggested, the university context could include various actors, such as teaching, courses set, and rules. Hence, it is apparent that the concept of learning environment is too complicated to measure in detail holistically. To add further insights into constructing the transitioning in-between learning space, I will focus on several actants in the general academic culture rather than cover all different aspects.

5.1 *Belong to a Collective Community in China*

Considering the meaning of in-between from the perspectives of the university context, I noticed that these Chinese students studied and lived in a highly connective environment. Students' learning and living at the university indicated a strong sense of collective features in this environment. They have more opportunities to interact with each other. Such interactions as a collective group made students in-between each other without a strong sense of their individuality. For instance, Liang shared his views on the collective features of his Chinese university.

> In China, most students in the same major had the same course plan. Students usually did not need to manage their course and learning plan independently ... Following other peers was enough in most situations.

Dong also reported a similar experience.

> In China, students usually lived together and were in the same class. Students had more connections in such a mode. The friendship was easy to be established compared to my Australian experiences. If I had problems with study and life, other students also helped me deal with them without barriers as we were in the same learning mode and life context.

These interview extracts provided evidence to shed light on Hofstede's (1986) argument that Chinese society had a strong sense of collectivist features.

116 CHAPTER 5

Zhuang summarised his views on the features of the Chinese university context in the following way:

> My Chinese university seems to be a semi-enclosed society. Students have their autonomy, but they still need to follow specific rules.

Learners in a highly collective context are always in between different members in a semi-fixed group. As Dong identified, one of the significant advantages of such a construction of in-between was the tight connections with other group members. However, many interviewees suggested some disadvantages in this situation. For instance, Rui felt that "the quality of students determined the quality of the learning context." Yuner shared her experiences:

> Some peers usually failed in their exams, but they seemed to not worry about it. Some students even did not submit assignments as usual.

Such feeling was not unique amongst research participants. Other interviewees also reported similar experiences. As Dong noted,

> Generally, my Chinese university environment was not suitable for study, and most classmates did not study very hard. In such a context, it was not easy to be independent. When other people play games, why should I study?

Notably, Xiang's interview provided more details about the learning context to explain why many peers did not focus on study in China.

> In China, many students found it difficult to be admitted to a university and accessible to graduate. Students had no pressures to study once they were admitted to a university ... Most students at my Chinese university lack enough motivation to study, and some are still passive learners because the university context is too flexible ... They only have pressured for one week before the final test.

The above extract suggests that students needed to study hard for preparing for the university entrance exam. Once they were admitted to a university, graduation seemed to be an easy task. As a result, they might lack learning pressures and motivation. Xiang's experiences were also found in the study conducted by Zhu (2016), who argued that many Chinese students were educated in a highly tight educational context in school due to the pressures of

Gao Kao. Hence, a hostile atmosphere potentially influenced many students' views of the learning context, impacting their behaviour. As Ramsden (1997) indicated, students' learning orientations and learning approaches were significantly influenced by the academic atmosphere of their learning context. Such experiences indicated that their collective learning context could lack an academic atmosphere when peers did not have positive attitudes towards daily study.

In this case, many learners were passively positioned in a negative in-between space in China. The in-between space in the Chinese context was mainly created by the collective features of the university context. In this space, as the data above showed, students interacted with each actant in a semi-closed setting where in-between activities usually occurred. However, when these students came to Australia, the sense of in-between became more complicated than their Chinese experiences.

5.2 *Isolated in an Individualistic Context in Australia*
The construction of the in-between learning space at the Australian university was based on students' multiple experiences of their interactions with the new context as intercultural learners. As the section title indicates, I noticed that many students became in-between learners who have both Chinese and Australian educational genes, as it were. When they were in China, as they suggested above, they were used to a collective context. Learning in this space, they spontaneously become a member of the specific fixed group. However, when they came to Australia, most of them were divided into different individuals even though they might study in the same TAP.

As findings in Chapter 4 suggested, many learners (e.g., Zhuang, Liang, Shuo, Dang, Qing, Hao, and Diao) felt that they became individuals after coming to Australia. It was difficult for them to belong to a similar fixed group as they had experienced in the previous Chinese context. For example, Zhuang shared:

> In Australia, I felt I have already started my life in an open society. I was not just a learner at university; I also needed to become more independent and manage every aspect of my life and study, especially for me in Australia. I needed to learn how to communicate with others, adapt to society, and deal with every problem that I faced.

Liang's experience also shed light on such changes:

> In Australia, I did need to arrange my life and study plan at the beginning of each semester at the Australian university, which I did not need to do

at my Chinese university. I thought this context had more challenges for me, but it also was perfect for my future.

According to these examples, it is evident that many students have realised changes from a member who was positioned in a collective context to an individual who needed to interact with different actants in a new context actively. Each nation has its particular cultural and social features, affecting students' identities and behaviours in cross-cultural transition (Dai, 2020). Zhuang and Liang's experiences indicated that the Australian academic context seemed to be individualistic (Hofstede, 1986), which potentially made them independent in learning. In the process of adapting to the new context, people reshaped their identities and constructed their own space to reflect their views towards the cross-cultural and societal changes they experienced (Dai, 2020). Although these students had various changes of identity as intercultural learners, they also developed individual spaces to reflect on their interactions with the new context.

At times, students' experiences of communicating with peers at their Australian universities reflected their effective and multiple negotiations in the new learning space. In the process of communicating with others, individuals produce their space. Some students felt that communication with other peers helped them engage in the Australian learning context in this study. For instance, Shuo mentioned his experiences in the following way.

> In my opinion, I thought most of my Australian students were very warm-hearted, and most of them want to help international students to adapt to the local environment. For example, when I started my university study, I could not entirely understand the course content. I asked some questions to Australian peers. They were accommodating and explained my questions, gave me suggestions. I thought they wished to help others no matter what the problems were. They tried their best to help each other in learning.

Hao also comparatively discussed her views on the differences between her Chinese and Australian peers in learning.

> Many Australian students usually appreciated other students' design. For Chinese students, they are used to compare their works with others unrealistically. Sometimes, a student notices other's work is better than his/her, he/she may be jealous of other students. In this case, it is not easy to communicate with each other. They do not want to share their ideas or knowledge with other students. Many Australian students seemed to be friendly and open-minded to discuss problems. I think every skill to

design something is just a method rather than a secret. When it is used in different designs, the effects or results may also be varied. Therefore, sharing ideas with others is so vital for a design major.

These extracts indicated a positive relationship between the interviewees and their peers at their Australian universities. In their minds, such positive communication could create a space that made them feel confident in learning in the new context. Specifically, as Hao's interview indicated, the comparative experiences demonstrated her views as a student in different learning spaces created by the different peer relationships. In contrast, some interviewees had different experiences. For instance, although they studied in the Australian context, they felt isolated and found it challenging to construct positive relationships with others. Dong shared her experience:

> I felt it was challenging to make friends in Australia. For example, when I had some learning questions, I wanted to ask other peers. However, some of them did not want to help me. I also felt it was not easy to communicate in-depth with Australian peers ... In Australia, I feel everyone becomes independent. I felt awkward engaging in a group in learning. Every student can select different courses depending on the individual situation, even though some TAP students were in the same major. I thought most Chinese students may still like a collective mode.

Dong's data extract indicated her isolation from the perspective of communication with peers in the new context. It seemed that she preferred to study in the Chinese collective space rather than in the individual focused context in Australia. In her mind, a contradiction between the Chinese and Australian contexts was generated. In adjusting to the new context, even though she has studied in Australia, she seemed to prefer the learning and lifestyles at her Chinese university. Such contradicted feelings made her became an individual who needed to adjust to an individualist context. However, she still preferred the collective Chinese mode, which positioned her mind between different contexts as an intercultural learner who kept reflecting, comparing and negotiating the cultural, social, and educational differences.

6   Conclusion

This chapter has illustrated the spectrum of a transitioning in-between learning space based on students' comparative experiences towards using ICTs, different assessment modes, different teaching strategies, and diverse university contexts and cultures between the Chinese and Australian stages of their programmes. These different elements in and across systems created an intercultural learning network that motivated students to construct their transitioning in-between learning space. According to the analysis, it is evident that the TAP provided a complex pathway for students to experience these educational differences, and this allowed them to shape their sense of in-between as intercultural learners. The two layers of in-between space created by the TAP setting influenced students' changing senses of identity, agency and belonging towards different educational and cultural contexts.

Through comparing the Chinese and Australian experiences, most students indicated a sense of in-between in their minds. Their learning experiences suggested that their learning usually happened in physical places without enough engagement with virtual space in the Chinese stage. When they moved to Australia, learning seemed to happen in an in-between space shaped by the connections between different educational contexts via multiple changes in teaching strategy, the use of ICT, assessment, and university context. Through continually shifting individual preferences and learning strategies in the new context, many students developed their sense of in-betweenness as intercultural learners in the transitional learning process.

Notably, with the influence of Covid-19, standard teaching/learning practices and university context have also undergone various changes. Most teaching and learning activities have been moved to the online mode, which also impacts assessment. On the one hand, many onsite exams have been changed to online tests. On the other hand, many practices or lab-based assessments have been cancelled. There are limited teaching and learning activities that now happen in physical places at universities. It seems that online learning in the virtual space has replaced the traditional model. The university campus has become desolate without previous vigour and vitality. International student mobility has also been changed due to travel bans between countries, which may negatively influence intercultural communication and learning. Even though teaching and learning could keep going in virtual space, most students who proposed experiencing different socio-cultural contexts may not have opportunities under the global pandemic. Many questions may need to consider: How does the Covid-19 pandemic influence or (re)shape intercultural learning in the future? How do the Covid-19 pandemic influence teaching and learning practices in the future?

To further interpret the concept of in-betweenness in cross-system transition, I will discuss my life and learning experiences as a former TAP learner, an immigrant diaspora, and a returnee. Based on the analysis of my journey, I would argue that people may experience in-betweenness when they encounter intercultural adjustment. Notably, the in-betweenness in the process of intercultural adjustment could happen in a macro-level cross-country setting or is abstractly considered a transition between a familiar and an unfamiliar setting in everyday life.

Notes

1 Parts of this chapter are based on (1) Dai, K., Matthews, K. E., & Shenshaw, P. (2020). Crossing the 'bridges' and navigating the 'learning gaps': Chinese students learning across two systems in a transnational higher education programme. *Higher Education Research & Development, 39*(6), 1140–1154; and (2) Dai, K., Lingard, B., & Musofer, R. P. (2020). Mobile Chinese students navigating between fields: (Trans)forming habitus in transnational articulation programmes? *Educational Philosophy and Theory, 52*(12), 1329–1340. Permission for re-use has been given by the publishers.
2 Parts of this section are based on Dai, K., Matthews, K. E., & Reye, V. (2020). Chinese students' assessment and learning experiences in a transnational higher education programme. *Assessment & Evaluation in Higher Education, 45*(1), 70–81. Permission for re-use has been given by the publishers.

CHAPTER 6

A Reflexive Journey as an In-Betweener

I think, therefore, I am.
我思故我在

∴

My experiences as a Chinese international student and a transnational learner across different fields could be a valuable point to help me reflexively analyse and understand my cross-fields learning journey. By inserting my reflexivity into the analysis and presenting the learning journey in a narrative-based style, I can understand research participants' learning stories and recall my previous TAP learning experiences. In doing so, as Milligan (2016) indicated, the researcher (I) then becomes a "knowledgeable outsider and subsequently an in-betweener" (p. 248). This chapter will recall my growing trajectory, which could illustrate how to shape a sense of in-betweenness across different learning stages.

1 Transitioning between Different Schools as a Domestic Diaspora[1]

When I recalled my learning trajectory, I noticed that I started my transitioning in-between learning journey when I completed primary school. Drawing upon Bourdieu's thinking tools (e.g., field, habitus, and capital), I briefly illustrate and analyse my learning journey to illuminate the process of shaping a sense of in-betweenness. I experienced different schools (e.g., private, elite public, urban fringe, and rural). Each field has its unique logic of practice; these shifts between various schools potentially made me experience different academic and social fields. The cross-field movement constantly (re)shapes my habitus depending on different logics of practices (Bourdieu, 1984, 1993). During this journey, various capitals (e.g., social, cultural, and economic) play different roles in either positive or negative ways (Bourdieu, 1986). These capitals systematically influenced my development. Notably, I may not positively develop a solid "educational capital" as my learning was not outstanding. However, I may gain various "social" and "culture" capitals as a domestic and diasporic

© KONINKLIJKE BRILL NV, LEIDEN, 2022 | DOI: 10.1163/9789004505131_006

A REFLEXIVE JOURNEY AS AN IN-BETWEENER

in-betweener through experiencing different schools. Although these shifts happened in China, moving between different school contexts still made me encounter "cross-cultural" barriers, and I needed to experience "intercultural adjustment" to survive.

I completed my primary learning in a public school and then moved to a private international school to start my secondary journey in 2000. This cross-context movement opened the door of my adventure. The school was located in another city and was a boarding school. This was my first time leaving my parents and family to study and live in a new city. The school faced a beautiful beach, and my dormitory seemed to be a holiday apartment with fantastic ocean views. I usually returned home at the end of each month, and my peers came from different parts of China. Some of them came from other countries, for example, Korea and Japan. This school offered K-12 comprehensive education by offering various activities and extracurricular training, including music, sport, and art. Each classroom had advanced equipment, such as providing computers for each student and having an internet connection. Such a setting may still be advanced in 2020. Teachers also came from different parts of China, and foreign teachers taught us English. Of course, the fee was much higher than in other schools. However, I was not interested in the study and paid attention to playing computer games. In year 8, I did not even know how to calculate plus and minus numbers. After completing year 8, my parents found a new school for me in my hometown and then I returned.

The new school is one of the top-ranked public elite schools with a high reputation in my city. The equipment was not advanced compared to the previous school, but it had a better learning environment. Most students had outstanding academic achievements. However, as my knowledge background was too weak, I could not "adjust" to such an academic-oriented context. When I attended the first test on Math and English, I had no ideas about the questions on the exam papers. After experiencing formal learning in different subjects, I realised that I could not understand the taught knowledge. I became an "outsider" of the new context even though I was an "insider" who physically sat in the classroom every day. After completing my year 9, I failed the high school entry exam (I only got about 350 out of 750; most schools asked at least 480 for students). The school had a particular policy for existing internal students and let me stay there, but I need to achieve specific academic requirements in year 10. Otherwise, I will be expelled.

Meanwhile, I also needed to sign a contract or an agreement with the school to promise to fulfil the requirement. Before discussing my future with my parents, I made a decision that I gave up the opportunity. Then, I had no idea where I will go next and what I will do. Students need to complete nine years of compulsory education in China, and theoretically, I did not need to study anymore. However, I felt strange if I did not study in high school as all my friends had started high school. I encountered a dilemma: on the one hand, I could not be admitted by any schools due to the low score of the entrance exam; on the other hand, I still wanted to keep studying, at least finishing high school.

After negotiating with my parents, I moved to an urban fringe school located in a small town near my city to resume my year 9. I was the only student who came from the city. Most peers came from the local town. I was an "Oppidan," and we were different in their minds, which resulted in me lacking a sense of belonging to the new context. I proposed to attempt the high school entry exam after another year of learning in this school. When I started at this school, I felt that I would fail again. Learning pressure was much higher than my previous elite school. Most students were highly competitive in doing exams. A similar situation happened again. In most courses, I could not understand taught content and started to give up. I did not know what will happen at the end of this year. I stayed in my dormitory most of the time. Teachers seemed to give up on me and knew I came from the city and did not belong to this community. They knew I would go back to the city to take the exam as my "Hu Kou" was not in the town. In this case, my score will not influence their examining rate in the high school entry exam.

Recalling this journey, I was absolutely an antipathetic outsider with a sense of disempowerment. After this year, I again failed the high school entry exam and would drop out of school soon if no high school allowed me to study. Luckily, heaven never seals off all the exits for me. My grandfather was a teacher in a rural high school located in my hometown, a small village in Shandong province. He helped me contact his school to see whether I could study there as an auditing student who would not take the Gao Kao as a local candidate. Finally, the head of school accepted my application and allowed me to study there. Then, I moved to a rural high school.

Initially, each day passed as if it was a year. I had never lived and studied in a rural village before. I cannot imagine what life will be like, and I was the only student from an urban city. I needed to change my habitus in this field as this field had very different practices compared with my previous schools and urban life study. Learning was very stressful, and I needed to take 12 classes from 6 am until 9:30 pm. All students needed to live in a dormitory, and usually, twelve students shared one room. We only had two rest days a month, and we usually needed to study from 5:30 am until 10:00 pm at school, which created a high-pressured atmosphere for most students. These practices in the rural school "field" made me feel disempowered in the initial stage. I clearly remembered that I was the last one out of 80 students in my class's high school entry exam score. Many teachers and students believed that I would quit soon as they thought I could not exist in this environment.

Similar to my previous learning experiences in the elite public school, I was not able to follow teaching, especially in Math, English, and Chinese, which are the three most important subjects (each subject is 150 marks, so a total of 450 out of 750) in the Gao Kao. Then, I focused on learning arts-integrated subjects (300 out of 750), for example, history and policy, because I could adopt "memorisation" as a valuable strategy to improve my score. After one year of learning, my Math, English, and Chinese had still have not improved to a reasonable level. However, other subjects showed significant improvement, which potentially enhanced my confidence to keep studying. At this stage, I realised that I would stay here until I complete my study rather than go back to my city. I wrote the following sentence in all my textbooks to remind and encourage myself: "since we have come here, let us stay and enjoy it" (既来之, 则安之). It seems that I was a "fish" out of the "education" or "learning" water for a long time (Hilgers & Mangez, 2005).

To improve my overall score, I started to pay more attention to the three key subjects. Facing examination pressures (note: in year 11, each month had a test and in year 12, each week has exams), I adopted several strategies to improve my score: (a) taking private tutoring (b) following "superstars" in English and Math in my class (c) learning these subjects in most courses. After one more year of learning (year 11), my Math, English, and Chinese had improved from an initial average 50 to 60 out of 120 in the first year to an average 80 to 90 out of 120. However, this achievement was still not competitive enough. To do so, I had to keep improving these subjects. I gave up all holidays and put nearly all my energy into learning, which made me feel that I seemed to become another person compared to my previous experiences as a problematic student. Luckily, with the help of teachers and peers, in year 12, I finally reached about 100 to 120 out of 150 in three key subjects and 220 to 240 out of 300 in the arts-integrated examination. My ranking jumped from the last one to an average 20 to 15 out of 60 students in my class. It seemed that I had positively adapted to the new field by (re)shaping my learning attitudes and adopting different approaches, which potentially improved my academic position and established a sense of belonging to this context.

Learning seems to be the only way to change future life for many students. My coordinator teacher (班主任) always told us that: "if you want to change your life and do not want to live in a small village, learning is the most achievable shortcut to go. Otherwise, you may still be the low class in society." Due to my Hu Kou in a capital city, I could get extra awarded marks in the Gao Kao compared to my classmates whose Hu Kou is usually registered in rural towns.

Although I could take advantage of this "institutionalised cultural capital" (Mu, 2018), I spontaneously adapted myself to this struggling atmosphere in the school in the same way as the other students. Most students pay full attention to everyday learning life from 5 am to 10 pm in the last year. Even during lunch or dinner time, most of the students were still learning while eating.

When I recalled this period, it seemed that we were all "crazy." In our minds, learning was our whole life. Notably, not all students insisted on learning and then gave up the journey. As mentioned above, in year 10, my class had 80 students; then, in year 11, the number was down to 60; finally, in year 12, 45 students remained. In comparison, my previous schoolmates in the city schools did not quit learning during the journey. Most students could complete their high school then started higher education in either Chinese or foreign universities. The high rate of wastage in the rural school shocked me, and I could not fully understand why this situation happened. Through discussing with peers, I noticed that the students who left school faced various issues, such as losing confidence in learning, financial difficulties, and family accidents. Later, I heard that many students still lived in a rural town and did not achieve their initial "dreams."

After completing three years of study in a rural school, I returned to my home city to attend Gao Kao. Based on the evaluation of previous university entry statistics and my mock exam scores, I realised that even though I could reach approximately 480 to 530 out of 750, this range was still not good enough to enter the tier 1 universities. Luckily, one of my previous secondary schoolmates told me about the TAP, which could be a reasonable way to go through. The development of TAP was in the initial stage in most Chinese universities, and it did not require students to have a very high score in the Gao Kao. However, it usually required students to have a solid English score as they will go overseas in the future. Therefore, I chose a TAP operated by an Art-Design focused university in my city. Compared to other candidates, my English was much better than theirs, reaching 110 out of 150. The lowest requirement for the programme was 80 out of 150. Therefore, I was admitted to the TAP without barriers. Although this "linguistic capital" may not be strong enough to support me to enter higher-ranked universities, it helped me enter another transnational "field," which started my transitioning in-between journey.

According to my learning story, it is apparent that I started my transitioning in-between journey once I completed primary school. I experienced different types of education through moving between private, public elite, and then rural schools. My habitus was constantly (re)shaped along with changes of identities, agency, and belonging. In this process, different types of "capitals" and "logic of practices" positively or negatively influenced me in either implicit or explicit ways (Bourdieu, 1990, 2000). The cross-field learning journey has had various "effects" on my longitudinal development (Lingard & Rawolle, 2004). This journey potentially shaped my sense of in-betweenness as a domestic diaspora who developed a solid resilience to deal with various challenges and adapt to different fields with a complex habitus. In short, during my school learning stage, I was constantly engaging in the cycle of "stress" and "adjust" without progressively experiencing "development." Luckily, I finally gained a little step forward, which allowed me to shape a sense of in-betweenness from domestic to global higher education fields.

2 Transitioning from China to Australia as a TAP Student

The transitioning in-between journey continued when I started my TAP. My position in this study is particular because I had experienced what I was researching and was an insider. As a researcher who had a TAP learning experience, I started my learning in 2007. From 2007 to 2009, I was studying at a Chinese university. This university was an Art-Design focused teaching institution that provided many TAPs with multiple international partners (e.g., Australia, the United States of America, Russia, and South Korea). I was admitted into the China-Australia programme. After reaching the IELTS requirement (average six or above) in 2009, I transferred to the Australian university, a research-teaching-focused, comprehensive institution, and started my last two years of study. My major was in Digital Design, which provided me with experiences similar to some of the students in my research. After completing the TAP, I completed my honours degree and achieved first-class honours, which helped me obtain a PhD offer to do further research.

On the one hand, my experiences had various similarities with my participants as we all studied in TAP settings in either the same or different programmes or universities. In this case, when I interviewed them, I quickly understood what they shared as I experienced many similar learning barriers and processes as they had. Hence, investigating their TAP learning experiences allowed me to recall my experiences and spontaneously compare their stories and mine. In this situation, I could be an insider. On the other hand, I could also be considered an outsider in the study. Although I had similar learning pathways and cultural backgrounds with my participants, many differences (e.g., time and spatial, programmes and majors, and even sociocultural developments) influenced our TAP experiences. Hence, when I interviewed the students, I was outside their contexts as I did not know how they experienced learning in a TAP and how they thought of themselves as TAP learners. This unique position reflected an issue of shifting the researcher's roles in the study.

My sense of agency, identity, and belonging were also dynamically (re)shaped in the cross-system transition.

2.1　*Adjustment in the Face of Stress*

When I recalled my own experiences in a TAP during my data collection and analysis, I surprisingly realised that my learning capabilities as a TAP learner had changed dramatically from China to Australia. My ability to deal with learning tasks and issues in my intercultural learning process was modified from stressfully out of control to smoothly under control. The TAP generates an intercultural academic discourse that challenges students' capabilities for adjustment to unfamiliar contexts. At different stages of the TAP, I made changes in my learning strategies to achieve my goals. As Bandura (1989) indicated, "people anticipate the likely consequences of their prospective actions, they set goals for themselves, and they plan courses of action likely to produce desired outcomes" (p. 1179). My experiences resonate with such a claim.

When I was successfully admitted to my TAP, being similar to most of my participants, I knew that I would go to Australia after completing two years' study and after achieving the IELTS requirement. However, I had no idea about the IELTS, my major, and my further study in Australia. All of these uncertainties made me feel somewhat unsure about my study and future. Learning in the TAP, I needed to achieve the IELTS requirement, which was my primary goal. Due to my limited understanding of the IELTS and weak English proficiency, I doubted whether I could meet the IELTS requirement. I also attended IELTS courses offered by my university to TAP students, and I also went to external training schools to take more individual sessions to reach the IELTS 6.0 overall. To achieve my goal, I took the IELTS exams four times. Although I finally reached the requirement, I felt that my energies were exhausted in that period, and it also broke my learning balance between IELTS and my discipline study.

When I came to Australia without worrying about the IELTS, compared to my participants' experiences, I had many similar issues with them in learning. More specifically, for instance, I needed to be familiar with listening to English-based teaching. My brain needed to work intensely and reflect on taught contents that seemed more advanced than what I learned in China. Even though I passed the IELTS, I realised that I needed to effectively study in a new context with different teaching and learning modes and rules. I distinctly remembered that my goal in the first semester was to obtain a "Pass" in each subject, which is similar to some of my research participants (e.g., Biang, Qing, Hao, and Dang). At that time, I never dreamed that high academic achievement in my study was possible. I thought that surviving the first semester without fail was the most significant success.

To deal with my learning barriers and achieve my proposed goals, I usually sought help from my previous Chinese lecturers, asking them how to create some special effects in Adobe Photoshop. Alternatively, I searched video tutorials via Chinese websites to learn detailed knowledge by myself. When I reflected on these experiences, I realised that I still had tight knowledge connections with the Chinese context as an overseas Chinese student in Australia, especially in the initial stage through new communication technologies. This experience coincided with Fei and Dang's stories, which indicate the importance of sociocultural and cultural connections between the home and the host-context (Rizvi et al., 2016). The diaspora mediates these connections (Rizvi et al., 2016; R. Yang & Welch, 2010). My initial unfamiliarity facilitated my growing process of intercultural adaptation through diasporic experiences.

After becoming familiar with the Australian context once I had completed my first semester, I started to consider whether I could become an academic achiever compared with my previous experiences? Bandura (1988) suggested that when people have resilient views about their capabilities to achieve their goals, they can become more persistent in their efforts. In my second semester, I tried to make some changes in learning to increase the possibilities of obtaining higher scores. For instance, I started to frequently communicate with my lecturers to discuss my assessments, which I did not do when I was in China and during the initial stage of the Australian study. Furthermore, I tried to seek English help from the university to improve my language proficiency to reach a professional level. I knew that the IELTS achievement and knowledge were no longer enough to support my study. By adopting such strategic changes in learning approaches, my GPA improved, and I achieved an average of "Distinction," which significantly improved my confidence in learning. Finally, when I graduated from my programme, I felt that I could be a successful student who could control and organise my study in the new system after experiencing dramatic changes in the new Australian academic context.

Based on the reflexive analysis of my journey and participants' experiences, the changes of agency towards different academic settings in the TAP discourse involve (re)shaping individual motivations and capabilities. I had various senses of agency in different intercultural academic discourses. For instance, many research participants and I transformed our learning approaches and strategies to adapt to the new educational contexts. However, Fei and Dong indicated that they could not study in Australia with positive attitudes because they seemed accustomed to the Chinese style. According to these different responses to the cross-system changes, it is evident that many students experienced a process of negotiation with the different educational contexts. In this process, their sense of agency to deal with learning issues also becomes multiple and complex. They might experience either positive or negative changes in this intercultural learning and adjustment journey. During the process of cross-system transition, my sense of identity has complex changed in an equally complex way.

2.2 *Who Was I? Who Am I?*

Who was I? As my narrative indicated above, I was a student with low academic achievement. I did not have the motivation to chase academic achievement. When I was in high school, I was not an academic achiever who could enter a top-ranked Chinese university. At that time, my parents and I were all worried about my future. After strategically analysing my situation, my parents and I decided to select the TAP to start my higher education because my score reached the academic requirement of that TAP. As parents, they wished me to be educated in a recognised university first and then create opportunities to explore something new. In my mind, the TAP offered me an opportunity to experience Chinese higher education. It seemed that the TAP was a life-saving straw for me. The parental and Gao Kao discourses profoundly influenced my identity as a high school student.

After starting my higher education journey, I became lazy in learning but active in playing. Studying in a context that lacked an excellent academic atmosphere, I had similar experiences to many of my research participants (e.g., Liang, Biang, and Chao) who ignored the study. Lave and Wenger (1991) indicated that the shape of identity is a process of interactions between the person and the sociocultural contexts that he/she lived in. Although I lived on the campus and attended lectures, my brain was not wholly devoted to studying. As many of my research participants mentioned, peers did not focus on learning, negatively influencing other students. As a young student who did not have robust capabilities to control me, I enjoyed my "holiday time" in a relaxed context, which made me feel comfortable. Even though I had been stressed about preparing for IELTS, I was not a "good" learner. The university context influenced my identity as a fresh university student.

Who am I? Compared to my previous self, I became a student who would achieve academically, a student who had a strong motivation to chase his academic goals, and a student. They can positively face and deal with challenges. As a member of the Chinese diaspora, I felt that I had some "translations" (Robins, 1991) in my life and study. Compared with my research participants' dynamic changes of identity in their TAP learning process, I also experienced such complex transitions when I was at the same stage. Precisely, my transitions happened in both study and daily life. In learning, I became a motivated learner from a demotivated student. I started to realise the importance of

A REFLEXIVE JOURNEY AS AN IN-BETWEENER   131

chasing outstanding academic achievements for my future. In my daily life, I also became a more independent adult who could manage various life issues.

As I mentioned above, I did not dream of achieving a high GPA and undertaking a PhD research study. I challenged myself with dealing with different types of differences from China to Australia in both study and life. With my increased confidence, I started to believe that I could do something that I had not tried before. As many participants said, teaching and learning practices were dramatically different from the Chinese approach in the Australian context. I needed to change my approaches and views to survive and develop myself further in the new environment. For instance, when I started my Australian study, I did not realise the importance of being an independent learner in the Australian context. I was also used to waiting for instructions, and as such, I missed a lot of valuable information. However, I gradually noticed that I had to change my strategies to be an active learner who needed to positively explore knowledge, especially when most lecturers were facilitators rather than dominators in teaching. By actively changing my views and attitudes towards study, I did notice that I became independent. Therefore, I can understand that my participants experienced multiple dynamic transformations from almost dependent to independent learners, given the changes in sociocultural and academic contexts in the transition from China to Australia.

The complex and multiple contexts spontaneously influence students' identities. Consequently, as a result, many students can transform their identities to fit into the new context based on strategically managing their life and study in these different discourses. In contrast, some students failed to rebuild their identities as intercultural learners when they had a strong sense of identity as traditional Chinese students. Students also indicated different preferences and belonging towards the two separate contexts through intercultural learning in the TAP setting. The following section will illustrate my changes in my sense of belonging as a TAP learner.

2.3   *Belonging to an "In-Between" Space*
Compared with participants' various senses of belonging as Chinese students in the Australian context, I will reflect upon my experiences. As McMillan and Chavis (1986) suggested, the following simple sentence can reflect the senses of belonging: "It is my group" and "I am part of the group." In my case, I experienced a smooth process of changing the sense of belonging, but I felt it was difficult to define where I belonged, even though I have studied in Australia for nearly eight years. When I considered my belonging as an intercultural learner, I think I belonged to an in-between space between the two different contexts.

132 CHAPTER 6

When I first landed in Australia, I was shocked by the different educational, natural, and social contexts. Like other participants, I also felt unfamiliar with the new environment; I was homesick and experienced loneliness. In that situation, my mind told me that I was a Chinese student in Australia, and I was an international student. I did not belong here, and my goal was to gain my degree. From the initial stage, such a feeling existed in my mind, and I had a strong sense of belonging to the Chinese context. This is because even though I was able to chase my academic dreams and work harder, I believed that the identity of an international student was still my label, and I did not belong to Australia. I aimed to graduate rather than adapt to the local sociocultural context. It seemed that although I was a student at an Australian university, I was not a member of society. In that period, once I completed my final assessment and exams in each semester, I booked the ticket and then went back to China. For me, it seemed that I was doing some cross-country business. I stayed in Australia for three months to complete my learning business and then went back to China for one- or two months holidays. Such experiences suggested that I initially had a strong sense of belonging to my home country as a member of various diasporas, which indicated my strong attachment to China (Rizvi et al., 2016).

After completing my degree and starting my research study, I realised that I seemed to be used to studying and living in the Australian context. This is because I had experienced several academic achievements, which did not happen in China. The successful experiences made me feel that only in Australia could my dreams come true. However, although I had adapted to the Australian context, especially in the academic setting, it seemed that I had more emotional contact with China. For instance, I usually communicate with my family and friends in China to discuss work, life and study issues via ICT-based tools, WeChat. The development of technology made the emotional distance of the diaspora became virtually shorter, which helped me keep more connections with my home country and family (Rizvi et al., 2016). Although I physically studied in Australia in this ICT-based context, I still had emotional solid and technologically mediated contacts with China.

With the rapid development of ICTs, I distinctly remembered that when I came to Australia in 2009, mobile technology and the Internet were not well developed and utilised compared with the current stage. In that period, the Internet quota was limited and expensive. Mobile technology was in the initial developing stage. Most communications with my homeland were based on traditional desktop-based personal computer (PC) applications or expensive telephone calls. However, the current situation is entirely different. As I mentioned, I can use WeChat to communicate with my friends and family easily via either PC or mobile devices. I can make unlimited international calls to select countries for a low fee. Such technological changes made me feel that the "time and space" distances have been compressed and facilitated by the new technologies (Harvey, 1999).

My daily observations and discussions with other Chinese students have similar experiences that communications with China have become unobstructed. Although my study did not focus on the ICT communications issues, I believe that such technological developments help diasporic students connect with their homelands in learning and daily life. When I recalled my experiences, I did feel that my and even other Chinese students' experiences of ICT-based communications in learning and life suggest that new technology played a crucial role in connecting them with the homeland (Rizvi et al., 2016).

Such feelings made me float in the two different contexts, which led to my in-between belonging. By exploring my research participants' stories and reflecting on my own experiences, I believe that it is difficult to say which society or system the intercultural learners (e.g., me) belong to. Different students presented various preferences towards these systems. I believed that intercultural learners' belonging is (re)constructed dynamically during their intercultural learning processes. This journey positions them between different educational contexts.

3 Shifting between Chinese and Australian Contexts

Chapter 5 has illustrated the contour of a transitioning in-between learning space from the perspectives of relationships between physical place and virtual space. The physical place is a metaphor to refer to a limited ICT-assisted or traditional learning context. As many students shared, learning activities in the Chinese stage seemed to happen in a physical place with limited virtually based experiences. In contrast, students' experiences indicated a strong sense of inbetweenness among the physical and virtual spaces in the Australian stage of their programmes. Their learning seemed to become in-between based. Moreover, they had many connections with China via ICT-based tools, which created a virtual space of knowledge transformation and cross-system communication. It seemed that when they studied and lived in a foreign context, the in-between features became much more apparent than in the home context.

3.1 *Shifting between Physical Place and Virtual Space*

When I considered my learning experiences in the move from China to Australia, I noticed that I had a similar journey as my participants in the Chinese context. When I was studying at my Chinese university nearly eight years ago, I did not have intensive ICT-based learning experiences in general. Although my major was also related to technology, especially the Internet-based tools (e.g., online learning system), it was not prevalent. I distinctly remembered that my university did not have even a functional online learning system. The university website did not have any educational content directly related to my study. The university website only displayed news and other general administrative information. Even on the campus, students did not have Wi-Fi access. It seemed that the development and applications of Internet-based technology were at a starting point. Therefore, I studied in a very traditional learning place without powerful ICT-based interventions due to the developmental issues with ICTs. I did not think that ICTs played an essential role in my study, and I felt that the Internet was for playing games rather than for learning.

However, when I heard about my interviewees' experiences six years later, it seemed the situation had not changed. They still experienced limited ICT-based learning, even though Internet-based technology has rapidly developed in the past years. Their experiences might indicate that with the constant development of ICTs, the TAP in the Chinese phase seemed not to pay enough attention to ICT-based learning. Although ICTs are no longer new for most Chinese students, the educational uses of ICTs in their daily study seemed to be at a low level, which limited these students' understanding of the actual value of ICTs as learning tools. However, when I came to Australia, I noticed that everything related to university life and study was based on ICTs, potentially reshaping my views towards ICTs and using ICTs as a learning mediation.

Considering my Australian experience, I did not have a strong sense of ICT-based in-between learning when I started my last two years in Australia. Although I could use Blackboard and other ICT-based tools when I started learning at my Australian university, I did not have strong connections with China via ICTs in both learning and living. I remembered that there were limited online resources or services that I could use to support my Australian study. Even though I watched some tutorial videos online, the quality was not good compared to the current vivid resources. The learning activities were Australia-based without enough support from China. It was impossible to video chat with families and friends via a mobile phone in daily life. I needed to make phone calls by paying expensive fees. Generally, I feel I was isolated from my homeland when I started my study in Australia.

With the development of ICTs, especially mobile technology and MOOCs, I have many in-between experiences now, especially while studying for my PhD programme. For learning, I attended many courses via live-video online platforms. For example, I learned NVivo and SPSS from professors at Peking

University via online training courses. Taking such courses, I now have a deep understanding of research methods and skills. Language barriers were not the primary issue for me to acquire knowledge from China. Such learning experiences offered me opportunities to know what has been taught in a top research-based Chinese university. I can reflect and compare what I learned from Australian and Chinese content. In doing so, I now have close connections with some aspects of the Chinese academic field. Such experiences are in line with a study conducted by Kim, Yun, and Yoon (2009), who found that the Internet is a hybrid space that allows diaspora to mediate and negotiate their home and host culture and society. In this process, although I am physically studying in Australia, I can easily access and connect with my home country. Such experiences made me aware that I am studying in the ICT-based in-between space where intercultural learners have to negotiate with new educational contexts.

Notably, with the rapid development of internet-based technology in China (e.g., mobile devices, 5G network, cloud computing, and artificial intelligence), the current situation may have changed dramatically and been different from eight or nine years ago. As mentioned above, due to the Covid-19 pandemic, most teaching and learning activities have been transferred to the internet. Many international students cannot travel to their host countries during this period, and they can only keep learning via an online platform. Academics also become "live broadcasters" who teach students from different parts of the world via the internet. In this virtual learning space, intercultural connections and communications are still happening. Students can access the learning contents and resources from different places at home. Even though they cannot physically move between different locations, it seems that they could virtually shift, shuttle, and transit among various cultures, knowledge, and information, which potentially positions themselves between different places and spaces. In short, although students and academics are now communicating with each other in a virtual space, they also shift and transfer between different sociocultural and educational contexts.

3.2 Shifting between Different Assessment Cultures

Assessments are approaches that evaluate students' learning and facilitate further efforts if possible but are also helpful tools to establish the transitioning in-between learning space. Considering my own experience of studying in different contexts, I believe that the changes in assessment methods were essential to motivate many Chinese students, including me, to change learning strategies and attitudes when we studied in the transitioning in-between space. Some students could adjust to the new assessment culture in the changing process, but many peers may have felt stressed in the new context. These various attitudes and strategies for dealing with assessment change suggested that individuals had different intercultural competence.

On the one hand, I had similar experiences with my participants in the Chinese context. When I was in my Chinese learning stage, I also did not pay enough attention to assessments. The assessment seemed to be just one academic symbol to show the programme had some educational features, rather than a proper strategy to motivate me to study hard. One of the reasons the assessment appeared to be of little value to many Chinese students was that the academic rules seemed to be not very strict. In this case, I was in an informal learning context that motivated learners to focus on exams without other types of assessments. Therefore, it was challenging to experience a multiple and dynamic in-between space of assessment in China.

On the other hand, I felt that these Chinese TAP students, including me, were the actual creators of the in-between space under the Australian assessment system. As I mentioned above, I did not care about the assessment when I was in China. However, after coming to Australia, I realised the importance of carefully completing each assignment. The workload increased, which made me feel stressed. Importantly, to deal with such stress, I started to think about every possible approach to help me complete each task. In this process, communication with the Chinese context was one of my essential strategies. For instance, I was not familiar with using Adobe Photoshop to edit pictures and create complicated effects. Learning-related knowledge via Chinese websites and resources helped me to solve various problems effectively. Through such strategies, first, there were no language barriers to learning knowledge in Chinese. Second, there were a lot of valuable resources, which I was able to use without problems. In doing so, I learned various skills and techniques through such communications in the virtual space in dealing with different assignment issues.

As many participants indicated, even though they did not have many experiences of overcoming assessment issues via in-between strategies in the Chinese stage, they did create and develop the in-between space by adopting different approaches to build a strong sense of agency in Australia. Such adaptations potentially reshaped most students' understanding of identity from passive listeners to active explorers moving from China to Australia. Importantly, learning activities, especially dealing with assessments, happened in a space that allowed students to interact dynamically with different people, resources, and places rather than rely on the textbook source. Therefore, the changes in assessment from China to Australia illustrated a route of creating a transitioning in-between learning space from a physical dominated space.

A REFLEXIVE JOURNEY AS AN IN-BETWEENER   137

Such in-betweenness included both a virtual-physical mode and home-host country knowledge interaction.

3.3   Teaching Strategies Positioned Me between Different Learning Modes

Based on my experiences, I generally agreed with the views of my respondents regarding the different teaching modes in the Chinese and Australian stages of the TAP. I felt that the different teaching styles from China to Australia made students engage deeply in the in-between space. Considering the in-between space of teaching in the Chinese stage, for instance, although many foreign lecturers visited my university and taught some fundamental content for students, I thought that the sense of teaching was still very Chinese in style. Most of my lecturers adopted similar teaching strategies to those interviewees reported in their programmes. It seems that such a teaching-based in-between space in the Chinese stage may not be strong enough to bring fresh learning experiences to learners.

After coming to Australia, I did not have a strong sense of non-adaptation to the new teaching experience than many research interviewees. In my programmes, many Australian lecturers were still adopting the traditional approaches to teaching. Students were also listening in most cases. However, I identified many differences in my learning journey. For instance, many lecturers became facilitators, especially in my last year of study, to create my graduate design works. They gave students enough autonomy to do their tasks. Based on my experiences, I think the teaching changes in the TAP also depended on the stage of learning. In the first two years, teaching usually focused on foundational knowledge that lecturers did need to teach carefully. In this case, the students seemed to be passive listeners. When they came to Australia, they started advanced stages of learning. In this stage, lecturers may use more open approaches to teach rather than merely deliver knowledge. Therefore, I felt that the transition of teaching mode from China to Australia reflected the stage of learning.

In this process, I also realised the issues of teaching strategies in the Australian context. Compared to other aspects of shaping an in-between space for these students (e.g., ICT and assessment), teaching strategies are more complicated because each student and lecturer is different. Therefore, it is challenging to clearly show how students approached the teaching differences via interactions between their home and host countries. However, as the data displayed, their views and opinions produced an in-between space that allowed them to critically evaluate the teaching quality and style depending on individual situations. For me, I had a similar contradictory sense in my learning process.

Depending on different situations, I may have different teaching styles, which also influenced my capability to deal with learning problems. Therefore, my mind was divided into two spaces.

However, I usually switched my views between the different teaching strategies and gained multiple and complex learning experiences in this hybrid context. It is essential for both Chinese and Australian lecturers to carefully consider students' learning requirements and design some teaching models that could help students adjust to becoming in-between learners who can benefit from this TAP intercultural learning process.

3.4 *Shifting between Different Contextual Features*

Generally, I had a similar learning journey to that of the research participants. However, I felt it was not very easy when I realised how to conceptualise my own in-between space after experiencing two different contexts.

In China, I was a member of a TAP rather than an individual who had many independent learning and life experiences. In the Chinese stage, I felt that every student was in-between in their programmes and universities. As Liang and Dong's interview data indicated, learning and living as a group was the default setting for most students who spontaneously had close connections with other group members. In this case, a semi-closed space was created smoothly, which perhaps ensured learners had a limited sense of independence in learning. After engaging in such a context for a long time, I felt in a fixed group. Theoretically, I am an individual who is different from any other students. Practically, I belong to a group that may have many similarities. Consequently, my sense of in-betweenness moved back and forth dynamically and circularly within the Chinese scope rather than engaging in the Australian context in depth.

After moving to the Australian university, I remembered trying to find my group, especially in the initial stage. However, I realised that it was impossible to have a fixed group anymore because everyone had different situations in both study and life. For example, different students started their Australian learning stage because of IELTS or other academic issues. Before coming to Australia, the students who passed IELTS could successfully begin their discipline study without language training in Australia. However, some students needed to learn English first, which delayed their discipline learning.

Furthermore, students usually rent rooms outside the university campus in different locations. Such a situation also made it somewhat difficult to contact each other frequently. In learning, every student could select various courses in one semester, even in the same major. Hence, it was not easy to study and live together, as was the case in the Chinese stage.

I also became independent in this context, even though I sought "collective" features in my daily life and study. This change made me step out of the previous collective space. I was not a group member who lived and studied in-between with other peers. In contrast, I became an individual that needed to survive independently in a new context. I needed to communicate with new actants (e.g., people, society, and culture) to establish an individual-based network, which helped me become influenced by collective and individual sociocultural contexts. Precisely, on the one hand, for instance, I needed to get used to being an "individual" learner who usually studied at university alone without secure connections with other classmates as a fixed cohort. On the other hand, I still had some links with the collective context. For example, even though I moved to Australia, I always wanted to live as a Chinese diaspora who could have strong connections with other Chinese people and community in the new context, in this case, the local Chinese cohort in Australia.

Considering the relationship with other people in the individualistic context, I felt isolated to some extent, especially in the undergraduate stage. Although I did not have a large, fixed group membership in my TAP, I usually studied with some Chinese friends in a small group. In contrast, I did not have any communication with local Australian students. It seemed that they were in the same group, but many Chinese students, including me, seemed to be another separate group on campus. Such experiences were also found by Hou (2011). She suggested that two fuzzy but apparent groups were labelled as "we" and "they" when Chinese students studied in a different context. In line with this finding, I noticed that I had the same sense of "we" as Chinese in the Australian university, but "they" as local students also had their own space.

However, as an intercultural learner, I had no choice to avoid the trend that they and we are mixed in a context that emphasises the individual. In this context, I felt that my mind was always in between the different settings. I did become independent in learning, but I struggled with the negotiations between these two contexts. I asked myself, who am I? Where do I belong to? To answer these questions, I would say that I am a person who had fluid identities and senses of belonging, but I may not belong to either the Chinese or Australian contexts. Thus, I am an in-between person who lives in an in-between space shaped by my hybrid understandings of communications within different settings. It seems that the TAP allowed me to experience two different sociocultural and educational systems. Meanwhile, it built an in-between space that facilitated students to become in-between human beings and shape hybridity. The negotiation between colonising and colonised subjects exists in cross-system intercultural transition (Bhabha, 1994; English, 2005; McLennan, 2003).

4 Conclusion

This chapter illustrated my in-between learning and life experiences across different stages, from school to university. As my learning story in different situations showed, I shifted between different educational contexts and progressively developed a sense of in-betweenness from a problematic teenager in the host context to an international student who studied between two educational settings. Notably, "intercultural adjustment" may not only happen when people move between countries but also exists in everyday life, which may have various micro-political changes depending on the features of different schools and universities. When a student shifted between different sociocultural and educational fields, he/she may spontaneously engage in developing a sense of in-betweenness with reflections of various senses of identity, agency, and belonging. The contextual features in different systems could create both cultural clashes and developmental opportunities for people. People could indicate various capabilities and resilience to respond to complex changes across sociocultural and educational contexts. They may immerse themselves in the cycle of stress-adaptation and gain either positive or negative changes. In short, people may always be in a status of "adjusting" from either micro or macro perspectives.

Note

1 Parts of this chapter are based on Dai, K. (2020), Learning between two systems: a Chinese student's reflexive narrative in a China-Australia articulation programme. *Compare, 50*(3), 371–390. Permission for re-use has been given by the publishers.

CHAPTER 7

Critical Reflections: Becoming Compatible

This study investigated a group of Chinese students' learning experiences in China-Australia TAPs. This research has added a student perspective to this under-researched field, allowing the student voices to be expressed in research interviews. To achieve this aim, I interviewed several students about their learning trajectories in TAPs. Furthermore, I attempted to explore how the TAP setting (re)shaped students' learning trajectories and how they made sense of their transnational intercultural learning journeys as TAP learners. In this chapter, I will answer each research question first. Then, implications are discussed.

1 Dynamically Transitioning between Different Systems

How do Chinese students experience intercultural learning in transnational articulation programmes? The findings illustrated different learning trajectories of Chinese students in their TAPs. Their experiences suggest that intercultural issues are "stressed as an important part of internationalisation" (Leask, 2004, p. 337). In the transitioning process, many students constantly negotiated between different academic systems to position themselves reasonably. The dynamic transitions can be reflected through the following aspects: national, institutional, and individual.

From the national level, these participants were transitioning between China and Australia. Existing research has suggested that those countries have differences regarding cultural, educational, and social settings (Hofstede, 1986; Ward & Kennedy, 1993a). When two different contexts with different rules, traditions, and standards work together, cross-system tensions are likely to spontaneously generate (Bhabha, 1994; Engeström, 1999). People who work in such mixed contexts need to realise and make sense of various cross-system differences to deal with the various tensions (Engeström, 1999). An in-between space created by students' various views and senses towards cross-system tensions becomes a platform for them to position themselves as in-betweeners (Bhabha, 1994). Students' different experiences in TAPs reflect how they negotiated with cross-system tensions. Their multiple approaches to dealing with cross-system differences indicated various shifts between cultural, social, and educational contexts.

© KONINKLIJKE BRILL NV, LEIDEN, 2022 | DOI: 10.1163/9789004505131_007

From the institutional level, these participants were transitioning between different educational approaches and academic cultures in TAPs, which could be situational differences. Chinese and Australian universities also have particular and idiosyncratic features. As students mentioned in this study, teaching strategies, Internet-based tools, assessments, university academic cultures revealed dramatic differences in their TAP across the two learning contexts. Although students were studying in an articulated model, they still needed to overcome cross-system barriers and reshape their approaches to survive in the two systems. In this case, many situational differences (different usages of ICTs, different assessment practices, contrasting teaching approaches, and different university cultures) created a learning space that ensured students constantly shifted between two systems, constituting them in-betweeners through the TAP setting. It is also important to note that educational institutions may also need to "adjust to" students who engage in the process of intercultural learning and adjustment, especially in TAPs. Although students may indicate different senses of identity, agency, and belonging while studying in multiple systems and institutions, educators and policymakers must consider students' diversity carefully when designing TAPs.

Third, at the individual level, these TAP students were transitioning between different roles as a unique cohort of diaspora. When facing situational differences in TAPs, students reflected various senses of agency, identity, and belonging, revealing how they made sense of themselves as TAP students in cross-system learning settings. Considering the changes of agency, many students (e.g., Hao, Diao, Shuo, Liang, Zhuang, and Qing) indicated positive experiences towards the cross-system learning differences and intercultural adjustment. They seemed to build up the confidence to adjust to intercultural learning as in-betweeners who knew how to handle educational differences emerged from the TAP transition process. Notably, as Hao's story suggested, she not only critically understood differences in learning between China and Australia but also fostered her capabilities to deal with problems in her cross-system study. In contrast, some students indicated a disempowered agency towards educational differences, such as Fei, who experienced a painful transition process, even though he considered himself an outstanding student in the Chinese context.

Concerning the sense of identity, most students' experiences illustrated a sense of in-betweenness that has been developed through TAP learning. On the one hand, many students (e.g., Qing, Shuo, Zhuang, Hao, and Liang) seemed to have a positive sense of in-betweenness. They could take advantage of cross-system differences, even though they experienced stress in their transition, especially in the initial stage. On the other hand, some students seemed to be unable to actively experience becoming in-betweeners who can strategically

CRITICAL REFLECTIONS: BECOMING COMPATIBLE 143

deal with the educational differences and then developed positive attitudes towards their changes as intercultural learners in a cross-system context.

Finally, influenced by the different senses of agency and identity, students also indicated different senses of belonging. For instance, some students (e.g., Hao, Diao, Zhuang, and Liang) could adjust to the Australian learning context. Then, they developed their belonging towards the new educational system, even though they studied in TAPs with many cross-system academic inconsistencies (e.g., teaching approaches, assessment modes, the usages of technology, and general university culture). Based on the positive sense of belonging, they may deeply engage in learning activities in the Australian context. In contrast, other students (e.g., Dong, Fei, and Rui) showed a dramatically different sense of belonging towards the new context and even their TAPs. For instance, although Dong was studying in her Australian stage, she indicated strong preferences for the Chinese educational system and learning approaches. This potentially reflected that she might not develop a sense of belonging to the new learning context. According to the students' dynamic learning experiences summarised above, it is apparent that their approaches and attitudes towards cross-system learning are multiple, varied and complex. This is because many students became ambivalent after experiencing the cultural, social, and educational differences, which provoked them to have a sense of in-betweenness in the cross-system setting. Consequently, a reciprocal relationship of in-betweenness between students and the TAP setting emerged from different learning stories.

As a researcher, their in-between learning trajectory evokes me to recall my growing up journey reflexively. As the narrative in Chapter 6 indicated, I shifted between various school contexts and then move from China to Australia. In the school learning stage, I became immersed in the process of shifting between different micro-level sociocultural contexts (e.g., from city to rural town; from private/public elite to rural school). These transitions progressively shaped my sense of in-betweenness, causing me to have different learning experiences and reflections on contextual changes. In this journey, I seemed to develop various types of identity, agency and belonging. I encountered various logics of practices in different fields, which could (re)shape my habitus. Different capitals also played positive or negative roles in my cross-field transition, which comprehensively impacted my learning life. In this process, as an agent, I become an in-between person who may have complex characters and various reactions towards the changes of micro-level sociocultural contexts. In short, even though I was studying in China without moving to Australia, learning in different sub-fields in education within China also made me engage in a journey of micro-level intercultural adjustment.

144   CHAPTER 7

Considering my learning journey in TAP, I am also an in-betweener with
fluid roles with different approaches to deal with the macro-level cross-system differences between China and Australia. As an outsider, I noticed that
many students in TAPs experienced both Chinese and Australian educational
features with endless negotiations within the two different systems. The TAP
setting practically established an in-between space to foster fluid identities,
oscillating agency, and multiple senses of belonging.

The TAP may not just have a series of well-documented goals and influences,
such as increasing the level of internationalisation of Chinese HE, offering Chinese students multiple pathways to study at the tertiary level, and positioning students as "profit machines" for both Chinese and foreign universities.
However, for students, as educational customers, although they also engage in
achieving some of the above aims, they may not be able to realise the changes
they may face in such TNHE. One of these changes is to have the possibility
of establishing the sense of in-betweenness after experiencing their TAP with
complex and dynamic attitudes. Hence, constructing the sense of in-betweenness could be either a planned or unintended consequence for students.

For individual students, they may have different motivations to study in
TAPs. If students initially have the intention to experience the cross-system
educational setting actively, they may indicate positive attitudes when they
spontaneously engage in the intercultural learning process. In contrast, if
students initially do not have a firm commitment to this learning transition,
they may engage in the process of being in-between without enough positive
experiences. For universities, policymakers, and educators may claim that
such educational settings could theoretically offer students multiple educational experiences. However, they may not explicitly identify the underlying
complexity of studying in such modes from students' perspectives, which is
the process of becoming in-betweeners who may immerse in a status of constant negotiations with different education contexts in an in-between learning space. Hence, developing a sense of in-betweenness for students could be
either an unintended or planned result of developing such TNHE depending
on different students' intentions to select TAPs as the learning pathway. Each
student may either positively engage in establishing in-betweenness or reflect
some negative responses towards this process.

The TAP objectively set up a learning context that positions students
between different education systems. Practically, students usually indicate different reactions towards the in-between learning space, which leads to various attitudes and experiences of having a sense of in-betweenness. In short,
although different stakeholders have various aims of running TAPs or other
TNHEs, for students, the development of the sense of in-betweenness could be

CRITICAL REFLECTIONS: BECOMING COMPATIBLE 145

one of the essential experiences in the learning process, and they may indicate different attitudes towards this unobservable result.

As the results showed, some students were able to engage in shaping a sense of in-betweenness positively. However, some of them did not want to involve in such a phenomenon actively. These students seemed to be too attached to their previous Chinese traditions of learning. From an insider perspective, I realised that my learning trajectory reflected a strong sense of in-betweenness. Based on careful reflection as outlined in previous chapters, my learning experiences indicated a complex process of being an in-betweener who negotiated continuously and renegotiated within different educational contexts, majors, tasks, and barriers in-between learning space. The role of in-betweener in qualitative research studies is fluid and dynamic, rather than fixed, single, and static (Milligan, 2016). My learning experiences illustrated a specific and exciting picture of my process of having a sense of in-betweenness from multiple perspectives, such as a school student, a TAP learner, a PhD researcher, and a member of the Chinese diaspora.

2 (Re)shaping Identity, Agency, and Belonging in Cross-System Transition

What changes do they experience in cross-system transition? As students' experiences indicated, they negotiated with various contextual features in cross-system transition, which indicated their identity changes, agency, and belonging.

Students' sense of identity is fluid and dynamic during the TAP transition. According to Hogg, Terry, and White (1995), identity is a mediation that connects society and individual behaviours. Therefore, individuals' behaviours reflect the relationship between their identity and the society that they stay in (Hogg et al., 1995). Based on the research findings outlined in Chapter 4, various identity changes suggest that students embraced fluid identities and learned with others in ways that had uncertain and unpredictable outcomes, as they were in a continual process of becoming. Importantly, their identities are "thus points of temporary attachment to the subject positions which discursive practices construct for us" (Hall & Du Gay, 1996, p. 6).

When discussing identity in the Chinese context, most students identified themselves as dependent and demotivated followers. This reflection indicates various features of Chinese culture, which has been widely discussed by many researchers (Allen, 1995; Li, 2003a, 2003b; Tweed & Lehman, 2002; Volet, 1999). For example, Allen (1995) suggested that the sense of hierarchy in traditional Chinese culture was significant. Profoundly respecting parents or teachers was considered an essential feature in the Chinese context, known as "a sign of obedience" (Li, 2003a, p. 147). In this study, many students selected the TAP and their majors relying on parental suggestions, which indicates that family influence is one of the substantial pull factors that motivated some students to study in TNHE (Liu et al., 2021). Furthermore, lecturers were usually seen as the authority in learning, so following them was considered a way to study from the perspective of traditional Chinese culture (Biggs, 1996c; Jin & Cortazzi, 2006). Many students were spontaneously used to being followers in many situations of their life and study.

The feature of students' identity in the Chinese stage is understandable. I had similar experiences with most participants. Most Chinese students were studying in a highly stressed context in high school because of university entry exams. The primary learning approach was to follow teachers to prepare for the exam via mock tests. This type of learning could be deeply implanted into students' minds. Such an experience possibly ensured that students have a potential consciousness that learning is to follow lecturers, practice tests repeatedly, and pass exams after being immersed in this context for a long time. This context potentially fostered students to become followers in many cases. After starting university, I felt that the high school learning experience was deeply inserted into my mind. I was used to following lecturers' teaching and waiting for "feeding knowledge" even though the university context is much more flexible than high school. The sense of identity as a follower or demotivator continued to influence me. However, when I reviewed the participants' experiences in Australia, I noted that their stories were different and more complicated.

When students moved to Australia, their identities underwent dramatic changes. As the results suggested, most students became independent and motivated explorers. These changes are similar to findings concluded by Wong (2012) and Gu (2016). They found that many Chinese students became independent in both learning and daily life after studying in different contexts for a period, for example, in Australia or the UK. However, students' changes in the current study offer more detailed insights and add further evidence to the current literature of understanding and theorising Chinese students' identity changes as intercultural learners.

On the one hand, many students actively enjoyed the change of identity from follower to explorer due to the educational changes (e.g., teaching strategies, assessments, and campus setting) in the Australian context, which could be a "learning shock" (Gu & Schweisfurth, 2006). For example, many lecturers usually motivated students to explore knowledge individually without detailed supervision; assessments were multiple and flexible; the university

CRITICAL REFLECTIONS: BECOMING COMPATIBLE 147

campus is open, and classes usually did not have a precisely fixed cohort. Many other scholars also found these positive experiences investigating Chinese students' cross-cultural learning in different culturally western contexts (e.g., Y. Gu, 2008; T. Wang & Shan, 2007; Wu, 2015; Zhu, 2016). Meanwhile, students' changes as optimistic explorers also challenge conventional understandings of the Chinese cohort, who are usually represented as passive learners (Samuelowicz, 1987). However, some students' stories provided evidence that could further refine these findings.

On the other hand, contrarily, some of them (e.g., Dong, Fei, Rui, and Dang) seemed to have passive attitudes towards accepting the reality that they had to become independent explorers in the new learning context. According to the research findings, they have been profoundly influenced by the Chinese context and indicated strong preferences for the Chinese model. For instance, Dang argued that being independent in learning as an Internet-assisted student seemed worthless; why pay expensive tuition fees to be trained in Australia where some lecturers seemed not to teach much detailed knowledge. It seemed that she would have preferred to study as a follower in Australia, and she did not want to be highly independent in her learning. For some of these students, a dilemma in their sense of identity emerged from these experiences.

Many students positioned themselves as passive in-between learners who physically studied in Australia with seeming independence but remained psychologically immersed in China with deeply dependent minds. This feature suggests that student's previous learning and life experiences significantly influenced their study in a new environment or mode (Biggs, 1996b; Dai, Matthews, & Renshaw, 2020; Yan, 2017; Zhu, Valcke, & Schellens, 2009). Such influences could be either positive or negative. For instance, several students' experiences (e.g., Dong and Rui) suggested that they seemed to still be followers in the Australian context, even though they did need to explore and learn knowledge by themselves actively. As these students mentioned, they also followed the lecturers' teaching as an effective learning strategy. These experiences did not make them feel much different from their Chinese experiences. Thus, they seemed to be shifting their identities fluidly between follower and explorer with contradicted minds and complex attitudes towards these educational differences. These fluid identities reflected that many students could flexibly change their roles and fit into the new context, which suggests that their identities were not fixed but dynamic (Hall, 1992).

It is worth noting that different students in different disciplines had a different sense of identity across the two educational contexts compared with these experiences. As Dang, who studied in Design, indicated, she was used to being a follower when studying in China. However, the Australian mode pushed her to become an independent explorer who had certain negative attitudes towards the new teaching and learning model. In contrast, some students (e.g., Dong and Rui) did not experience many differences in in-class learning between China and Australia, which is always lecturer-guided in the Business-related major. As a consequence, they seemed always to be followers in their study, but with some differences. Their experiences suggested that the shape of identity is affected across nations, cultures, and societies (Jenkins, 2008). Moreover, these students' learning approaches were also involved and flexible across different contexts, rather than fixed as rote learners who preferred memorisation, indicating that many students could make changes to their learning in different educational and cultural contexts (Kember, 2016).

The above examples indicated that the person's context profoundly influences the sense of identity. These multiple experiences about changing made me deeply immersed in the status of in-betweenness. According to Rizvi (2011), mobility potentially (re)constructs social identities. Being in-between such mixed and complicated situations, their learning journey in TAP is a process that lets them endlessly engage in an in-between space, where they needed to deal with various issues that emerged from cross-system differences. In this in-between process, students live and study in a circle of uncertainty-negotiation-change, which seems to be much more complicated than the model of stress-adaptation-development.

Considering the sense of agency, many students are between empowerment and disempowerment towards the academic differences in the TAP learning processes. Most students seemed to be empowered towards discipline exams in the Chinese stage but felt disenfranchised about passing the IELTS. Most students paid considerable attention to IELTS as it significantly influenced their learning in Australia. Their learning experiences of IELTS in the Chinese stage indicated a struggling sense of agency, which potentially indicated that learning IELTS needed to be the priority. In contrast, students' views and approaches towards discipline learning indicated their empowered sense of agency. Many students were confident about passing related academic tasks of discipline subjects as they believed that exams were easily passed. These shifts between IELTS focus and discipline course learning suggest that many students have different learning goals and approaches.

These findings echo several previous studies, which found that many Chinese students struggled with English preparation in TAPs (e.g., Bai & Y. Wang, 2020; Feng, 2016; Gao et al., 2012; Yu, 2014; Wilson-Mah & Thomlinson, 2018). According to Gao et al. (2012), most TAPs set up a benchmark of English tests (e.g., IELTS) to conduct their foreign study stage. However, the language requirement could become a significant barrier for many students who may

CRITICAL REFLECTIONS: BECOMING COMPATIBLE 149

not have a strong English learning background. As Yu (2014) and Feng (2016) found, English and IELTS were considered a key barrier for many Chinese students preparing to complete their TAPs. In contrast, there was a practical imbalance between learning English/IELTS and discipline knowledge for some students in their first two years of study at Chinese universities. Many students did not prepare well in the Chinese stage for later Australian learning (Y. Wang & Bai, 2020).

From the perspective of in-betweenness, this imbalanced focus might indicate learning quality in some TAPs. Such an imbalanced situation in my study happened as well. When I started my TAP, I had no idea about the IELTS. My programmes arranged extra IELTS courses for TAP students to help us learn how to pass them. However, I felt so emasculated when learning it, as language learning seemed much more complicated than discipline knowledge. Under such circumstances, I wished to get rid of the extra stress from the IELTS. In doing so, most of my energies were utilised to pass IELTS. Many students, including me, went to IELTS training schools outside the university in the second year to boost their IELTS scores. Hence, we passively lost the opportunities to learn discipline courses for quite a long time. As the final exams approached, we returned to study and could hardly remember the textbooks and other passing resources.

Another critical issue that may make IELTS become a barrier is students' English proficiency. For example, I was not very good at English when I was in high school. Therefore, I did not have the solid fundamental knowledge to pass IELTS easily. Consequently, I had to pay more attention to IELTS as I knew it significantly influenced the opportunity for my Australian visa, my university offer, and my time. Consequently, although I passed IELTS, I felt that the time was mainly spent dealing with it. However, even though many students might pass IELTS, they lost the primary direction they should have focused on, which is the discipline knowledge. Practically, it seemed that learning the discipline knowledge started after students moved to foreign universities. This finding reflects a similar concern as claimed by Zhuang and Tang (2012) in their study. They were worried that the language requirement and English barriers could negatively influence teaching and learning practices when Chinese universities cooperatively operate such programmes with foreign partners. As they suggested, many students may not have a high enough English proficiency to fulfil the language requirement when they started such programmes. Hence, they did need to pay more attention to achieve language scores to start their foreign learning stages, but this was detrimental to their engagement with discipline knowledge.

Concerning students' sense of agency in the Australian context, the story becomes much more complicated. On the one hand, several research findings partly affirm the current transition adjustment theoretical model: stress-adaptation-development (e.g., Gill, 2007; Kim, 1988). In the initial stage, most students aimed to survive in the new system, as they were not familiar with the new context and did not have the proper skills to deal with Australian learning and teaching approaches. Their experiences were generally consistent with previous research findings that Chinese students usually faced various stresses when they moved to a new context (Gu et al., 2010; Zhu, 2016).

Many students actively developed their approaches to adjust to the Australian learning context by continually negotiating with the new context. Their negotiations are the processes of adjustment to the new context (Gill, 2007). These students' experiences could indicate that although they struggled with the influence of previous experiences in the new context, they could actively deal with issues they faced. Finally, many of them positively transferred from the initial struggle to adjustment to the new context. These findings offer further shreds of evidence to previous studies, which identified that many Chinese students could adapt to the Western educational system and mode after staying in the new contexts for a period (Briguglio & Smith, 2012; Dai, 2020; Dai et al., 2020; Gu, 2016; Gill, 2007; Quan, He, & Sloan, 2016; Wong, 2012).

However, as this study found, not all students achieved positive development through experiencing stress. For instance, Fei's experiences have indicated that he felt disappointed and disempowered to deal with the issues in learning at the Australian university. He started language learning with a struggling and conflicted mind. Such adverse experiences highly influenced his performances and experiences in formal discipline learning. As his experiences illustrated, he felt it difficult to deeply engage in the Australian learning modes, which meant he was constantly stressed. As a result, although he insisted on studying in Australia, he became passive in surviving in the new context. This is worrying, given that he was an outstanding student in China. Such gaps seemed to destroy his positive attitudes towards intercultural learning and adjustment. In this case, he did not want to adjust but wished to escape from this context. It seems that he constantly faced stress and negotiated with different issues negatively. Although he may have achieved specific development, such growth seemed to be micro to some extent. His experiences challenged the theoretical assumptions that people can always deal with cross-cultural issues actively and finally adapt to the new context (Gill, 2007; Kim, 1988).

My experiences partly resonate with these students who achieved positive transformations in TAP. Although I did not need to learn IELTS first when I came to Australia, I felt that I could not engage deeply in learning in the Australian classroom. For instance, when my lecturer asked students to design a poster creatively but did not teach us how to do it, I felt disempowered and struggled, as I was used to following lecturers to create something step by step.

CRITICAL REFLECTIONS: BECOMING COMPATIBLE

I did not even know how to use Photoshop professionally. To deal with such learning issues, I asked my peers in China to help to create posters, or I used "Mei Tu Xiu Xiu" (美图秀秀). It is an image editing software for recreational purposes in China, rather than a professional design tool, to complete my assignment. Such experiences indicate that although I felt disempowered in doing assignments when I was in the initial stage in Australia, I could develop my solutions to help me overcome problems. As I mentioned above, as a member of the Chinese diaspora who lives in a technological era, I could seek help from the "home context" and use special Chinese tools to deal with learning issues in the English language context in Australia. Although it seemed unprofessional, this experience enabled me to genuinely engage and survive in my initial stage at the Australian university.

In contrast, some participants became immersed in the sense of disempowerment towards cross-system learning and adjustment for a long time, even for some across their whole period of studying overseas. Not all students had the same learning experiences. Some students felt it was challenging to deal with the cross-system differences to some extent. Due to various reasons (e.g., language barriers and different teaching strategies), these students had various negative attitudes towards the new learning systems. These factors were also found in many cognate extant studies (e.g., Ai, 2017; Dai, Matthews, & Reyes, 2020; Heng, 2018a; Zhou & Todman, 2009). One of the apparent features that emerged from students' experiences is that they were deeply immersed in their previous Chinese learning experiences. It seems that they preferred the Chinese educational model and internally rejected adjusting themselves to the new context with fresh views as intercultural learners. This negative sense towards intercultural differences also made them feel much stressed.

Facing the various changes in Australia, they critically compared the teaching and learning differences between the two contexts from their own experiences. For instance, Dong identified that the teaching strategies in the Australian stage were not supportive of her study, as lecturers seemed to not teach enough knowledge in a didactical approach. In this process, she passively studied the new system rather than actively adapted to it, which appears to challenge the existing adjustment model. She was strongly conditioned to the Chinese strategies, even though she adjusted to the Australian context reluctantly. These students showed a strong disempowered sense of agency towards their intercultural learning and adjustment. These experiences could suggest that these students oscillated between active and passive engagements in dealing with cross-system barriers.

Compared with these students' experiences, although I generally felt positive in dealing with learning issues in my cross-system study, I experienced a challenging journey in TAP and doctoral training. In my PhD journey, I was in-between the sense of empowered and disempowered agency towards a series of issues (see Dai & Hardy, 2021). Specifically, as I changed my area from design to education, I started an unpredictable adventure during my PhD journey. For example, I became immersed in shifting research directions. When I started my PhD, my primary research interests were about blended learning. After one and half years studying in this field, I noticed that I could not find in-depth and original research points, even though I had passed the first-year milestone. Then, I moved to investigate ICTs in education for another year. However, when I participated in the second internal milestone, I was asked to change the research topic to intercultural learning and adjustment again. Although I insisted on overcoming different problems when I faced new difficulties, such experiences made me feel frustrated and disappointed, even though I realised my study was nonetheless promising. In line with Park's (2018) argument of a sense of agency, such changes of research focus made me immersed in-between "mentally difficult to do" but "physically have to change."

According to the discussion above, it is clear that students' senses of agency to deal with different academic tasks, educational changes, and cultural differences have oscillated with dynamic changes. The interactions between the students and their educational context significantly influenced their senses of agency (Bandura, 2006). Their negotiations with new contexts indicate that the adjustment process is not linear but dynamic and complicated with constant shifts between current contexts (Gill, 2007; Gu et al., 2010; Heng, 2018a, 2018c). The academic setting of TAP demanded that students constantly negotiate with different issues in respect of their learning. Students reflected multiple senses of agency towards such cross-system differences. Our experiences paint a vivid picture of the shifting agency between acting positively and being frustrated. These negotiations in different contexts also result in students experiencing dynamic changes in their sense of belonging.

The sense of belonging reflects how these students considered their fit with different contexts through experiencing TAPs. According to Tinto, a sense of belonging reflects students "subjective sense of affiliation and identification with the university community" (as cited in Hoffman, Richmond, Morrow, & Salomone, 2002, p. 228). It indicates "the experience of personal involvement in a system or environment so that persons feel themselves to be an integral part of that system or environment" (Hagerty, Lynch-Sauer, Patusky, Bouwsema, & Collier, 1992, p. 173). As the findings indicated, some students revealed a strong sense of belonging to the Australian learning context. They were able to positively engage in the cross-system learning in TAP, even though they faced various issues.

However, some participants indicated a strong sense of isolation in the new context. They experienced disappointing learning experiences that negatively

CRITICAL REFLECTIONS: BECOMING COMPATIBLE 153

influenced their sense of belonging as intercultural learners in the Australian context. Even though they were studying in Australia to complete their TAP and obtain degrees, they had a strong sense of belonging to the previous Chinese educational context and even Chinese society, as they felt very much disempowered to achieve success intercultural adjustment in Australia. These experiences potentially offered some insights into the diasporic experience. Students (e.g., Fei and Dong) believed that they belonged to their "homeland" no matter how long they stayed in the new context (Rizvi et al., 2016). Although Fei and Dong's stories indicated their strong sense of non-belonging and non-adaptation to the Australian context, their experiences showed a particular case of diaspora's "emotional connections" with their home country. The struggling "diasporic experiences" made them have a strong sense of belonging to their homeland.

This sense of belonging indicated that many students were between the boundaries of two sociocultural contexts (Bhabha, 1994; Feng, 2009). Standing on the boundary, they seemed to "dance" between the two systems. Some students actively played between different contexts, but some could not perform well interchangeably. This research has demonstrated how learning in TAPs opens the door to have a sense of in-betweenness. The ways to approach the cross-system differences indicate how students position themselves as in-betweeners, who spontaneously belong to an in-between learning space, the third space in Bhabha's terms.

Considering my own story, a sense of belonging underwent several rounds of change during my learning process and right through until now. When I was in China, I did not realise that the sense of belonging was an issue, as I grew up in China without living outside the country. Therefore, I believed that I belonged there. Although I physically lived and studied in a new context after coming to Australia, I still had a strong sense of belonging to China. Meanwhile, facing differences and issues in my learning process in my undergraduate study made me feel that learning and living in China were more comfortable than in Australia. Therefore, I believed that I did not want to stay in Australia after obtaining my degree. To escape from the sense of non-belonging in Australia, I booked flight tickets in the middle of each semester. Once I submitted all assignments, I went back to China. At that stage, it seemed that I was temporarily working in Australia for three months and then back to China for a holiday. I knew I was just an overseas student who would return to China after completing my study. Such feelings existed in my mind until I had completed my honours study.

Before conducting my PhD study in Australia, I wished to apply for a position in other countries. However, the Australian university offered a position for me soon after getting my application. Considering my familiarity with the local context, I decided to stay in Australia. As I learned more during the PhD study, I started to genuinely engage in my research and local life, as I knew completing the PhD would be a long process, and I needed to change to accept the new context and lifestyle. To stay in Australia for future work, I applied for Australian PR during my PhD. During the waiting period for the decision, I realised that I might become a person who could officially and permanently work and live in two countries. When I obtained the visa, I felt that I am not just a TAP or PhD student, but I am a Chinese migrant shifting between China and Australia.

The sense of belonging changed across different stages of the TAP for most students. Factors that influenced a sense of belonging were also multiple, including both internal and external elements. Although this study did not holistically investigate these factors in-depth, students' reactions towards the cross-system educational differences provided some evidence to reveal their changes of belonging from a learning perspective. My experience was extended by studying in the PhD stage, which potentially offered me further changes in my sense of belonging. After studying in Australia for nearly ten years, how could I stay here for such a long time if I say I do not belong here? If I say I belong here in Australia, I still feel that I do not belong here, as I still have solid psychological connections with my own country where I grew up. Through learning in TAP, my culture and ideology are mixed by Chinese and Australian cultures and contexts, which makes me believe that I am now in-between these countries, where I seem to transfer between different contexts with a sense of belonging each setting. In short, it seems that I may be transitioning in between different contexts.

The in-between journey continues in my life after completing my doctoral journey. In April 2019, after being awarded as one of the postdoc fellowships in the China International Postdoc Exchange Programme, I moved back to China and started my new research journey at Peking University in Beijing. This journey positioned me between different contexts again. As I had not studied in China for many years, I was unfamiliar with the existing university and research contexts. Learning is different from research. I need to (re)adjust to the Chinese context after the research training in Australia. This process also has many unexpected issues, such as new research discourse, evaluation system, and publishing rules.

Distinct from Australia, China has its unique system and rules in social science, a unique "academic field" with particular logics of practices. Even though every country has its features, the logic of practice in the Chinese field has dramatic differences compared to others in the above aspects. For me, it seems that I am an "academic stranger" in the Chinese field. The postdoc journey is a process of (re)negotiation between Chinese and Australian fields. In this process, I needed to maintain my advantages as an international returnee and (re)

CRITICAL REFLECTIONS: BECOMING COMPATIBLE   155

build a research "habitus" for the Chinese context, further strengthening my sense of in-betweenness. The movement between different fields pushes me to work and live in an in-between space with hybrid senses of identity, agency and belonging.

3 The Contour of the In-Between Learning Space in TAP

What factors influence their intercultural learning in transnational articulation programmes? Students' dynamic changes of identity, agency, and belonging and the TAP setting have interactive relationships. The educational and sociocultural differences between TAP partners potentially map the contour of the in-between learning space for students to (re)position themselves as international sojourners. On the one hand, students' learning experiences reflected how they continuously negotiated with different contexts, manifesting in-betweenness. On the other hand, various educational differences (e.g., use of ICTs, assessment, teaching strategies, and university context) between TAP partners played essential roles in (re)shaping students' agency, identity, and belonging in each system.

According to the analysis of students' applications of ICTs, I surprisingly found that most students had dramatically different uses of the Internet to transition from China to Australia. According to the findings, the Internet-based tools were not adopted to support students' learning activities but utilised mainly for entertainment in the Chinese context. This finding concurs with many previous studies that found limited use of Internet-based tools for academic purposes. Many students mainly used them for social communications (e.g., Shao, 2012; Tegegne & Chen, 2003). The research findings regarding ICT infrastructure in the Chinese context indicated that although many Chinese universities have established ICT-based learning environments, the quality of ICTs seemed to have various problems that negatively influenced students' ICT tools for learning purposes. As a result, in the first two years of study in the Chinese stage, ICTs were not effectively adopted as learning mediation. This aspect potentially shaped students' limited technology-based study experiences, even though they are a digital generation in the modern technological era. This finding partly concurs with Hou (2011)'s results that many students in a China-UK TAP started to use more Internet-based tools to support their study after moving to the UK because of the better availability and accessibility of ICTs in the UK context.

According to this evidence, it seems that the applications of ICTs in TAP students' learning from China to overseas places a demand upon students, which might lead to a "technological (or digital) shock" when they move from one to another context. This technological shock pushed many students to (re)shape their habitus to fit into the new logic of practice. This process could be a process of "technological (or digital) adjustment." This point also indicates that it is challenging to offer a "one-fit-all" digital learning environment for students with different educational and sociocultural backgrounds (Chang & Gomes, 2020). Thus, educators and universities must realise these differences in digital practices.

Many of them were between a physical place and virtual space when they transferred from a limited ICT-based context to a highly ICT-assisted mode. Meanwhile, ICTs seemed to become much more critical for students' learning in Australia. They needed to adjust to the new ICT-based context and seek support from China and other resources via the virtual worldwide network. Their experiences might reveal that the rapid development and extensive applications of ICTs locate diaspora between different countries and cultures (Rizvi et al., 2016). In doing so, a blended learning space (re)shapes many students to become in-between learners who are immersed simultaneously in both physical and virtual learning spaces. This finding could align with Lei and Guo's (2020) study investigating Chinese international doctoral graduates' experiences in China after completing their overseas learning. They suggested that by taking advantage of digital technology, many graduates could develop new ways of being and belonging as the virtual transnational diaspora. As this study indicated, many transnational students actively used different digital tools and resources to support their everyday learning when they encountered barriers, especially in the Australian context. In this process, they shift between different virtual spaces and progressively develop multiple virtual intercultural competences as "fish in many waters" (Stahl, Soong, Mu, & Dai, coming soon).

As the findings indicated, assessment played a crucial role in influencing students' intercultural learning experiences in TAPs. As an essential element in education, assessment directly influences what and how students learn to some extent (Tang, 1991). In the Chinese stage, textbook-based exams were the dominant assessment approach in most students' learning, indicating the feature of Chinese education: the examination has become a symbol of Chinese education (Li, 2001). Distinct from the examination focused mode in China, assessment became multiple and continuous in the Australian stage, which pushed students to become active in their daily study to deal with different tasks. Textbooks become less critical in the Australian stage, and many students did not even have textbooks. This approach motivated students to expand their explorations rather than rely on memorising textbooks (J. Wang, 2016a). Facing these assessment changes, many students struggled, but they could survive and then adjust to this different assessment context. They spontaneously adopted multiple approaches to deal with different types of assessment, for example, using Internet-based tools.

The different assessment modes shift students between various tasks, learning strategies, and stress. This experience challenged the stereotyped views of Chinese students and affirmed that Chinese students could interchangeably adopt or even oppose learning approaches depending on their particular learning context (Biggs, 1996c; Li, 2009). The assessment differences from China to Australia reconstructed students' agency and identity as in-between learners and indicated a relationship between the assessment mode and the application of ICTs. As many students' learning experiences indicated, when they studied in an assessment model that was mainly based on textbook-based summative exams, they tended not to utilise ICTs as learning assisted tools frequently in their learning. Under this assessment mode, learning seemed to happen in physical places of the classroom and the textbook. However, when they studied in a setting with multiple and continuous assessments, students seemed to be more likely to use ICTs and the Internet to deal with different assignments. In this case, we might say they studied in a place and a space constructed by both physical and virtual elements. Along with the changes in assessment modes from China to Australia, teaching strategies were also essential in continually shaping and (re)shaping students' agency, identity, and belonging.

Teaching, assessment, and learning have impacts on each other. The research findings indicate that many lecturers in the Chinese stage usually adopted didactic teaching approaches focusing on the textbook-based knowledge that could be tested in exams. In this case, many students became followers without many opportunities for independent exploration, as teaching was mainly based on textbook-based knowledge with limited usage of ICTs. The findings related to teaching and ICTs generally suggested that faculty factors directly impacted students' usage of ICTs as learning mediation (Khan, 2017). Other studies also identified these features (e.g., Shao, 2012; Wong, Cooper, & Dellaportas, 2015; Wu, 2015), finding that many Chinese lecturers did not usually teach through adopting various ICT-based strategies. Lecturers were usually at the centre of the classroom. Similar results were found by T. Wang and Shan (2007), who compared a group of Chinese postgraduate students' learning experiences in China and Australia. Learning in this model, students usually passively accepted knowledge rather than actively participated in teaching and learning and lacked independence and creativity (Cortazzi & Jin, 1997). After studying in Australia, many students suggested that their lecturers seemed to be facilitators who adopted multiple teaching strategies, which meant that students could have more individual exploration in learning by adopting different approaches.

158   CHAPTER 7

However, even though this strategy motivates students to become autonomous and the centre of their learning, as many students reflected, such an approach can lack in-depth teaching. Sometimes the students seemed not to learn detailed knowledge, and they learned more content from the Internet than their lecturers, which seemed not to be valuable to many of them. This finding resonates with results concluded by Wong et al. (2015). They noticed that many Chinese students worried about the quality of teaching in Australia because their lecturers usually did not teach knowledge in detail. As a result, many students preferred to study in the Chinese teaching modes. Based on these findings, it is necessary to consider balancing lecturers' teaching practices, Chinese students' learning preferences, and academic requirements (Heffernan et al., 2010).

According to these differences, there is a dilemma in respect of teaching and learning strategies in TAPs. Similarly, Zhuang and Tang (2012) also identified that many lecturers in China-UK programmes usually taught in traditional teacher-centred approaches without enough English-based teaching activities in the Chinese phase. In this case, it was difficult for students to be familiar with the student-centred learning mode in the UK context. These findings concur with results concluded by Ng and Nyland (2016). They found that many Chinese lecturers did not know how Australian lecturers teach in the Australian context in a China-Australia TAP and vice versa. In this case, many lecturers usually taught students using their usual approaches without consideration for appropriate articulation between teaching approaches across the two HE systems.

If the above aspects reflect specific academic elements, the university context can be a holistic environmental factor that creates different cultures for these students in their TAPs. As the findings indicated, the Chinese university had a strong sense of collective culture in learning and living. In the Australian context, it seems that individualism is distinct. Most students had their learning plan and usually lived in different places, which reduced interactions and influences between students. These experiences concur with Hofstede's (2001) general account of collectivism and individualism. In a collectivist context, people could belong to a tightly knit group, and they usually follow group norms to conduct their activities. In contrast, the individualistic context usually emphasises self-regulation and individual orientated behaviours (Hofstede, 2001). The different settings and university contexts reflected the different sociocultural features of China and Australia, respectively.

Findings in this study have suggested that many students in the Australian phase had to become more individual in orientation. This finding is different from Hou (2011), who found that the TAP setting allows students to learn as a

CRITICAL REFLECTIONS: BECOMING COMPATIBLE

group in a foreign university. According to TAP features, theoretically, students can move to Australia and learn together, which is similar to their Chinese experiences. However, as my research indicated, practically, it was challenging for the students to study and live as a TAP group in the Australian context. This was due to several factors, for example, the achievement of IELTS, course selection, and open campus settings. These students experienced the change from being a member of a fixed group to be an individual without group-based solid connections. Such a change positioned students between a sense of group members and individuals.

According to these contextual features, it is worth noting that each system or approach has both advantages and disadvantages. These differences potentially create an in-between space for TAP students to engage in globalisation, internationalisation, and intercultural adjustment with a sense of in-betweenness (Dai, 2020; Rizvi, 2005; Turner, 1969). However, these differences could become a double-edged sword in TAPs. On the one hand, students could immerse themselves in "academic gaps" between the Chinese and Australian partners. Two universities usually operate TAPs based on various agreements. According to Knight (2001), a programme should be designed progressively year by year rather than disordered as separate parts. The consistency of academic arrangements and practices could provide a fluent pathway for students to follow. However, many students lost in differences and gaps between partners, which is an "academic weakness" in TNHE (Ding, 2020).

On the other hand, students can benefit from these differences. As many students suggested, TAP offers opportunities for them to experience cross-system differences, which could be a valuable aspect of the transition. If TAP has the same setting as regular programmes, the value of transnational education may lose. Thus, in the cross-system transitioning journey, students should critically absorb the essence and reject the dross, which traditional Chinese proverbs could explain: "Qu Chang Bu Duan" (取长补短). In short, TAP students should be "Compatible" (兼容并包) towards different educational and sociocultural features. As R. Yang and Shen (2020) suggested, the Chinese HE system needs to understand and integrate different sociocultural and educational contexts strategically and critically. Dealing with cultural ignorance becomes necessary for academics, educators, and students. Becoming a "ferryman" who could be "transitioning in-between" different sociocultural and educational contexts will help these stakeholders shape a cosmopolitan sense of identity, agency, and belonging. Students need to have an amphibious mind when they encounter cross-system differences (Chen, 2020). Strategically dealing with issues in transnational learning has significant influences on student development.

160   CHAPTER 7

4   Intercultural Adjustment as a Way of Transitioning In-Between

Overall, Chinese students in this study indicated various intercultural learning and adjustment trajectories in their TAPs. Notably, they dynamically experienced TAP learning processes while constantly negotiating different academic systems to position themselves in reasonable roles with a sense of in-betweenness. Students' learning experiences indicated that existing models might not holistically theorise international students' intercultural adjustment (Burnett & Gardner, 2006). According to findings in this study, it is apparent that many students transitioned in-between two different systems under TAPs. Although some students' trajectories of intercultural learning and adjustment reflect the process of stress-adaptation-development, the complex picture of negotiation between two systems illustrates a transitioning in-between journey. This conceptual lens seems to be a complementary theoretical lens for analysing and understanding the trajectories of intercultural adjustment and individuals changes of identity, agency and belonging that TAP student experienced in cross-system transition.

Moreover, these shreds of evidence could add further insights into Heng's (2018c) argument that some students may experience different lines of intercultural adjustment rather than only the "ascent" trajectory. Most students may be unfamiliar with their TAPs and also intercultural learning. They could have different expectations for the future. After engaging in the learning journey, they started negotiations with multiple senses of agency. On the one hand, some students' experiences reflect the trend of "uneven ascent."

On the other hand, students who shared experiences of "negative adjustment" illustrate other types of trajectories. Specifically, some students may hold positive attitudes towards their intercultural learning journey in Australia. However, the reality makes them disempowered and feeling lost in the new context, leading to more minor or ordinary adjustments than the positive cohort. A wave trajectory with different ends (see Figure 1) may illustrate these complex trajectories:

Notably, the process of learning and adjustment may be psychologically "negative." However, many students may still gain what they proposed to achieve, for example, dual degrees from Chinese and foreign and international experiences, which could be a "positive" achievement (or cultural capitals) at a "material" level. This positive achievement will play a significant role in students' future career development. As indicated in Chapter 3, gaining foreign degrees could be the first goal for many students when studying overseas via TAPs. They did not have a clear understanding of "intercultural adjustment" in the initial stage. No matter how they experience different cultures, if they could finally gain degrees, such achievements may still be considered positive

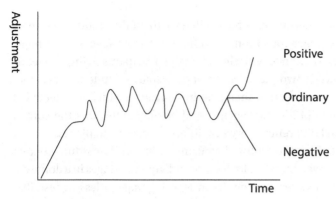

FIGURE 1   A wave trajectory with different ends

development of the intercultural movement. My learning experiences from school to university could also indicate the above trajectory, describing human development in different stages or intercultural adjustment. In each stage, I negotiate with various barriers and struggles with an end. Then, I start the line again in a new context or stage with another end. This cyclic journey continues in my life.

Drawing upon Bhabha's (1994) concept of third space and Deleuze and Guattari's (1987) smooth and striated space, I argue that such TNHE, for example, the TAP in this study, potentially created an in-between learning space for students to experience cross-system transitions. Notably, according to students' different views towards Chinese and Australian contexts, each context might be seen as a striated learning space. In each striated space, students needed to follow specific rules in their learning processes. Meanwhile, students smoothly developed their approaches to studying in different striated spaces. This process potentially established the specific smooth spaces that allowed them to deal flexibly with different rules in a striated space. As students' experiences suggested, some of them could develop their smooth spaces actively in each context. It seemed that their smooth spaces were more potent than a local striated space, which could indicate their intercultural trajectory of stress-adaptation-development (Gill, 2007; Kim, 1988, 2001).

However, some students were negatively influenced by striated spaces. Practically, they may still prefer to be a "traditional" Chinese student who was genuinely used to the Chinese educational system. Although they tried to establish their smooth spaces, striated spaces created many barriers to overcoming problems. Finally, a group of students could flexibly shift between striated and smooth spaces in one context (e.g., China). However, when they moved from China to Australia, they could also shift as intercultural learners between these two contexts and developed new smooth spaces in the Australian context.

In contrast, some other students felt challenged to establish suitable smooth spaces in their cross-place transitions (or different striated spaces). This might also be a diasporic experience with the research participants living and learning effectively between two places and multiple spaces. Students developed their sense of in-betweenness in such a multiplex mode, which is reflected by their various changes of identity, agency, and belonging towards the contextual and educational differences between different spaces and places.

Apart from describing intercultural adjustment in a cross-cultural context, the concept of in-betweenness could describe individual changes in a domestic, micro-level, and cross-system setting. As my learning trajectories are described in Chapter 6, it is apparent that I experienced the process of shaping my sense of in-betweenness via transitioning between different schools and then countries. Like many research participants in this study, I also studied in different places (e.g., public and elite schools in the city and rural schools in small towns, China and Australia) that provided me with various memories of each place. Then, in the transition process, I also became an in-betweener who studied in an in-between space rather than being solidly grounded in one place.

The transition between schools and countries makes me feel that I seem to not mentally belong to either China or Australia but in an in-between space. It combines and mixes different educational, social, and cultural features, even though I need to physically study and live in one context or country like many other people. My sense of agency also shifted between senses of disempowerment and empowerment in dealing with the differences between various macro/micro sociocultural and educational changes. As a result, my sense of identity becomes complicated in these continually negotiating processes between different contexts. Finally, my sense of in-betweenness is dynamically shaped with fluid changes depending on the context I live and study. The intercultural adjustment could happen in both domestic and international transitions.

In the process of cross-system transition, students (re) become intercultural learners between different smooth and striated spaces that were mapped by the combination of different educational systems. They were not restricted to specific places and spaces; instead, they studied in-between these geographical and spatial contexts with dynamic changes of agency, identity, and belonging. Enabled by ICTs, these places and spaces were mixed through TAPs. The sense of in-betweenness students potentially developed might be seen as an unintended consequence of the lack of clear and close articulation between the Chinese and Australian parts of the TAP. Paradoxically, this unintended consequence probably prepared these students well for cosmopolitan futures. This sense could be a psychical response in either virtual or physical cross-system and intercultural transitions.

To sum up, it is worth noting that the TAP may create multi-layers of in-between spaces for students. First, the TAP setting is an in-between learning space with various places (e.g., China and Australia). Second, each place has its specific striated space to rule and frame students' learning activities. In each place, students reflected various attitudes and different abilities to adjust to different striated spaces, and in the process, developed their smooth spaces. Third, when they moved from China to Australia, students were immersed in a more complicated space. They not only shifted their places but also engaged in a new striated space. In this case, they began to develop new smooth spaces to survive in this new striated space. During this process, they were just in between smooth and striated spaces in the Australian context and between Chinese and Australian HE systems via networked space created and facilitated by Internet-based technologies. These complex experiences could further indicate that human behaviour and development have innumerable links with the sociocultural contexts in which they live (Heng, 2018c). In the journey of learning overseas, these Chinese students are navigating between different sociocultural and educational settings (Heng, 2020). As a result, they studied various places and spaces in diverse contexts with a sense of in-betweenness. A diagram (see Figure 2) is experimentally developed to depict the possible trajectory of intercultural transitioning in-between, which could be adopted to explain the domestic or international cross-system movement. This diagram could represent the status of intercultural adjustment at a macro level or indicate individuals' coping strategies with struggles and barriers in various "zigzags" in the cross-system movement.

As Figure 2 shows, home and host (or familiar/unfamiliar) contexts have their boundaries. When people move from one to another, they may transit between the boundary across the two systems. In this process, they do not fully fit into the host context. In contrast, they may dynamically shift between different contexts in an in-between position. The boundary of the two systems might become blurry. Thus, the crossing experience might become a journey of transitioning in-between. Notably, the crossing might happen all the time

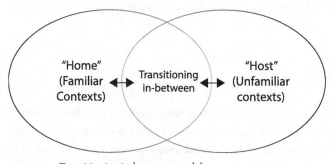

FIGURE 2   Transitioning in-between model

and everywhere in both the real physical world and the virtual community. The transitioning in-between may also happen in different situations and contexts when people encounter physical or virtual movement between different places and spaces.

When I was writing this book, Covid-19 became a pandemic. Intercultural learning and communication also had significant changes compared to how people could freely move between countries. The role of Internet-based tools becomes irreplaceable in communication under this situation as people cannot gather and need to keep social distance. The Internet-based video conference tools (e.g., Zoom and Skype) have become the essential mediation to support virtual learning and communication, which may not have happened before in human history. This health crisis impedes international students' movement among countries, negatively influencing their intercultural learning experiences and communication. In this case, they cannot physically immerse themselves in their host countries to experience the culture, education, and society. To reduce these negative influences, international students who cannot go to their host countries could learn via Internet-based tools. Academics can stay at home and keep teaching students who are in different parts of the world. Seminars and conferences are all moved to the online mode. The Internet-based tools systematically create an in-between space that allows people to engage in intercultural interactions and transition between different contexts virtually. It seems that the demands and practices of virtually in-between intercultural learning and communication have reached a "historical peak." These changes may (re)shape intercultural communication. Education to be internationalised at home via curriculum reforms (Leask & Green, 2020) or "at a distance" (Mittelmeier, Rienties, Gunter, & Raghuram, 2020).

Meanwhile, the quality of education under these changes may differ from traditional modes that have people and resources physically move between nations. As Leask (2004) suggests, the internationalisation of higher education means students and educators' mobility. Using ICTs in different ways to support teaching and learning practices in a cross-cultural context, the connotations of internationalisation could have various meanings and functions in different situations and eras.

5   Implications

A series of implications relevant for different stakeholders could be suggested based on students' lived experiences and views towards learning in TAPs. Universities should offer relevant courses about cross-system learning and cultural differences in education for students to help them develop intercultural competence. Compared with normal learning pathways at university, TAPs or other types of TNHE seem to offer different channels for students to start their higher education. However, as Ding (2020) suggested, due to the quality issues in TNHE, these models may be "marginal" in the landscape of Chinese higher education even though the number of TNHE has rapidly increased in recent years in both top-ranked and regional universities. Chasing academic profits seems to be the priority, which may negatively influence the sustainable development of TNHE. When designing TAPs, it is essential to comprehensively examine language issues, teaching approaches, course content connections, assessments, and other learning-related problems that may bring barriers to transformative learning. Better articulation is required.

Academics, programme designers, and policymakers who practically engage in designing and operating TAPs should collaborate as partners to enhance the quality of cross-system learning. Knowing students' learning experiences from both home and host institutions is essential to adopt suitable teaching approaches and manage the programmes. In doing so, it might be necessary to carefully assess cross-system collaborations and enhance communications between home and host partners (Bordogna, 2019; Ding, 2019, 2020; Heffernan, Wilkins, & Butt, 2018; Y. Wang & Bai, 2020). If the quality of collaboration cannot be guaranteed and making profits is still the dominant purpose for TNHE, it may not have the potential for sustainable development in the future (Bennell, 2019; Healey, 2019). Specifically, these stakeholders need to communicate and collaborate in operating TAPs constantly. The quality assurance system should be established between partners. Notably, academics and programme designers should be aware of potential differences between partners. It is vital to strategically change teaching approaches depending on student requirements and cultural backgrounds.

For students, it is essential to be aware of the issues of in-betweenness in such TAPs. The sense of in-betweenness may start to grow when these students began their intercultural learning journeys in TAP, but they may not be able to identify and realise this bud. The sense of in-betweenness could be developed along with their learning activities from home (familiar contexts) to host (unfamiliar contexts) across their trajectory of intercultural adjustment. In this process, most students could study in an in-between learning space where they may need to continuously negotiate with cultural, social, and educational differences. Consequently, they may find a position or develop an individual in-between space, allowing them to either positively adjust to the new context or reluctantly survive between their preferred environment and stressed context. Therefore, students must prepare for shaping a sense of in-betweenness, which means that they may need to flexibly shift their senses of agency, identity, and belonging.

CHAPTER 8

Conclusion

To the best of the author's knowledge, although various research studies have been conducted in TNHE about the Chinese context, this book could be the first monograph illustrating Chinese students' intercultural learning experiences and adjustment in TAPs. The TAPs create an in-between learning space, allowing students to experience different cultures, societies and educational systems. Students' views, learning trajectories, and the author's reflexive narratives have added a series of insights into the under-researched domain of students' experiences in TNHE. Students' journeys revealed that their learning experiences in TAPs were complex and dynamic. Students' intercultural learning and adjustment in TAPs is not a straightforward process, which leads to development. Instead, it is a process of experiencing and fostering an unintended sense of in-betweenness with twists and turns in constant (re)shapes of the sense of identity, agency, and belonging.

Moreover, this study found that ICTs, teaching strategies, assessment modes, and university/class settings are considered vital elements that influenced students' learning methods, attitudes, adjustment, and establishing the TAP in-between learning space. Based on the analysis of their trajectories in TAPs, the author has attempted to propose a "transitioning in-between" model to conceptualise a possible way of understanding intercultural learning and adjustment.

Several limitations and future research directions should be aware. This analysis provided in this book mainly focuses on student's voices without adding other stakeholders' views into the analysis. Thus, it is worth comprehensively investigating other stakeholders' understandings in a comparative approach to illustrate a more systematic picture of TAP and TNHE. Notably, TNHE can be a product of globalisation and internationalisation. Influenced by the Covid-19 and also many other geopolitical conflicts and incidents between different countries, it may be essential to critically examine whether TNHE and even the internationalisation of HE can be sustainable in the future or not. The Covid-19 pandemic may be controlled soon; this crisis's influence on the international TNHE collaboration remains unclear. The potential changes happening in the world may (re)define student mobility, intercultural learning, and communication.

Furthermore, this study mainly relies on interview data to understand students' learning trajectory. In the future, it may be better for researchers to conduct more quantitative or mixed-method studies, which may offer new

© KONINKLIJKE BRILL NV, LEIDEN, 2022 | DOI: 10.1163/9789004505131_008

CONCLUSION 167

insights from different perspectives. For instance, the number of TAPs in China is approximately more than 1,000, and there are also many other types of TNHE, for example, branch campuses and affiliated institutions. How do students understand their cross-system learning in different types of TAPs? How do they experience an intercultural adjustment in other TNHE models? What are the similarities and differences of intercultural learning and adjustment among these different TNHEs? Whether students and academics in other types of TNHE also have a sense of in-betweenness or not? How do they navigate themselves when they encounter cross-system collaboration and differences? Thus, more comprehensive and comparative studies may examine these questions. As the author knows, many researchers in both China and other contexts are doing related research. It may also be necessary for these scholars to create a network in the future to share their thoughts about the development of TNHE in different sociocultural and educational contexts.

References

Adler, P. S. (1975). The transitional experience: An alternative view of culture shock. *Journal of Humanistic Psychology, 15*(4), 13–23.

Ahearn, L. M. (2001). Language and agency. *Annual Review of Anthropology, 30*(1), 109–137.

Ai, B. (2017). The communication patterns of Chinese students with their lecturers in an Australian university. *Journal of Educational Studies, 43*(4), 484–496.

Allen, A. (1995). Confucius rules OK? Cultural influences on distance learners in Asia. In A. Tait (Ed.), *Putting the student first: Learner-centred approaches in open and distance learning* (pp. 1–19). Open University, East Anglia Region.

Alred, G., Byram, M., & Fleming, M. (2003). *Intercultural experience and education.* Channel View Publications Ltd.

Altbach, P. G. (2004). Globalisation and the university: Myths and realities in an unequal world. *Tertiary Education & Management, 10*(1), 3–25.

Altbach, P. G., & Knight, J. (2007). The internationalisation of higher education: Motivations and realities. *Journal of Studies in International Education, 11*(3–4), 290–305.

Altbach, P. G., Reisberg, L., & Rumbley, L. E. (2009). *Trends in global higher education: Tracking an academic revolution.* A report prepared for the UNESCO 2009 World Conference on Higher Education. The United Nations Educational, Scientific and Cultural Organisation.

Alvesson, M., & Sköldberg, K. (2000). *Reflexive methodology – New vistas for qualitative research.* Sage Publications.

Amin, A. (2002). Spatialities of globalisation. *Environment and Planning A: Economy and Space, 34*(3), 385–399.

Anderson, L. E. (1994). A new look at an old construct: Cross-cultural adaptation. *International Journal of Intercultural Relations, 18*(3), 293–328.

Appadurai, A. (1996). *Modernity at large: Cultural dimensions of globalisation* (Vol. 1). University of Minnesota Press.

Appadurai, A. (2000). Grassroots globalisation and the research imagination. *Public Culture, 12*(1), 1–19.

Arthur, L. (2010, November). *Insider-outsider perspectives in comparative education.* Paper presented at the Seminar presentation at the Research Centre for International and Comparative Studies, Graduate School of Education, University of Bristol, Bristol.

Bai, L., & Wang, Y. (2020). Pre-departure English language preparation of students on joint 2 + 2 programs. *System, 90*, 1–11. https://doi.org/10.1016/j.system.2020.102219

Bai, L., & Wang, Y. X. (2021). Pre-departure academic preparation: international students' experiences of disciplinary study on 2 + 2 joint programmes. *Globalisation, Societies and Education*, 1–13. doi:10.1080/14767724.2021.1904384

Bandura, A. (1988). Self-regulation of motivation and action through goal systems. In V. Hamilton, G. H. Bower, & N. H. Frijda (Eds.), *Cognitive perspectives on emotion and motivation* (pp. 37–61). Springer Netherlands.

Bandura, A. (1989). Human agency in social cognitive theory. *American Psychologist, 44*(9), 1175–1184.

Bandura, A. (2001). Social cognitive theory: An agentic perspective. *Annual Review of Psychology, 52*(1), 1–26.

Bandura, A. (2006). Toward a psychology of human agency. *Perspectives on Psychological Science, 1*(2), 164–180.

Bannier, B. J. (2016). Global trends in transnational education. *International Journal of Information and Education Technology, 6*(1), 80–84.

Beck, U. (1994). The reinvention of politics: Towards a theory of reflexive modernisation. In U. Beck & A. Giddens (Eds.), *Reflexive modernisation* (pp. 1–55). Polity Press.

Bennell, P. (2019). Transnational higher education in the United Kingdom: An up-date. *International Journal of Educational Development, 67*, 29–40.

Bennett, M. (1986). A developmental approach to training for intercultural sensitivity. *International Journal of Intercultural Relations, 10*(2), 179–196.

Bennett, M. (2010). A short conceptual history of intercultural learning in study abroad. In W. Hoffa & S. Depaul (Eds.), *A history of U.S. study abroad: 1965-present* (pp. 419–449). Special publication of *Frontiers: The Interdisciplinary Journal of Study Abroad*.

Berry, J. (1997). Immigration, acculturation, and adaptation. *Applied Psychology, 46*(1), 5–34.

Bhabha, H. K. (1994). *The location of culture*. Routledge.

Biggs, J. (1994). Asian learners through Western eyes: An astigmatic paradox. *Australian and New Zealand Journal of Vocational Education Research, 2*(2), 40–63.

Biggs, J. (1996a). Approaches to learning of Asian students: A multiple paradox. In J. Pandey, D. Sinha, & D. P. S. Bhawuk (Eds.), *Asian contributions to cross-cultural psychology* (pp. 180–199). Sage.

Biggs, J. (1996b). Enhancing teaching through constructive alignment. *Higher Education, 32*(3), 347–364.

Biggs, J. (1996c). Western misperceptions of the Confucian-heritage learning culture. In D. Watkins & J. Biggs (Eds.), *The Chinese learner: Cultural, psychological and contextual influences* (pp. 45–67). Hong Kong University Press.

Biggs, J. (1998). Learning from the Confucian heritage: So size doesn't matter? *International Journal of Educational Research, 29*(8), 723–738.

Blasco, M. (2012). On reflection: Is reflexivity necessarily beneficial in intercultural education? *Intercultural Education, 23*(6), 475–489.

Bochner, S. (1972). Problems in culture learning. In S. Bochner & P. Wicks (Eds.), *Overseas students in Australia* (pp. 65–81). New South Wales University Press.

Bodycott, P., & Lai, A. (2012). The influence and implications of Chinese culture in the decision to undertake cross-border higher education. *Journal of Studies in International Education, 16*(3), 252–270.

Bordogna, C. M. (2019). The development of social capital between operational academics delivering transnational collaborative programme partnerships. *Studies in Higher Education,* 1–13. doi:10.1080/03075079.2019.1605502

Bordogna, C. M. (2020). Advocating and administering critical realism in a study of transnational educational collaborative partnerships. *Higher Education Research & Development,* 1–15. doi:10.1080/07294360.2019.1704691

Boud, D., Cohen, R., & Sampson, J. (1999). Peer learning and assessment. *Assessment & Evaluation in Higher Education, 24*(4), 413–426.

Boud, D., & Soler, R. (2016). Sustainable assessment revisited. *Assessment & Evaluation in Higher Education, 41*(3), 400–413.

Bourdieu, P. (1984). *Distinction: A social critique of the judgement of taste.* Harvard University Press.

Bourdieu, P. (1986). The forms of capital. In J. Richardson (Eds.), *Handbook of theory and research for the sociology of education* (pp. 241–258). Greenwood Press.

Bourdieu, P. (1990). *The logic of practice* (R. Nice, Trans.). Polity Press.

Bourdieu, P. (1993). *Sociology in question.* Sage.

Bourdieu, P. (2000). *Pascalian meditations* (R. Nice, Trans.). Polity Press.

Braun, V., & Clarke, V. (2006). Using thematic analysis in psychology. *Qualitative Research in Psychology, 3*(2), 77–101.

Brennan, T. (2006). *Wars of position: The cultural politics of left and right.* Columbia University Press.

Briguglio, C., & Smith, R. (2012). Perceptions of Chinese students in an Australian university: Are we meeting their needs? *Asia Pacific Journal of Education, 32*(1), 17–33.

Brooks, R., & Waters, J. (2011). *Student mobilities, migration and the internationalization of higher education.* Palgrave Macmillan.

Brubaker, R. (2005). The 'diaspora' diaspora. *Ethnic and Racial Studies, 28*(1), 1–19.

Burnapp, D. (2006). Trajectories of adjustment of international students: U-curve, learning curve, or third space. *Intercultural Education, 17*(1), 81–93.

Burnett, C., & Gardner, J. (2006). The one less travelled by: The experience of Chinese students in a UK university. In M. Byram & A. Feng (Eds.), *Living and studying abroad* (pp. 64–90). Multilingual Matters Ltd.

Casey, E. S. (1997). *The fate of place: A philosophical history.* University of California Press.

Chan, S. (1999). The Chinese learner – A question of style. *Education + Training, 41*(6/7), 294–305.

Chang, S., & Gomes, C. (2020). *Digital experiences of international students: Challenging assumptions and rethinking engagement.* Routledge.

Chen, H. J. (2020). *Shaping an amphibious mind in cross-system learning journey.* Paper presented at the 40th anniversary of re-establishing the subject of education at Peking University.

Cheng, B., & Yang, P. (2019). Chinese students studying in American high schools: International sojourning as a pathway to global citizenship. *Cambridge Journal of Education, 49*(5), 553–573.

Cheng, X. (2000). Asian students' reticence revisited. *System, 28*(3), 435–446.

Chirkov, V., Vansteenkiste, M., Tao, R., & Lynch, M. (2007). The role of self-determined motivation and goals for study abroad in the adaptation of international students. *International Journal of Intercultural Relations, 31*(2), 199–222.

Cohen, L., Manion, L., & Morrison, K. (2007). *Research methods in education* (6th ed.). Routledge.

Connelly, F. M., & Clandinin, D, J. (2006). Narrative inquiry. In J. L. Green, G. Camalli, & P. B. Elmore (Eds.), *Handbook of complementary methods in education research* (pp. 375–385). American Educational Research Association.

Corrin, L., Bennett, S., & Lockyer, L. (2010, May 3–4). *Digital natives: Everyday life versus academic study.* Paper presented at the 7th International Conference on Networked Learning.

Cortazzi, M., & Jin, L. (1996). Cultures of learning: Language classrooms in China. In H. Coleman (Ed.), *Society and the language classroom* (pp. 169–206). Cambridge University Press.

Cortazzi, M., & Jin, L. (1997). Communication for learning across cultures. In D. McNamara & R. Harris (Eds.), *Overseas students in higher education: Issues in teaching and learning* (pp. 76–90). Routledge.

Creswell, J. W. (2007). *Qualitative inquiry and research design: Choosing among five approaches* (2nd ed.). Sage Publications.

Creswell, J. W. (2009). *Research design: Qualitative, quantitative, and mixed methods approaches* (3rd ed.). Sage Publications.

Cushner, K., & Karim, A. (2004). Study abroad at the university level. In D. Landis, J. Bennett, & M. Bennet (Eds.), *Handbook of intercultural training* (3rd ed., pp. 289–308). Sage Publications.

Dai, K., Lingard, B., & Reyes, V. (2018). 'In-betweeners': Chinese students' experiences in China-Australia articulation programs. *Scottish Educational Review, 50*(1), 36–55.

Dai, K. (2020). Learning between two systems: A Chinese student's reflexive narrative in a China-Australia articulation programme. *Compare: A Journal of Comparative and International Education, 50*(3), 371–390.

Dai, K., & Garcia, J. (2019). Intercultural Learning in transnational articulation programs. *Journal of International Students, 9*(2), 362–383.

Dai, K., & Hardy, I. (2021). The micro-politics of cultural change: A Chinese doctoral student's learning journey in Australia. *Oxford Review of Education, 47*(2), 243–259.

REFERENCES

Dai, K., Matthews, K. E., & Renshaw, P. (2020). Crossing the 'bridges' and navigating the 'learning gaps': Chinese students learning across two systems in a transnational higher education programme. *Higher Education Research & Development, 39*(6), 1140–1154.

Dai, K., Matthews, K. E., & Reyes, V. (2020). Chinese students' assessment and learning experiences in a transnational higher education programme. *Assessment & Evaluation in Higher Education, 45*(1), 70–81.

Dale, R., & Robertson, S. L. (2002). The varying effects of regional organisations as subjects of globalisation of education. *Comparative Education Review, 46*(1), 10–36.

Deardorff, D. K. (2006). Identification and assessment of intercultural competence as a student outcome of internationalization. *Journal of Studies in International Education, 10*(3), 241–266.

de Wit, H. (2002). *Internationalisation of higher education in the United States of America and Europe: A historical, comparative, and conceptual analysis.* Greenwood.

de Wit, H. (2020). Internationalization of higher education. *Journal of International Students, 10*(1), i–iv. https://doi.org/10.32674/jis.v10i1.1893

de Wit, H., Hunter, F., Howard, L., & Egron-Polak, E. (2015). *Internationalisation of higher education.* European Parliament, Directorate-General for Internal Policies.

Deleuze, G. (1994). *Difference and repetition.* Athlone Press.

Deleuze, G. (2006). *Nietzsche and philosophy.* Continuum.

Deleuze, G., & Guattari, F. (1987). *A thousand plateaus: Capitalism and schizophrenia* (B. Massumi, Trans.). University of Minnesota Press.

Dewey, J. (1963). *Experience and education.* Collier-Macmillan.

Ding, X. (2018). Capacity building or market demand? Transnational teaching in China. *Higher Education Policy, 31*(2), 267–287.

Ding, X. (2019). Marginal revolution: The impact of transnational education on higher education in host countries: A case study of China. *Higher Education Policy, 32*(3), 419–440.

Ding, X. (2020). Marginal revolution: The impact of transnational education on higher education in China. *International Higher Education, 101* (8), 1–3.

Djerasimovic, S. (2014). Examining the discourses of cross-cultural communication in transnational higher education: From imposition to transformation. *Journal of Education for Teaching, 40*(3), 204–216.

Dowling-Hetherington, L. (2020). Transnational higher education and the factors influencing student decision-making: The experience of an Irish university. *Journal of Studies in International Education, 24*(3), 291–313.

Dwyer, S. C., & Buckle, J. L. (2009). The space between: On being an insider-outsider in qualitative research. *International Journal of Qualitative Methods, 8*(1), 54–63.

Elliott, J. (2005). *Using narrative in social research: Qualitative and quantitative approaches.* Sage.

Ellis, R. A., & Goodyear, P. (2016). Models of learning space: Integrating research on space, place and learning in higher education. *Review of Education, 4*(2), 149–191.

Engeström, Y. (1987). *Learning by expanding: An activity-theoretical approach to developmental research.* Orienta-Konsultit Oy.

Engeström, Y. (1999). Activity theory and individual and social transformation. In Y. Engeström, R. Miettinen, & R. Punamäi (Eds.), *Perspectives on activity theory* (pp. 19–38). Cambridge University Press.

Engeström, Y. (2001). Expansive learning at work: Toward an activity theoretical reconceptualisation. *Journal of Education and Work, 14*(1), 133–156.

English, L. M. (2005). Third-space practitioners. *Adult Education Quarterly, 55*, 85–100.

Fang, W. (2012). The development of transnational higher education in China: A comparative study of research universities and teaching universities. *Journal of Studies in International Education, 16*(1), 5–23.

Feng, A. (2009). Becoming interculturally competent in a third space. In A. Feng, M. Byram, & M. Fleming (Eds.), *Becoming interculturally competent through education and training* (pp. 71–91). Multilingual Matters.

Feng, Q. (2016). How to integrate English language teaching and academic study in Chinese-foreign joint bachelor's degree programmes in local universities: The case of Hubei Engineering University. *Journal of Language Teaching and Research, 7*(5), 1029–1035.

Feng, Y. (2013). University of Nottingham Ningbo China and Xi'an Jiaotong-Liverpool University: Globalisation of higher education in China. *Higher Education, 65*(4), 471–485.

Furnham, A., & Bochner, S. (1986). *Culture shock: Psychological reactions to unfamiliar environment.* Methuen.

Gao, C., Feng, Y., & Henderson, F. (2012). On joint-programmes in China – Development, challenges and suggestions. *On the Horizon, 20*(4), 293–304.

Gao, X. (2006). Understanding changes in Chinese students' uses of learning strategies in China and Britain: A socio-cultural re-interpretation. *System, 34*(1), 55–67.

Gieryn, T. F. (2000). A space for place in sociology. *Annual Review of Sociology, 26*(1), 463–496.

Gieve, S., & Clark, R. (2005). 'The Chinese approach to learning': Cultural trait or situated response? The case of a self-directed learning programme. *System, 33*(2), 261–276.

Gill, S. (2007). Overseas students' intercultural adaptation as intercultural learning: A transformative framework. *Compare: A Journal of Comparative and International Education, 37*(2), 167–183.

Goodyear, P. (2006). Technology and the articulation of vocational and academic interests: Reflections on time, space and e-learning. *Studies in Continuing Education, 28*(2), 83–98.

REFERENCES 175

Grimshaw, T. (2007). Problematising the construct of 'the Chinese learner': Insights from ethnographic research. *Educational Studies, 33*(3), 299–311.

Gu, Q. (2009). Maturity and interculturality: Chinese students' experiences in UK higher education. *European Journal of Education, 44*(1), 37–52.

Gu, Q. (2016a). Chinese students in the UK. In S. Guo & Y. Guo (Eds.), *Spotlight on China: Chinese education in the globalised world* (pp. 107–128). Sense Publishers.

Gu, Q. (2016b). (Re)constructing identities beyond boundaries: Revisiting insider-outsider perspectives in research on international students. In M. Crossley, L. Arthur, & E. McNess (Eds.), *Revisiting insider-outsider research in comparative and international education* (pp. 185–206). Symposium Books Ltd.

Gu, Q., & Maley, A. (2008). Changing places: A study of Chinese students in the UK. *Language and Intercultural Communication, 8*(4), 224–245.

Gu, Q., & Schweisfurth, M. (2006). Who adapts? Beyond cultural models of the Chinese learner. *Language, Culture and Curriculum, 19*(1), 74–89.

Gu, Q., Schweisfurth, M., & Day, C. (2010). Learning and growing in a foreign context: Intercultural experiences of international students. *Compare: A Journal of Comparative and International Education, 40*(1), 7–23.

Gu, Y. (2008). Chinese learner: My lived experiences of studying in Mainland China and Australia. *Critical Perspectives on Accounting, 19*(2), 217–221.

Gudykunst, W. (1988). Uncertainty and anxiety. In Y. Kim & W. Gudykunst (Eds.), *Theories in intercultural communication* (pp. 123–156). Sage Publications.

Gullahorn, J. T., & Gullahorn, J. E. (1963). An extension of the U-curve hypothesis. *Journal of Social Issues, 19*(3), 33–47.

Hagerty, B. M., Lynch-Sauer, J., Patusky, K. L., Bouwsema, M., & Collier, P. (1992). Sense of belonging: A vital mental health concept. *Archives of Psychiatric Nursing, 6*(3), 172–177.

Hall, S. (1990). Cultural identity and diaspora. In J. Rutherford (Ed.), *Identity: Community, culture difference* (pp. 222–237). Lawrence and Wishart.

Hall, S. (1992). The question of cultural identity. In S. Hall, D. Held, & T. McGrew (Eds.), *Modernity and its futures* (pp. 274–316). Polity Press.

Hall, S., & Du Gay, P. (1996). *Questions of cultural identity.* Sage Publications.

Han, X. (2017). The challenges and benefits of transnational higher education: A case study of Sino-Foreign Cooperation University in China. In C. S. Collins (Ed.), *University-Community engagement in the Asia Pacific: Public benefits beyond individual degrees* (pp. 41–55). Springer International Publishing.

Han, X. (2019). Cross-field effect and institutional habitus formation: Self-reinforcing inequality in Chinese higher education system. *Journal of Education Policy, 34*(2), 267–294.

Harvey, D. (1999). Time-space compression and the postmodern condition. In M. Waters (Ed.), *Modernity: Critical concepts* (Vol. 4, pp. 98–118). Routledge.

He, L. (2016). Transnational higher education institutions in China. *Journal of Studies in International Education, 20*(1), 79–95.

He, L., & Liu, E. (2018). Cultural influences on the design and management of transnational higher education programmes in China: A case study of three programmes. *International Journal of Educational Management, 32*(2), 269–283.

He, L., & Wilkins, S. (2018). Achieving legitimacy in cross-border higher education: Institutional influences on Chinese international branch campuses in Southeast Asia. *Journal of Studies in International Education, 22*(3), 179–197.

Healey, N. M. (2019). The end of transnational education? The view from the UK. *Perspectives: Policy and Practice in Higher Education*, 1–11. doi:10.1080/13603108.2019.16 31227

Heffernan, M., & Pimpa, N. (2019). Globally transformative student experience: Challenges and opportunities in learning and teaching in the transnational business education program. In A. M. de Albuquerque Moreira, J. J. Paul, & N. Bagnall (Eds.), *Intercultural studies in higher education: Policy and practice* (pp. 225–253). Springer International Publishing.

Heffernan, T., Morrison, M., Basu, P., & Sweeney, A. (2010). Cultural differences, learning styles and transnational education. *Journal of Higher Education Policy and Management, 32*(1), 27–39.

Heffernan, T., & Poole, D. (2005). In search of 'the vibe': Creating effective international education partnerships. *Higher Education, 50*(2), 223–245.

Heffernan, T., Wilkins, S., & Butt, M. M. (2018). Transnational higher education: The importance of institutional reputation, trust and student-university identification in international partnerships. *International Journal of Educational Management, 32*(2), 227–240.

Held, D., McGrew, A., Goldblatt, D., & Perraton, J. (2000). Global transformations: Politics, economics and culture. In C. Pierson & S. Tormey (Eds.), *Politics at the edge: The PSA yearbook 1999* (pp. 14–28). Palgrave Macmillan.

Hellawell, D. (2006). Inside-out: Analysis of the insider-outsider concept as a heuristic device to develop reflexivity in students doing qualitative research. *Teaching in Higher Education, 11*(4), 483–494.

Henderson, M., Selwyn, N., Finger, G., & Aston, R. (2015). Students' everyday engagement with digital technology in university: Exploring patterns of use and 'usefulness.' *Journal of Higher Education Policy and Management, 37*(3), 308–319.

Heng, T. T. (2017). Voices of Chinese international students in USA colleges: 'I want to tell them that ....' *Studies in Higher Education, 42*(5), 833–850.

Heng, T. T. (2018a). Coping strategies of Chinese international undergraduates in response to challenges in U.S. colleges. *Teachers College Record, 120*(3), 1–42.

Heng, T. T. (2018b). Different is not deficient: Contradicting stereotypes of Chinese international students in US higher education. *Studies in Higher Education, 43*(1), 22–36.

REFERENCES

Heng, T. T. (2018c). Exploring the complex and non-linear evolution of Chinese international students' experiences in USA Colleges. *Higher Education Research & Development, 37*(6), 1141–1155.

Heng, T. T. (2019). Understanding the heterogeneity of international students' experiences: A case study of Chinese international students in U.S. universities. *Journal of Studies in International Education, 23*(5), 607–623.

Heng, T. T. (2020). Chinese students themselves are changing. *Journal of International Students, 10*(2), 539–545.

Henze, J., & Zhu, J. (2012). Current research on Chinese students studying abroad. *Research in Comparative and International Education, 7*(1), 90–104.

Hilgers, M., & Mangez, E. (Eds.). (2015) *Bourdieu's theory of social fields: Concepts and applications.* Routledge.

Hoffenburger, K., Mosier, R., & Stokes, B. (1999). Transition experience. In J. H. Schuh (Ed.), *Educational programming and student learning in college and university residence halls* (pp. 33–50). Association of College and University Housing Officers-International (ACUHO-I).

Hoffman, M., Richmond, J., Morrow, J., & Salomone, K. (2002). Investigating "sense of belonging" in first-year college students. *Journal of College Student Retention: Research, Theory & Practice, 4*(3), 227–256.

Hofstede, G. (1980). Culture and organisations. *International Studies of Management & Organisation, 10*(4), 15–41.

Hofstede, G. (1984). *Culture's consequences: International differences in work-related values.* Sage Publications.

Hofstede, G. (1986). Cultural differences in teaching and learning. *International Journal of Intercultural Relations, 10*(3), 301–320.

Hofstede, G. (2001). *Culture's consequences: Comparing values, behaviours, institutions, and organisations across nations.* Sage Publications.

Hofstede, G., Hofstede, G. J., & Minkov, M. (2010). *Cultures and organisations: Software of the mind* (3rd ed.). McGraw-Hill.

Hogg, M. A., Terry, D. J., & White, K. M. (1995). A tale of two theories: A critical comparison of identity theory with social identity theory. *Social Psychology Quarterly,* 255–269.

Hou, J. (2011). *Learning on two campuses: Students' transition experiences in a China-UK Articulation programme* [Doctoral thesis]. Northumbria University.

Hou, J., & McDowell, L. (2013). Learning together? Experiences on a China–UK articulation programme in engineering. *Journal of Studies in International Education, 18*(3), 223–240.

Hou, J., Montgomery, C., & McDowell, L. (2011). Transition in Chinese-British higher education articulation programmes – Closing the gap between East and West? In J. Ryan (Ed.), *China's higher education reform and internationalisation* (pp. 104–120). Routledge.

Hou, J., Montgomery, C., & McDowell, L. (2014). Exploring the diverse motivations of transnational higher education in China: Complexities and contradictions. *Journal of Education for Teaching, 40*(3), 300–318.

Hu, M., Eisenchlas, S. A., & Trevaskes, S. (2019). Factors affecting the quality of transnational higher education in China: A qualitative content analysis on Chinese host universities' self-appraisal reports. *Journal of Higher Education Policy and Management, 41*(3), 306–321.

Hu, M., & Willis, L. D. (2017). Towards a common transnational education framework: Peculiarities in China matter. *Higher Education Policy, 30*(2), 245–261.

Huang, F. (2003a). Policy and practice of the internationalisation of higher education in China. *Journal of Studies in International Education, 7*(3), 225–240.

Huang, F. (2003b). Transnational higher education: A perspective from China. *Higher Education Research and Development, 22*(2), 193–203.

Huang, F. (2008). Regulation and practice of transnational higher education in China. In L. Dunn & M. Wallace (Eds.), *Teaching in transnational higher education: Enhancing learning for offshore international students* (pp. 57–66). Routledge.

Huang, F. (2011). Transnational higher education in Japan and China: A comparative study. In D. W. Chapman, W. K. Cummings, & G. A. Postiglione (Eds.), *Crossing borders in East Asian higher education* (pp. 265–282). Springer Netherlands.

Huang, F. (2014). *The internationalisation of China's higher education: Foci on its transnational higher education.* Paper presented at the Report of the Hiroshima International Seminar on Higher Education.

Jenkins, R. (2008). *Social identity* (3rd ed.). Routledge.

Jin, L., & Cortazzi, M. (2006). Changing practices in Chinese cultures of learning. *Language, Culture and Curriculum, 19*(1), 5–20.

Jokila, S. (2015). The internationalisation of higher education with Chinese characteristics: Appadurai's ideas explored. *Asia Pacific Journal of Education, 35*(1), 125–139.

Jones, C., & Shao, B. (2011). *The next generation and digital natives: Implications for higher education.* Higher Education Academy.

Kelly, P. (2016). Constructing the insider and outsider in comparative research. In M. Crossley, L. Arthur, & E. McNess (Eds.), *Revisiting insider-outsider research in comparative and international education* (pp. 57–74). Symposium Books Ltd.

Kember, D. (1996). The intention to both memorise and understand: Another approach to learning? *Higher Education, 31*(3), 341–354.

Kember, D. (2000). Misconceptions about the learning approaches, motivation and study practices of Asian students. *Higher Education, 40*(1), 99–121.

Kember, D. (2016). Understanding and teaching the Chinese learner: Resolving the paradox of the Chinese learner. In R. B. King & A. B. I. Bernardo (Eds.), *The psychology of Asian learners* (pp. 173–187). Springer.

Khan, M. A. (2017). A theoretical analysis of factors influencing student's decision to use learning technologies in the context of institutions of higher education. *Advances in Social Sciences Research Journal, 4*(1), 165–178.

Kim, Y. (1988). *Communication and cross-cultural adaptation: An integrative theory.* Multilingual Matters.

Kim, Y. (2001). *Becoming intercultural: An integrative theory of communication and cross-cultural adaptation.* Sage Publications.

Kim, Y., & Ruben, B. (1988). Intercultural transformation: A systems theory. In Y. Kim & W. Gudykunst (Eds.), *Theories in intercultural communication* (pp. 299–321). Sage Publications.

Knight, J. (1993). Internationalisation: Management strategies and issues. *International Education Magazine, 9*(6), 21–22.

Knight, J. (1997). Internationalisation of higher education: A conceptual framework. In J. Knight & H. de Wit (Eds.), *Internationalisation of higher education in Asia Pacific Countries.* European Association for International Education.

Knight, J. (2004). Internationalisation remodelled: Definition, approaches, and rationales. *Journal of Studies in International Education, 8*(1), 5–31.

Knight, J. (2006). Cross border education: An analytical framework for programme and provider mobility. In J. C. Smart (Ed.), *Higher education: Handbook of theory and practice* (pp. 345–395). Springer.

Knight, J. (2007). Cross-border tertiary education: An introduction. In *Cross-border tertiary education: A way toward capacity development.* OECD and World Bank.

Knight, J. (2016). Transnational education remodeled toward a common TNE framework and definitions. *Journal of Studies in International Education, 20*(1), 34–47.

Knight, J., & Liu, Q. (2019). International program and provider mobility in higher education: Research trends, challenges, and issues. *Comparative & International Education, 48*(1), 1–17.

Knight, P. T. (2001). Complexity and curriculum: A process approach to curriculum-making. *Teaching in Higher Education, 6*(3), 369–381.

Kolb, A. Y., & Kolb, D. A. (2005). Learning styles and learning spaces: Enhancing experiential learning in higher education. *Academy of Management Learning & Education, 4*(2), 193–212.

Kosmützky, A., & Putty, R. (2016). Transcending borders and traversing boundaries: A systematic review of the literature on transnational, offshore, cross-border, and borderless higher education. *Journal of Studies in International Education, 20*(1), 8–33.

Kroeber, A. L., & Parsons, T. (1958). The concepts of culture and of social system. *American Sociological Review, 23*(5), 582–583.

Kuh, G. D., & Love, P. G. (2000). A cultural perspective on student departure. In J. M. Braxton (Ed.), *Reworking the student departure puzzle* (pp. 196–212). Vanderbilt University Press.

Lamberton, G., & Ashton-Hay, S. (2015). Preparing Chinese international business students for the transition to undergraduate study in Australia. *Journal of Research in International Education, 14*(2), 155–171.

Latour, B. (2005). *Reassembling the social: An introduction to actor-network-theory.* Oxford University Press.

Lave, J., & Wenger, E. (1991). *Situated learning: Legitimate peripheral participation.* Cambridge University Press.

Leander, K. M., Phillips, N. C., & Taylor, K. H. (2010). The changing social spaces of learning: Mapping new mobilities. *Review of Research in Education, 34*(1), 329–394.

Leask, B. (2004). Internationalisation outcomes for all students using information and Communication Technologies (ICTs). *Journal of Studies in International Education, 8*(4), 336–351.

Leask, B., & Green, W. (2020). Is the pandemic a watershed for internationalisation? *University World News.* https://www.universityworldnews.com/post.php?story=20200501141641136

Lefebvre, H. (1991). *The production of space.* Blackwell.

Lei, L., & Guo, S. (2020). Conceptualizing virtual transnational diaspora: Returning to the 'return' of Chinese transnational academics. *Asian and Pacific Migration Journal, 29*(2), 227–253.

Leung, M. W., & Waters, J. L. (2013). British degrees made in Hong Kong: An enquiry into the role of space and place in transnational education. *Asia Pacific Education Review, 14*(1), 43–53.

Levatino, A. (2017). Transnational higher education and international student mobility: Determinants and linkage. *Higher Education, 73*(5), 637–653.

Li, J. (2001). Chinese conceptualisation of learning. *Ethos, 29*(2), 111–137.

Li, J. (2003a). The core of Confucian learning. *The American Psychologist, 58*(2), 146–147.

Li, J. (2003b). US and Chinese cultural beliefs about learning. *Journal of Educational Psychology, 95*(2), 258–267.

Li, J. (2009). Learning to self-perfect: Chinese beliefs about learning. In K. K. Chan & N. Rao (Eds.), *Revisiting the Chinese learner: Changing contexts, changing education* (pp. 35–70). Springer.

Li, S., & Wang, Z. (2009). Thirty years' transnational education in China – Based on 11 provinces and municipalities. *Journal of South China Normal University (Social Science Edition), 2*, 96–99.

Lien, D., & Keithley, A. (2020). The determinants of international branch campuses. *Studies in Higher Education, 45*(2), 452–463.

Lin, J. (2016). Chinese-foreign cooperation in running schools. *Chinese Education & Society, 49*(4–5), 229–230.

Lin, J., & Liu, Z. (2007a). Importing quality higher educational resources through Chinese-Foreign cooperation in running schools. *US-China Education Review, 4*(3), 1–7.

REFERENCES

Lin, J., & Liu, Z. (2007b). Reasonably introduction and effective utilisation of quality education resources in Sino-foreign cooperation in running schools. *Educational Research, 5*, 36–39.

Lincoln, Y. S., & Guba, E. G. (1985). *Naturalistic inquiry*. Sage Publications.

Lingard, B., & Rawolle, S. (2004). Mediatizing educational policy: The journalistic field, science policy, and cross-field effects. *Journal of Education Policy, 19*(3), 361–380.

Liu, W. (2020). The Chinese definition of internationalisation in higher education. *Journal of Higher Education Policy & Management, 43*(2), 230–245.

Liu, W., & Lin, X. (2016). Meeting the needs of Chinese international students: Is there anything we can learn from their home system? *Journal of Studies in International Education, 20*(4), 357–370.

Liu, D., DeWinter, A., Harrison, P., & Wimpenny, K. (2021). Motivation factors in student decisions to study transnational higher education in China: A comparative study of two Anglo-Sino programmes. *Journal of Marketing for Higher Education*, 1–21. doi: 10.1080/08841241.2021.1900487

Lysgaand, S. (1955). Adjustment in a foreign society: Norwegian Fulbright grantees visiting the United States. *International Social Science Bulletin, 7*, 45–51.

Marginson, S. (2008). Global field and global imagining: Bourdieu and worldwide higher education. *British Journal of Sociology of Education, 29*(3), 303–315.

Marginson, S. (2011). Higher education in East Asia and Singapore: Rise of the Confucian model. *Higher Education, 61*, 587–611.

Marton, F., Dall'Alba, G., & Tse, L, K. (1996). Memorising and understanding: The keys to the paradox. In D. Watkins & J. Biggs (Eds.), *The Chinese learner: Cultural, psychological and contextual influences* (pp. 69–83). Hong Kong University Press.

Matthews, K. E., Andrews, V., & Adams, P. (2011). Social learning spaces and student engagement. *Higher Education Research & Development, 30*(2), 105–120.

McLennan, G. (2003). Sociology, eurocentrism and postcolonial theory. *European Journal of Social Theory, 6*(1), 69–86.

McLoughlin, C. (1999). Culturally responsive technology use: Developing an online community of learners. *British Journal of Educational Technology, 30*(3), 231–243.

McMillan, D. W., & Chavis, D. M. (1986). Sense of community: A definition and theory. *Journal of Community Psychology, 14*(1), 6–23.

McNess, E., Arthur, L., & Crossley, M. (2016). 'Ethnographic dazzle' and the construction of the 'other': Shifting boundaries between the insider and the outsider. In M. Crossley, L. Arthur, & E. McNess (Eds.), *Revisiting insider-outsider research in comparative and international education* (pp. 21–38). Symposium Books Ltd.

Merton, R. K. (1972). Insiders and outsiders: A chapter in the sociology of knowledge. *American Journal of Sociology, 78*(1), 9–47.

Mezirow, J. (1991). *Transformative dimensions of adult learning*. Jossey-Bass.

Mezirow, J. (2000). *Learning as transformation: Critical perspectives on a theory in progress.* Jossey-Bass.

Milligan, L. (2016). Insider-outsider-inbetweener? Researcher positioning, participative methods and cross-cultural educational research. *Compare: A Journal of Comparative and International Education, 46*(2), 235–250.

Mittelmeier, J., Rienties, B., Gunter, A., & Raghuram, P. (2020). Conceptualizing internationalization at a distance: A "third category" of university internationalization. *Journal of Studies in International Education,* 1–17. doi:10.1177/1028315320906176

Mok, K. H., & Han, X. (2016). The rise of transnational higher education and changing educational governance in China. *International Journal of Comparative Education and Development, 18*(1), 19–39.

Mok, K. H., & Ong, K. C. (2014). Transforming from 'Economic Power' to 'Soft Power': Transnationalisation and internationalisation of higher education in China. In Q. Li & C. Gerstl-Pepin (Eds.), *Survival of the fittest: The shifting contours of higher education in China and the United States* (pp. 133–155). Springer.

Mok, K. H., & Xu, X. (2008). When China opens to the world: A study of transnational higher education in Zhejiang, China. *Asia Pacific Education Review, 9*(4), 393–408.

Mok, K. H., Han, X., Jiang, J., & Zhang, X. (2018). International and transnational education for whose interests? A study on the career development of Chinese students. *Higher Education Quarterly, 72*(3), 208–223.

Montgomery, C. (2010). *Understanding the international student experience.* Palgrave Macmillan.

Montgomery, C. (2016). Transnational partnerships in higher education in China: The diversity and complexity of elite strategic alliances. *London Review of Education, 14*(1), 70–85.

Moufahim, M., & Lim, M. (2015). The other voices of international higher education: an empirical study of students' perceptions of British university education in China. *Globalisation, Societies and Education, 13*(4), 437–454.

Mu, G. M. (2014a). Chinese Australians' Chineseness and their mathematics achievement: The role of habitus. *The Australian Educational Researcher, 41*(5), 585–602.

Mu, G. M. (2014b). Heritage language learning for Chinese Australians: The role of habitus. *Journal of Multilingual and Multicultural Development, 35*(5), 497–510.

Mu, G. M. (2018). *Building resilience of floating children and left-behind children in China: Power, politics, participation, and education.* Routledge.

Naidoo, V. (2009). Transnational higher education: A stock take of current activity. *Journal of Studies in International Education, 13*(3), 310–330.

Neri, S., & Wilkins, S. (2019). Talent management in transnational higher education: Strategies for managing academic staff at international branch campuses. *Journal of Higher Education Policy and Management, 41*(1), 52–69.

REFERENCES

Ng, J., & Nyland, B. (2016). Internationalisation of higher education and global learning. In T. Barkatsas & A. Bertram (Eds.), *Global learning in the 21st century* (pp. 231–250). Sense Publishers.

Ng, J., & Nyland, B. (2017). Critical examination of internationalisation: A case study of a collaboration between an Australian and a Chinese university. *European Journal of Higher Education, 8*(1), 52–66.

Oberg, K. (1960). Cultural shock: Adjustment to new cultural environments. *Practical Anthropology, 7*(4), 177–182.

Otten, M. (2003). Intercultural learning and diversity in higher education. *Journal of Studies in International Education, 7*(1), 12–26.

Park, J. (2011). Metamorphosis of Confucian heritage culture and the possibility of an Asian education research methodology. *Comparative Education, 47*(3), 381–393.

Park, J. (2018). Higher education knowledge production in postcolonial-neoliberal Asia. In J. Jung, H. Horta, A. Yonezawa (Eds.), *Researching higher education in Asia: Quality, excellence and governance* (pp. 51–71). Springer.

Patton, M. Q. (2014). *Qualitative research & evaluation methods: Integrating theory and practice*. Sage Publications.

Planel, C. (2016). Mind the gap: Reflections on boundaries and positioning in research in international and comparative education. In M. Crossley, L. Arthur, & E. McNess (Eds.), *Revisiting insider-outsider research in comparative and international education* (pp. 95–112). Symposium Books Ltd.

Prensky, M. (2001). Digital natives, digital immigrants. *On the Horizon, 9*(5), 1–6.

Punch, K. (2009). *Introduction to research methods in education*. Sage Publications.

Pyvis, D. (2011). The need for context-sensitive measures of educational quality in transnational higher education. *Teaching in Higher Education, 16*(6), 733–744.

Pyvis, D., & Chapman, A. (2004). *Student experiences of offshore higher education: Issues for quality*. Australian Universities' Quality Agency (AUQA) Occasional Paper. AUQA.

Qin, Y. (2021). *Building cross-border joint universities in China: A study of organizational dilemma* (1st ed.). Routledge. https://doi.org/10.4324/9780429319594

Qin, Y., & Te, A. Y. C. (2016). Cross-border higher education in China: How the field of research has developed. *Chinese Education & Society, 49*(4–5), 303–323.

Quan, R., He, X., & Sloan, D. (2016). Examining Chinese postgraduate students' academic adjustment in the UK higher education sector: A process-based stage model. *Teaching in Higher Education, 21*(3), 326–343.

Ramsden, P. (1979). Student learning and perceptions of the academic environment. *Higher Education, 8*(4), 411–427.

Relph, E. (1976). *Place and placelessness*. Pion.

Renshaw, P., & Volet, S. (1995). South-East Asian students at Australian universities: A reappraisal of their tutorial participation and approaches to study. *The Australian Educational Researcher, 22*(2), 85–106.

Rizvi, F. (2000). International education and the production of global imagination. In N. Burbules & C. Torres (Eds.), *Globalisation and education: Critical perspectives* (pp. 205–227). Routledge.

Rizvi, F. (2005). Rethinking "brain drain" in the era of globalisation. *Asia Pacific Journal of Education*, 25(2), 175–192.

Rizvi, F. (2009). Global mobility and the challenges of educational research and policy, in T. Popkewitz & F. Rizvi (Eds.), *Globalization and the study of education* (108th yearbook of the National Society for the Study of Education) (pp. 268–289). Wiley-Blackwell.

Rizvi, F. (2011). Theorising student mobility in an era of globalisation. *Teachers and Teaching*, 17(6), 693–701.

Rizvi, F., & Lingard, B. (2010). *Globalising education policy*. Routledge.

Rizvi, F., Louie, K., & Evans, J. (2016). *Australia's diaspora advantage: Realising the potential for building transnational business networks with Asia*. Australian Council of Learned Academies.

Robins, K. (1991). Tradition and translation: National culture in its global context. In J. Corner & S. Harvey (Eds.), *Enterprise and heritage: Crosscurrents of national culture* (pp. 21–44). Routledge.

Rutherford, J. (1990). The third space-interview with Homi Bhabha. In J. Rutherford (Ed.), *Identity: Community, culture, difference* (pp. 207–221). Lawrence & Wishart.

Samuelowicz, K. (1987). Learning problems of overseas students: Two sides of a story. *Higher Education Research and Development*, 6(2), 121–133.

Sarbaugh, L. E. (1988). A taxonomic approach to intercultural communication. In Y. Kim & W. Gudykunst (Eds.), *Theories in intercultural communication* (pp. 22–38). Sage Publications.

Savin-Baden, M., McFarland, L., & Savin-Baden, J. (2008). Learning spaces, agency and notions of improvement: What influences thinking and practices about teaching and learning in higher education? An interpretive meta-ethnography. *London Review of Education*, 6(3), 211–227.

Savvides, N., Al-Youssef, J., Colin, M., & Garrido, C. (2016). Methodological challenges: Negotiation, critical reflection and the cultural other. In M. Crossley, L. Arthur, & E. McNess (Eds.), *Revisiting insider/outsider research in comparative and international education* (pp. 113–129). Symposium Books Ltd.

Schumann, J. H. (1986). Research on the acculturation model for second language acquisition. *Journal of Multilingual & Multicultural Development*, 7(5), 379–392.

Scouller, K. (1998). The influence of assessment method on students' learning approaches: Multiple choice question examination versus assignment essay. *Higher Education*, 35(4), 453–472.

Searle, W., & Ward, C. (1990). The prediction of psychological and sociocultural adjustment during cross-cultural transitions. *International Journal of Intercultural Relations*, 14(4), 449–464.

REFERENCES   185

Seidman, I. (2006). *Interviewing as qualitative research: A Guide for researchers in edu-cation and the social sciences* (3rd ed.). Teachers College Press.

Shaffer, L. F., & Shoben, E. J. (1956). *The psychology of adjustment.* Houghton Mifflin.

Shah, M., Nair, S., & de la Harpe, B. (2012). Intentionally (or not) ignored: Engaging transnational students in surveys and feedback. *Studies in Learning, Evaluation Innovation and Development, 9*(1), 66–73.

Shao, B. (2012). *University students' use of technologies in China* [Doctoral thesis]. The Open University.

Sin, I. L., Leung, M. W., & Waters, J. L. (2019). Degrees of value: Comparing the contextual complexities of UK transnational education in Malaysia and Hong Kong. *Compare: A Journal of Comparative and International Education, 49*(1), 132–148.

Singh, M. (2009). Using Chinese knowledge in internationalising research education: Jacques Rancière, an ignorant supervisor and doctoral students from China. *Globalisation, Societies and Education, 7*(2), 185–201.

Smalley, W. A. (1963). Cultural shock, language shock, and the shock of self-discovery. *Practical Anthropology, 10*, 49–56.

Soja, E. W. (1996). *Third space: Journeys to Los Angeles and other real-and-imagined places.* Blackwell.

Sugimoto, K. (2006). Australia's transactional higher education in the Asia-Pacific region: Its strategies and quality assurance. In F. Huang (Ed.), *Transnational higher education in Asia and the Pacific Region* (pp. 1–19). RIHE International Publication Series No. 10.

Tan, C. (2013). For group, (f)or self: Communitarianism, Confucianism and values education in Singapore. *The Curriculum Journal, 24*(4), 478–493.

Tan, C. (2015). Beyond rote-memorisation: Confucius' concept of thinking. *Educational Philosophy and Theory, 47*(5), 428–439.

Tan, C. (2016). Confucius and creativity. *Journal of Genius and Eminence, 1*(1), 84–89.

Tan, C. (2017a). Confucianism and education. In G. Noblit (Ed.), *Oxford Research Encyclopedia of Education* (pp. 1–18). Oxford University Press.

Tan, C. (2017b). A Confucian conception of critical thinking. *Journal of Philosophy of Education, 51*(1), 331–343.

Tang, K. (1991). *Effects of different assessment procedures on tertiary students' approaches to studying* [Doctoral thesis]. University of Hong Kong.

Taylor, C. (1989). *Sources of the self: The making of the modern identity.* Harvard University Press.

Taylor, E. (1994a). Intercultural competency: A transformative learning process. *Adult Education Quarterly, 44*(3), 154–174.

Taylor, E. (1994b). A learning model for becoming interculturally competent. *International Journal of Intercultural Relations, 18*(3), 389–408.

Teddlie, C., & Yu, F. (2007). Mixed methods sampling: A typology with examples. *Journal of Mixed Methods Research, 1*(1), 77–100.

Tegegne, A. T., & Chen, C. B. (2003). Student use of internet in China: A study on Huazhong University of Science and Technology (HUST). *Pakistan Journal of Information and Technology, 2*(1), 25–29.

Teichler, U. (2009). Internationalisation of higher education: European experiences. *Asia Pacific Education Review, 10*(1), 93–106.

Temple, P. (2008). Learning spaces in higher education: An under-researched topic. *London Review of Education, 6*(3), 229–241.

Tian, X., & Martin, B. (2014). Curriculum design, development and implementation in a transnational higher education context. *Journal of Applied Research in Higher Education, 6*(2), 190–204.

Tu, C. (2001). How Chinese perceive social presence: An examination of interaction in online learning environment. *Educational Media International, 38*(1), 45–60.

Tuan, Y. (1977). *Space and place: The perspective of experience.* University of Minnesota Press.

Turner, V. (1967). *The forest of symbols: Aspects of Ndembu Ritual.* Cornell University Press.

Turner, V. (1969). Liminality and communitas. In V. Turner (Ed.), *The ritual process: Structure and anti-structure* (pp. 358–374). Aldine.

Tweed, R. G., & Lehman, D. R. (2002). Learning considered within a cultural context: Confucian and Socratic approaches. *American Psychologist, 57*(2), 89–99.

van Damme, D. (2001). Quality issues in the internationalisation of higher education. *Higher Education, 41*(4), 415–441.

van der Wende, M. C. (2003). Globalisation and access to higher education. *Journal of Studies in International Education, 7*(2), 193–206.

Verbik, L., & Lasanowski, V. (2007). International student mobility: Patterns and trends. *World Education News and Reviews, 20*(10), 1–16.

Vertovec, S. (2001). Transnationalism and identity. *Journal of Ethnic and Migration Studies, 27*(4), 573–582.

Volet, S. (1999). Learning across cultures: Appropriateness of knowledge transfer. *International Journal of Educational Research, 31*(7), 625–643.

Volet, S., & Renshaw, P. (1996). Chinese students at an Australian university: Adaptability and continuity. In D. Watkins & J. Biggs (Eds.), *The Chinese learner: Cultural, psychological and contextual influences.* (pp. 205–220). Hong Kong University Press.

Wang, C., Whitehead, L., & Bayes, S. (2017). 'They are friendly, but they don't want to be friends with you': A narrative inquiry into Chinese nursing students' learning experience in Australia. *Journal of Nursing Education and Practice, 7*(8), 27–36.

Wang, F., Clarke, A., & Yu, W. (2016). Empty success or brilliant failure: An analysis of Chinese students' study abroad experience in a collaborative Master of Education Programme. *Journal of Studies in International Education, 20*(2), 140–163.

REFERENCES

Wang, J. (2016). *Activity theoretical perspectives on international Chinese students' (ICSs')
issues with their learning in Australia: The adapted Change Laboratory Approach
(CLA)* [Doctoral thesis]. RMIT University.

Wang, T. (2008). Intercultural dialogue and understanding: Implications for teachers.
In L. Dunn & M. Wallace (Eds.), *Teaching in transnational higher education: Enhancing learning for offshore international students* (pp. 57–66). Routledge.

Wang, T. (2016). Intercultural dialogue framework for transnational teaching and
learning. In B. Krishna & F. Charlotte (Eds.), *Campus support services, programmes,
and policies for international students* (pp. 223–242). IGI Global.

Wang, T., & Shan, X. (2007). *A qualitative study on Chinese postgraduate students' learning experiences in Australia.* Paper presented at the Proceedings AARE 2006, Ade-
laide, SA, Australia.

Wang, Y., & Bai, L. (2020). Academic acculturation in 2 + 2 joint programmes: Students'
perspectives. *Higher Education Research & Development*, 1–16. doi:10.1080/0729436
0.2020.1775556

Ward, C., Bochner, S., & Furnham, A. (2001). *The psychology of culture shock* (2nd ed.).
Routledge.

Ward, C., & Kennedy, A. (1992). Locus of control, mood disturbance, and social dif-
ficulty during cross-cultural transitions. *International Journal of Intercultural Relations, 16*(2), 175–194.

Ward, C., & Kennedy, A. (1993a). Where's the "culture" in cross-cultural transition?
Comparative studies of sojourner adjustment. *Journal of Cross-Cultural Psychology,
24*(2), 221–249.

Ward, C., & Kennedy, A. (1993b). Psychological and socio-cultural adjustment during
cross-cultural transitions: A comparison of secondary students overseas and at
home. *International Journal of Psychology, 28*(2), 129–147.

Wilkins, S., Butt, M. M., & Annabi, C. A. (2017). The effects of employee commitment in
transnational higher education: The case of international branch campuses. *Journal
of Studies in International Education, 21*(4), 295–314.

Wilkins, S., & Huisman, J. (2011). International student destination choice: The influence of home campus experience on the decision to consider branch campuses.
Journal of Marketing for Higher Education, 21(1), 61–83.

Wilson-Mah, R., & Thomlinson, E. (2018). Mind the gap: Chinese diploma student
views of bridges and barriers to transferring into a Canadian university. *Higher Education Research & Development, 37*(3), 635–648.

Winkelman, M. (1994). Cultural shock and adaptation. *Journal of Counselling & Development, 73*(2), 121–126.

Wong, G. (2012). *Learning context in Australian universities-perceptions of Chinese
accounting students* [Doctoral thesis]. Deakin University.

Wong, G., Cooper, B. J., & Dellaportas, S. (2015). Chinese students' perceptions of the teaching in an Australian accounting programme – An exploratory study. *Accounting Education, 24*(4), 318–340.

Wu, H. (2019). Three dimensions of China's 'outward-oriented' higher education internationalization. *Higher Education, 77*(1), 81–96.

Wu, Q. (2015). Re-examining the 'Chinese learner': A case study of mainland Chinese students' learning experiences at British Universities. *Higher Education, 70*(4), 753–766.

Xu, X., & Kan, Y. (2013). Cross-border higher education in China in the globalised world: The perspective of the World Trade Organisation's general agreement on trade in services. *KEDI Journal of Educational Policy, 10*(2), 199–220.

Xue, W. (2016). Chinese-Foreign cooperation in running schools in the process of quality construction – Some thoughts based on the report of the third-party evaluation in higher education. *China Higher Education Research, 2*, 12–19.

Yan, K. (2017). *Chinese international students' stressors and coping strategies in the United States.* Springer.

Yang, C., Wu, H., Zhu, M., Brian, G., & Southwell. (2004). Tuning in to fit in? Acculturation and media use among Chinese students in the United States. *Asian Journal of Communication, 14*(1), 81–94.

Yang, H., & Lesser, B. (2017). Internationalising the university: A case study of a Canada-China Programme. *Creative Education, 8*(3), 359–372.

Yang, R. (2002). *Third delight: The internationalisation of higher education in China.* Routledge.

Yang, R. (2008). Transnational higher education in China: Contexts, characteristics and concerns. *Australian Journal of Education, 52*(3), 272–286.

Yang, R., & Welch, A. R. (2010). Globalisation, transnational academic mobility and the Chinese knowledge diaspora: An Australian case study. *Discourse: Studies in the Cultural Politics of Education, 31*(5), 593–607.

Yang, R. (2014). China's strategy for the internationalisation of higher education: An overview. *Frontiers of Education in China, 9*(2), 151–162.

Yang, R. (2016). Internationalisation of higher education in China. In S. Guo & Y. Guo (Eds.), *Spotlight on China: Chinese education in the globalised world* (pp. 35–49). Sense Publishers.

Yang, R., & Shen, Y. T. (2020). Integrating Chinese and Western knowledge is one of important goals for Chinese higher education. *Guangming Daily.*
http://www.china.com.cn/opinion/theory/2020-04/21/content_75956781.htm

Yoshikawa, M. J. (1988). Cross-cultural adaptation and perceptual development. In Y. Kim & W. Gudykunst (Eds.), *Cross-cultural adaptation: Current approaches* (pp. 140–148). Sage Publications.

Young, T. J., & Schartner, A. (2014). The effects of cross-cultural communication education on international students' adjustment and adaptation. *Journal of Multilingual and Multicultural Development, 35*(6), 547–562.

Yu, Q. (2014). *Various items causing IELTS test-takers low performance in Mainland China: An international joint education programme solution.* Paper presented at the 2014 International Conference on Global Economy, Finance and Humanities Research.

Zhao, X. (2017). *Qualitatively different ways of experiencing learning: A phenomenographic investigation of international economics and trade undergraduates' conceptions of learning in a Chinese-Australian cooperative programme* [Doctoral thesis]. University College London.

Zhao, X., & Hu, Y. (2020). A phenomenographic study of Chinese undergraduates' conceptions of learning in transnational programs. *Sage Open.* doi: 10.1177/2158244020967034

Zhou, Y., Jindal-Snape, D., Topping, K., & Todman, J. (2008). Theoretical models of culture shock and adaptation in international students in higher education. *Studies in Higher Education, 33*(1), 63–75.

Zhou, Y., & Todman, J. (2009). Patterns of adaptation of Chinese postgraduate students in the United Kingdom. *Journal of Studies in International Education, 13*(4), 467–486.

Zhu, C., Valcke, M., & Schellens, T. (2009). A cross-cultural study of online collaborative learning. *Multicultural Education & Technology Journal, 3*(1), 33–46.

Zhu, J. (2016). *Chinese overseas students and intercultural learning environments.* Palgrave Macmillan.

Zhuang, L., & Tang, X. (2012). Sino-UK transnational education in China: Rhetoric versus reality. *Journal of Technology Management in China, 7*(2), 218–234.

Ziguras, C. (2003). The impact of the GATS on transnational tertiary education: Comparing experiences of New Zealand, Australia, Singapore and Malaysia. *The Australian Educational Researcher, 30*(3), 89–109.

Ziguras, C. (2016). Globalisation and the transformation of Asian higher education. In C. S. Collins, M. N. N. Lee, J. N. Hawkins, & D. E. Neubauer (Eds.), *The Palgrave handbook of Asia Pacific higher education* (pp. 73–88). Palgrave Macmillan.

Ziguras, C., & McBurnie, G. (2011). Transnational higher education in the Asia-Pacific region: From distance education to the branch campus. In S. Marginson, S. Kaur, & E. Sawir (Eds.), *Higher education in the Asia-Pacific: Strategic responses to globalization* (pp. 105–122). Springer Netherlands.

Index

adaptation   XII, 25, 27, 29, 30, 34, 38–40, 42, 63, 70, 73, 74, 79, 86, 87, 89, 90, 129, 136, 140, 148, 150, 153, 160, 161

agency   1, 23, 36, 38, 42, 49, 60, 61, 64, 66, 68, 72, 74, 76, 77, 79, 92–94, 103, 120, 126, 128, 129, 136, 140, 142–145, 149, 151, 152, 155, 157, 159, 160, 162, 165, 166

assessment   XI, 17, 50, 68, 72, 82, 92, 104–108, 110, 114, 119, 120, 121, 129, 132, 135, 136, 137, 142, 143, 146, 155–157, 165, 166

Australia   XII, 1, 7, 9, 15, 18, 20–22, 24, 30, 49, 55, 58–60, 64–66, 68–75, 77–80, 82–91, 93–97, 99–102, 104–107, 111–115, 117, 119, 120, 127, 128, 130–139, 141–144, 146–148, 150, 151, 153–163

belonging   1, 36, 38, 42, 48, 49, 66, 68, 85, 86, 88–90, 92–94, 103, 120, 124–126, 128, 131–133, 139, 140, 142–145, 152–157, 159, 160, 162, 165, 166

China   XI, XII, 1, 5–7, 9, 10–14, 18, 20, 21, 25, 26, 30, 32, 33, 42, 49, 53–56, 58, 60–66, 68–76, 78, 80–83, 87–91, 93–99, 101–105, 107, 109, 112–117, 123, 124, 127–129, 131–138, 141–144, 147, 148, 150, 151, 153–158, 161–163, 167

Chinese learner   30, 86

collectivist   30, 115, 158

community   1, 6, 46, 89, 92, 115, 124, 139, 152, 164

Confucian Heritage Culture (CHC)   31–36, 109, 110

culture   3, 4, 6, 10, 18, 27–31, 33, 35–45, 51, 54, 56, 65, 68, 85, 91, 92, 94, 102, 103, 109, 110, 115, 120, 122, 135, 139, 142, 143, 145, 146, 148, 154, 156, 158, 160, 164, 166

development   1, 3, 4, 6, 7, 9–12, 14, 15, 17, 25, 34, 38–41, 48, 50, 52–54, 74, 79, 87, 90–93, 95, 121, 122, 126, 127, 132–135, 144, 148, 150, 156, 159–161, 163, 165, 166

diaspora   XII, 25, 31, 42, 43, 49, 77, 80, 84, 85, 89, 90, 100, 120, 122, 127, 129, 130, 132, 135, 139, 142, 145, 151, 153, 156

globalisation   XI, XII, 1–7, 10, 11, 16, 25, 43, 47, 48, 159, 166

growth   3–5, 11, 12, 39, 40, 42, 74, 87, 150

identity   XII, 1, 2, 6, 35, 36, 38, 40, 42, 48, 49, 66, 68, 79, 80, 82–84, 92–94, 103, 118, 120, 128, 130–132, 136, 140, 142, 143, 145–148, 155, 157, 159, 160, 162, 165, 166

in-between/third space   XII, 19, 23, 43–49, 51, 92, 94, 95, 153, 161, 163

in-betweener   1, 19, 23, 24, 26, 122, 123, 141, 142, 144, 145, 153, 162

in-betweenness   40, 43, 94, 97, 120–122, 127, 133, 137, 138, 140, 142–145, 148, 149, 153, 155, 159, 160, 162, 163, 165–167

individualist   30, 114, 117–119, 139, 158

Information and Communication Technology (ICT)   4, 6, 9, 48, 49, 68, 70, 73, 74, 77, 83, 84, 88, 94–96, 98, 99, 101, 102, 104, 108, 119, 120, 132–135, 137, 142, 152, 155–157, 162, 164, 166

intercultural adjustment   10, 19, 24, 25, 31, 37–40, 42, 43, 51–53, 64, 66, 68, 71, 77–79, 90, 121, 123, 140, 142, 143, 153, 159–163, 165, 167

intercultural learning   2, 18, 19, 24–27, 29, 33, 35, 37–43, 51, 63, 64, 66, 67, 70–72, 74, 77–79, 83, 84, 86, 89, 90, 94, 102, 107, 108, 114, 120, 128, 120, 131, 133, 138, 141, 142, 144, 150–152, 155, 156, 160, 164–166

International English Language Testing System (IELTS)   60–65, 75, 79, 127–130, 138, 148–150, 159

internationalisation   1, 2, 4–6, 10–16, 19, 25, 27, 31, 42, 43, 141, 144, 159, 164, 166

learning experiences   1, 7–9, 15, 17–20, 22–25, 32, 34, 36, 42–44, 49, 50, 54, 55, 58, 59, 61–64, 68, 74, 75, 77–79, 86, 90, 94–97, 99, 101, 107, 108, 112, 114, 120–122, 125, 127, 133–135, 137, 138, 141, 143, 145, 148, 151, 152, 155–157, 160, 161, 164–166

learning trajectory   1, 122, 143, 145, 166

INDEX

narrative inquiry   20

place   1, 7, 23, 27, 38, 44–51, 58, 79, 85, 91, 93–100, 102–104, 107, 115, 120, 133–136, 155, 156, 158, 162–164

qualitative study   20, 21, 24

reflexivity   23, 24, 40, 122

space   XII, 1, 6, 19, 23, 27, 36, 37, 41–51, 72, 91–107, 110–112, 114–120, 131, 133, 135–139, 141, 142, 144, 145, 148, 153, 155–157, 159, 161–166

stress   XII, 30, 38–40, 42, 52, 54, 59, 61, 63, 64, 68–72, 79, 88, 90, 99, 105–107, 114, 124, 127, 128, 130, 136, 140–142, 146, 148–151, 157, 160, 161, 165

student mobility   27, 50, 120, 166

teaching approach   77, 78, 106, 109–111, 114, 142, 143, 150, 157, 158, 165

transitioning   XI, 1, 20, 27, 30, 36, 42, 44, 49, 51, 52, 70, 80, 85, 92–94, 102–104, 108, 114, 115, 119, 120, 122, 126, 127, 133, 135, 136, 141, 142, 154, 159, 160, 162–164, 166

Transnational Articulation Programme (TAP)   XI, 1, 2, 121, 141, 155

Transnational Higher Education (TNHE)   XI, 1, 2, 6–19, 25, 33, 54, 121, 144, 146, 159, 161, 165–167

Printed in the United States
by Baker & Taylor Publisher Services